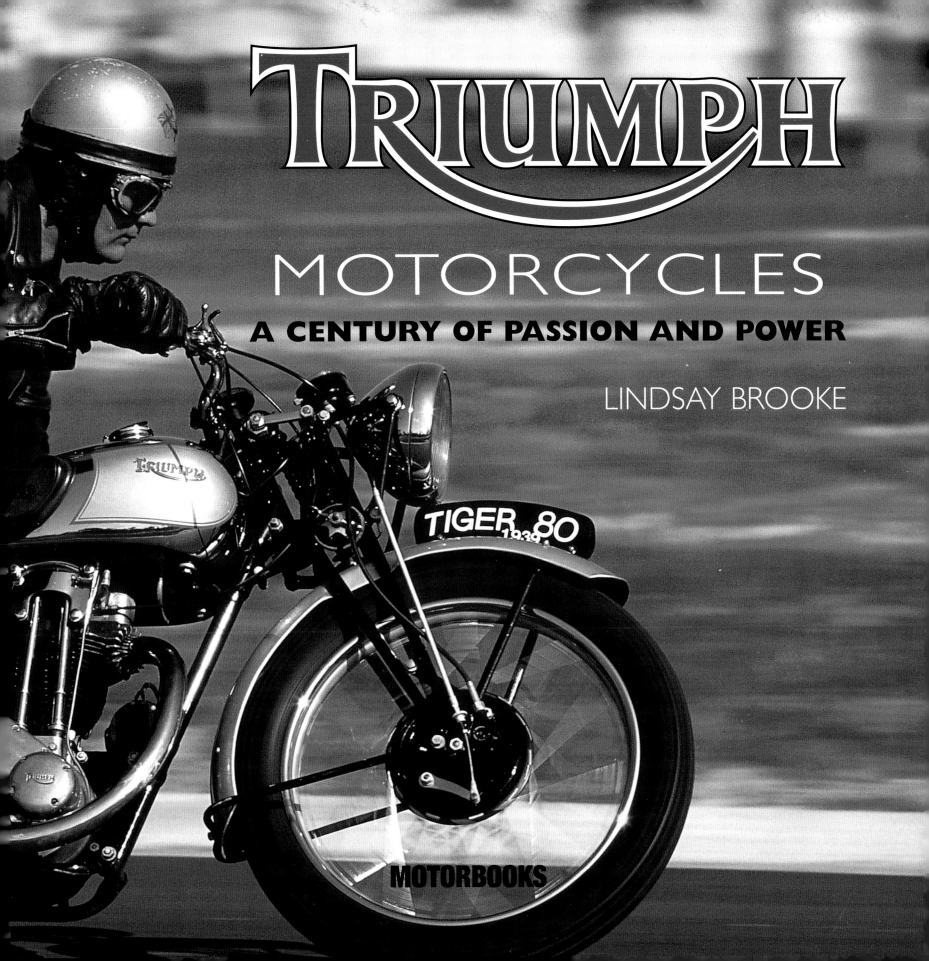

TRIUMPH

MOTORCYCLES

A CENTURY OF PASSION AND POWER

LINDSAY BROOKE

TIGER 80 1939

MOTORBOOKS

First published in 2002 by Motorbooks, Galtier Plaza, Suite 200, 380 Jackson Street, St. Paul, MN 55101 USA

MBI Publishing Company books are also available at discounts in bulk quantity for industrial or sales-promotional use. For details write to Special Sales Manager at MBI Publishing, Galtier Plaza, Suite 200, 380 Jackson Street, St. Paul, MN 55101-3885 USA.

Library of Congress Cataloging-in-Publication Data Available

ISBN-13: 978-0-7603-0456-3
ISBN-10: 0-7603-0456-4

Front cover, top left: The 1965 T120R Bonneville benefited from an improved fork, a better stand, and the now-classic teardrop "sports" mufflers. *Jeff Hackett.* **Top right:** Mike Benolken's exquisitely restored 1940 Speed Twin showing large 8-inch headlamp and "pedestrian slicer" fender-mounted front license plate. *Jeff Hackett.* **Bottom left:** The 955i Daytona continues to get refinements to keep it firmly in the superbike game. *Lindsay Brooke.* **Bottom right:** The outrageous X75 Hurricane was conceived in 1969 by BSA Inc. executive Don Brown, who commissioned Craig Vetter to design and build the prototype. *Jeff Hackett*

Frontispiece: A 1965 Bonneville.

Title page: The 1939 Tiger 80 on test for *Classic Bike* magazine. *EMAP archive*

Back cover: The 1968 Bonneville exemplifies the classic Triumph twin. *Jeff Hackett*

Edited by Chad Caruthers
Designed by Stephanie Michaud
Layout by Katie Sonmor

Printed in Hong Kong

CONTENTS

This book is dedicated to four wonderful people who made an indelible mark on me and on motorcycling, and all passed away during the course of this project:

Carol Baver, whose warmth, humor, and encyclopedic knowledge of the Triumph and Moto Morini parts books made visiting my favorite Triumph shop, Hermy's Tire and Cycle in Port Clinton, Pennsylvania, so much fun.

Doug Hele, whose brilliance as Triumph's greatest development engineer was surpassed only by his gentlemanly persona and his respect for colleague and competitor alike.

Jack "Big D" Wilson, whose Triumphs set world speed records at Bonneville for more than 30 years and who never met a fast motorcycle he didn't think could go faster.

Bruce Finlayson, whose enthusiasm for this sport and its machinery should be an example for us all.

INTRODUCTION

The year 2002 is Triumph's centennial anniversary, making it the world's oldest motorcycle marque still in production. What a glorious achievement, considering only one other company that was making bikes prior to 1904—that old nemesis from Milwaukee—is alive today. One has to marvel at the rich history and ongoing durability of this legendary British brand. Those of us who love Triumphs and can't get enough of them certainly do.

Triumph reached the magic one hundred year milestone despite challenges and outright calamity that sunk hundreds of lesser competitors. Robust engineering propelled the company during the industry's formative years, days when the horse was still king of the road. New technology and added features allowed Triumph to carry on when other bikemakers failed as the wave of cheap automobiles arrived in Britain and Europe. From the very beginning, sporting successes helped define Triumphs as machines that excelled on the track as well as on the road.

When Jack Sangster purchased the company in 1936 and put the brilliant Edward Turner in command, Triumph's image and financial success soared. Turner quickly injected an undeniable style into the product range by creating the beautiful 250-cc, 350-cc, and 500-cc Tiger singles. His blockbuster 1938 Speed Twin and its high-performance sibling, the 1939 Tiger 100, turned the two-wheel world upside down. For the next three decades, the compact, agile, powerful, and versatile British parallel twin dominated motorcycling. Its legacy lives on today as the reborn twenty-first century Bonneville.

Triumph's story is also about survival in the face of adversity, some of it self-inflicted. The disastrous Model P launch was the company's first major product blunder, but Triumph recovered. Hitler's bombers scored a direct hit on the Coventry factory in 1940, but they couldn't kill Triumph. Neither could the punishing Meriden workers' blockade from 1973–1974, nor the fire that ravaged the Hinckley factory in March 2002. Triumph even survived ownership by BSA, whose management was clearly the worst in the industry during the 1960s and 1970s.

As the Triumph brand enters its second century, John Bloor's resurrected enterprise is already into its second decade and moving from strength to strength. Having started with the single Hinckley factory, two modular engine types, and a handful of models in 1991, Triumph now encompasses multiple production facilities, five unique engine families, and a dozen model variants—with much more to come.

Triumph's future will reveal bikes with unique design, engineering, and style, but it also will embrace the heritage that made the name so valuable to Bloor twenty years ago. Now is the perfect time to look back at a century of passion and power (with a few hiccups along the way) and to celebrate a tough, timeless motorcycle marque that keeps getting better with age.

TRUSTY
TRIUMPH

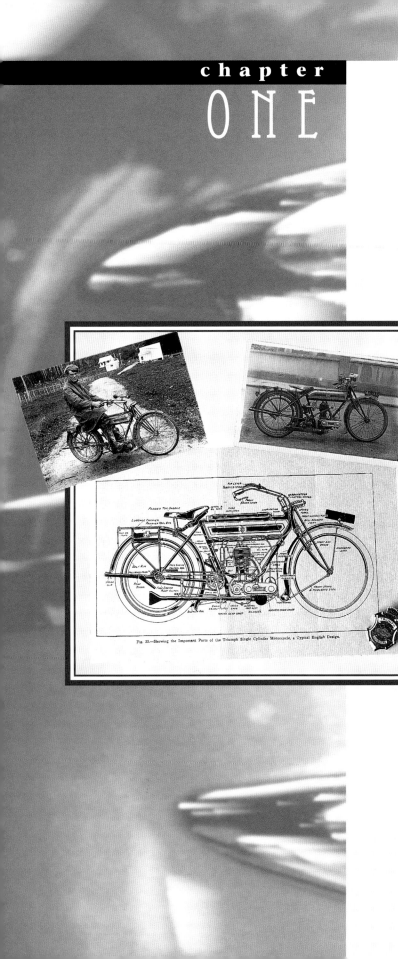

Fig. 31.—Showing the Important Parts of the Triumph Single Cylinder Motorcycle, a Typical English Design.

Thumb the starter button of a new Triumph Daytona and its fuel-injected 955-cc heart leaps instantly to life. From inside the bike's skintight fairing comes the faint whistle of straight-cut primary gears; from behind comes a muted warble from the exhaust silencer. As the engine settles into a steady idle, the overall sonic quality, typical of modern liquid-cooled motorcycles, is not unlike a large sewing machine.

Blip the throttle hard, and the Daytona snarls. The tachometer needle dances around its dial, startling a passer-by. Snick the gear lever into first, feed in the feathery clutch, and the Triumph's 128 horsepower hardly notices it's hauling a rider. You're off. Shifting up through 5,000 rpm—not quite halfway to redline—the unmistakable sound of a three-cylinder superbike reverberates off the flanks of passing cars. This bike wants to *go*.

A fistful of throttle catapults the metallic-blue Daytona forward, slicing through lazy commuter traffic and past the city limits. The bike feels muscular, the exhaust note rising to a manic howl. The noise splits the rural solitude, evoking Triumph's fabulous road-racing triples of thirty years ago.

The open road beckons Triumph's latest, fastest, and most exciting road burner as it has for a century. Experiencing the new Daytona for the first time is an exhilaration that has been shared by countless motorcyclists of previous eras—on Tigers in the 1940s, Thunderbirds in the 1950s, Bonnevilles in the 1960s, and Tridents in the 1970s. Indeed, Triumph's sporty character has been one of the marque's strongest allures throughout its 100-year history.

The Triumph Brand Is Born

Because of the skills needed to master the early twentieth-century motorcycle and the general noise and commotion that riding one caused, motorcyclists of that day faced plenty of detractors. Most of the critics were landed gentry who were firmly in favor of four-legged horsepower. When *The Motor Cycle*'s columnist Ixion saw an approaching horse, he would cut his engine and try to find cover in the nearest hedge or alleyway to avoid being attacked by the horse's rider!

The respected journal *Engineering* even joined in. It characterized motorcycling as "a form of entertainment that can appeal only to the most enthusiastic of mechanical eccentrics." The publication's editors doubted the staying power of the motorcycle, wondering "whether the motorcycle will, when the novelty has worn off, take a firm hold of public favor."

That the editors were proved wrong can to some degree be attributed to the strength of Triumph's products. By 1906, motorcycle sales in Britain had hit their first slump. The "novelty" appeared to be waning. It became clear that the marques with the greatest reliability were the most likely to survive. While some of its early competitors disappeared, Triumph's annual production rose from 500 motorcycles in 1905 to 1,000 machines in 1907. By 1909, the year's output topped 3,000 units. The company was on its way to success, a fact that Triumph's founder could hardly have imagined when he launched the firm in 1885.

Siegfried Bettmann was 20 years old when he landed in London in 1883. It was the twilight of the Victorian Era, a period when the British Empire was at its zenith and Britain's economy was booming. Germany's recent unification had encouraged many of its citizens to emigrate, and many German entrepreneurs, including Bettmann, headed for Britain to seek their fortunes.

Upon arrival in Britain, Bettmann tried his hand at a couple of jobs before settling on becoming a bicycle manufacturer. The bicycle was booming, as it was quickly revolutionizing personal transportation in cities and towns. Bettmann contracted with a Birmingham factory to build bicycles for him. Before he could sell them, however, the bikes needed a brand name.

"For a long time my customers, who were practically all on the Continent, talked of the bicycle as being the 'Bettmann,'" he wrote in a 1949 retrospective. Opting against using his surname—possibly because, given the political and social views of the day, he felt a Jewish name on a product might hamper sales in certain markets—Bettmann wanted a label that would immediately be accepted in Britain and that "could be understood in all European languages."

The name he selected was Triumph.

Triumph Means Motorcycles

Bettmann needed someone to design his bikes and manage his factory, and he found such a person in Maurice Schulte, another German immigrant and a trained mechanical engineer. The forward-looking Schulte helped Bettmann raise capital to fund Triumph's start-up, which amounted to £500 (about $2,500) from Bettmann's parents and £150 (about $750) from Schulte's family. Bettmann and

Siegfried Bettmann, the German who came to Britain in 1883 to sell bicycles and ended up founding Triumph two years later. *Mick Woollett archive*

Maurice Schulte was Bettman's chief engineer. He masterminded Triumph's first motorcycle in 1902 and its first engine in 1905. He's shown in 1911 with a 3 1/2-horsepower model. *Mick Woollett archive*

Triumph's earliest brand, used from the birth of the Triumph Cycle Co. in 1887, was typical of a British bicycle maker. It was a very regal-looking shield or crest topped off by a formal crown and noting the company's Coventry location. By 1907, as Triumph exports began to grow, the shield was modified with the words America, Europe, and Australia.

The shield was used as Triumph's primary trademark through 1929, though some supplemental logos were employed along the way. In 1905 came fuel-tank transfers with *Triumph* in stylized block letters, bisected by a long thin trumpet. For a few years this was applied on some models, forward of the central crest.

In 1908, a company artist designed the basic typeface for what would later become Triumph's best-known logo. This style, with the serif letters in proportion but without the sweeping R, appeared sporadically in advertising and company documents. Its first use with the sweeping R came in 1914, on the cover of the factory parts and accessories booklet. This was the exact same logo, with its outlined letters, that was adopted by Edward Turner as the Triumph Engineering Co.'s official brand in 1936. It's the one best known to enthusiasts worldwide as the classic Triumph logo, and during the day of the 1914 parts booklet, it looked extremely modern.

However, that logo was used only sporadically for the next 22 years, according to Triumph literature expert David Gaylin. Its primary role seemed to be in public promotions of various new models in the mid-1920s (including the Model P), where it appeared on large banners and a few posters. But the classic logo did not yet surface on any motorcycle, asserts Gaylin.

Meanwhile, continued success in foreign markets prompted a major redesign of the brand for 1929. The old bicycle shield was replaced by a "globe." Variants of this logo graced fuel tanks through 1933. A similar design was used for years by Triumph cars, with the H sporting a tail that underlined the word Triumph.

A sweeping-R logo, albeit with thinner typefaces that lacked the outlined letters of the famous version, finally appeared on the motorcycles in 1931. It was embossed in two locations on the sloper engine range—on the right side of the cylinder head rocker box—and on each side of the oil-bearing crankcases near the front. For the Val Page-designed model range of 1934, the sweeping-R trademark became Triumph's official brand. A thinner-font version was used on engine castings, fuel tanks, and knee pads.

At the same time, the classic version with the wider, outlined letters was broadly used in company advertising and show literature. When the Turner-designed line-up was launched in 1936, this logo became the company's mainstay through Meriden's demise in 1983. It was then licensed by Les Harris during his production of the T140 from 1984 through 1988.

When John Bloor's Hinckley-built Triumphs debuted in 1990, they wore a modernized version of the classic logo. This current form has squarish letters, and the tail of its sweeping-R ends just ahead of the letter H instead of connecting to it. The earlier style brand lives on, however. Mr. Bloor retains full worldwide trademark rights to the logo that made Triumph famous.

Three examples of early logos: the 1903 to 1906 shield; 1932-33 globe variant; 1934 to mid-1936 "swooping R". David Gaylin archive

Factory illustrations of the original 1902 Triumph (top) and the first model with Triumph designed and built engine, 1905. The 1902 machine was basically the company's bicycle frame with a 2 1/2-horsepower Belgian-made Minerva single hung from the front downtube. The 1905 model was completely new. Its 363-cc sidevalve single made 3.0 horsepower at 1,500 rpm. *Lindsay Brooke archive*

Schulte were now in the bicycle business, and in 1887 they set up a factory on Much Park Street in Coventry, the center of the new cycle industry. Their black-enameled Triumphs sold well, so well that in 1896, Bettmann opened a subsidiary factory in his birthplace of Nuremberg, Germany.

Schulte, though, was more interested in powered cycles than pedaled ones, and he quickly turned Bettmann's attention in the same direction. In 1897, the pair imported a German-made Hildebrand and Wolfmüller, one of the world's first motorcycles, to Britain for public demonstration. A year later, they were cobbling together their own power-assisted bicycle.

After winning the 1908 Isle of Man TT, Triumphs proved their mettle in the toughest reliability runs and hill climbs. Company advertising followed the action, as this 1913 ad from the British weekly *The Motor Cycle* shows.

A postcard showing "Fred," a Royal Signals Corpsman on his trusty Type H. The hand-written message on the back is signed "Somewhere in France." Triumph produced over 30,000 Type H singles for the Allied forces during World War I, about 20,000 of them for the British Army. All were countershaft three-speed models. Some Type A clutch-hub models were also sent to duty. The Triumphs proved themselves outstandingly reliable among dispatch riders, who often had to dodge German shellfire on the move. *David Gaylin archive*

So it was that in 1902, the first motorcycle to wear a Triumph badge hit the streets. It was basically the company's heaviest bicycle frame and was powered by a Belgian-made 2 1/4-horsepower Minerva single clipped onto the front downtube. A compartment that held the fuel tank and ignition components hung from the top tube. The 240-cc engine directly drove the rear wheel via a leather belt.

For the next three years, Bettmann and Schulte made improvements to their creation. At about the time when Britain's national speed limit was raised from 12 miles per hour to a stratospheric 20 miles per hour, the frame was strengthened to accept larger and more powerful J.A.P. and Fafnir engines. Nevertheless, the performance of these pioneering Triumphs was about equal to a modern-day moped, and a rider would have a hard time maintaining a walking pace on a steep uphill climb.

"The Triumph Motor Cycle is not an experiment, but an article of proven value," asserted a 1905 magazine ad for Triumph. It is made throughout in our own works, by experienced workmen only, no female whatever being employed."

The Early Days of Triumph Motorcycles

The proud owner of a new 1914 Triumph Type A would have been confident that his 3 1/2-horsepower 550-cc sidevalve single was sired from the company's racing experience. Six years prior, a Triumph-mounted Jack Marshall won the single-cylinder class at the 1908 Isle of Man TT, which was already the most grueling motorcycle race in the world. It was the first TT victory by a machine built, frame and engine, by the same manufacturer. Marshall, who'd placed second in the inaugural 1907 TT on a Triumph, set the fastest lap mark of 42.48 miles per hour. His 476-cc racer met all the requirements for TT bikes that year, as it was fitted with a standard silencer and 2-inch tires.

Marshall's Triumph was also plenty efficient, easily squeezing out the required 100 mile per gallon fuel consumption (he actually averaged 114) and completing the 158-mile race with gasoline to spare. Triumph riders also took third, fifth, seventh, and tenth places, a remarkable achievement.

In those pioneering years, the TT and other endurance events were becoming battlegrounds for the world's motorcycle makers, who used racetrack successes to advertise their products' durability and speed. The first

THE FIRST PARALLEL TWIN

Say parallel twin or vertical twin to a motorcycle history buff, and the likely reply will be, "Triumph." But while the British marque certainly popularized the engine format in the late 1930s, other makers pioneered its production. The advantages of twin-cylinder power were not lost on Mauritz Schulte.

In 1909, Schulte purchased a Bercley for evaluation and it convinced him that a vertical cylinder arrangement, rather than a Vee or horizontally opposed, gave the best packaging, and neatest appearance. Three years later, Schulte designed Triumph's first twin, which began its initial bench tests in the spring of 1913. The prototype was unveiled to writers from *The Motor Cycle* in July of that year, timed with an eye toward publicity before the upcoming Olympia Show.

Like the Belgian engine, Triumph's 600-cc sidevalve prototype was designed to be mounted across the bike's frame. Both iron cylinders were cast together, as a pair, with wide cooling fins on the top half. Another Bercley-inspired feature was cross-flow breathing, which arranged the exhaust and the intake valves ahead of and behind the cylinders, with the exhaust ports facing forward.

Schulte's design, however, differed from the Bercley in a number of key areas. Rather than using a built-up crankshaft with 360-degree throws and a center main bearing, the Triumph's was a one-piece forging. Its big-end journals were set 180 degrees apart, like countless Japanese parallel twins of decades later. At the crank's center was a helical gear that drove the camshaft. A large, stamped-steel flywheel was fitted on the right side, outboard of the crankcase. Ironically, the cases were horizontally split—a design that the Japanese also would use decades later for improved oil retention.

On the factory's test bench, the new twin claimed to produce 4 1/4 horsepower—a full 3/4 horsepower more powerful than Triumph's single. The engine was slated to go with a new three-speed countershaft gearbox and chain final drive, features that would make it even more appealing to sporting solo riders and sidecarists. However, the outbreak of World War I in 1914 changed Triumph's plans, as the

The 1913 prototype vertical twin was influenced by a Belgian motorcycle engine. Note horizontally split crankcases. The outbreak of World War I killed the project. Mick Woollett archive

British Army wanted single-cylinder machines in big volumes. The twin project was shelved.

Had it gone into production, Triumph's twin might have been overshadowed by a far more advanced parallel twin from across the English Channel. In 1913, Peugeot shocked the motorcycle world with its new Grand Prix engine, featuring double-overhead camshafts, four valves per cylinder and "unit" (integral crankcase and gearbox) construction. With a 65x82-mm bore and stroke, the Peugeot produced about 28 horsepower at a revvy 5,000 rpm.

The Great War also stopped development of this technological marvel. A year after the Armistice was signed, another parallel twin made its debut at the 1919 Paris Motorcycle Show. It was the French-made Lutece, a machine that boasted 1,000 cc and shaft drive. It was produced in small quantity through 1926.

It would take until 1933 before the Triumph badge finally adorned a production vertical twin—the 650-cc model 6/1.

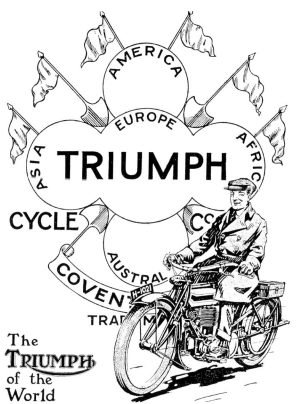

The TRIUMPH of the World

Shown here is a 1919 magazine ad reinforcing the brand to the postwar world. The famous Triumph "sweeping-R" logo first appeared in print in a 1914 company advertisement, and was used sporadically until its official adoption by the Triumph Engineering Co. in 1936.

motorcycle race at Britain's famous Brooklands speed circuit in February 1908 was won by Gordon McMinnies, an Oxford undergrad whose 476-cc Triumph clocked a blistering 53.55 miles per hour. The following year, 3 1/2-horsepower Triumphs took the only gold medals in the inaugural Scottish Six-Days Trials, heralded as the world's most severe test of man and machine.

A year later, in the Isle of Man, Triumph swept five of the top ten places, including a third-place by Billy Creyton on one of the factory's 3 1/2-horsepower TT Racer models. In 1911, Billy Newsome, riding a modified Triumph, set the world's one-hour speed record at Brooklands.

Such performances quickly spread the company's reputation worldwide. In 1912, a Triumph single in the hands of Italian rider Gio Ravelli won the motorcycle class of the famous Targa Florio road race. The next year, a pair of 3 1/2-horsepower Triumphs finished first and second in the Championship of Japan, held on a 12-mile course at Kobe. The winning machine averaged nearly 60 miles per hour.

All of these competition successes were based on upgraded and enlarged versions of Triumph's basic 3-horsepower single. Launched in 1905, this single was the first engine designed and produced by Triumph. From the time the company made its first motorized bicycle, in 1902, Triumph had bought its engines from three outside specialists: Belgium's Minerva, Germany's Fafnir, and Britain's ubiquitous J.A. Prestwich (J.A.P.). The original 363-cc (78x76-mm bore and stroke) sidevalve thumper served as the foundation of the company's model range through the 1920s, much as the original Speed Twin did years later. It progressively grew to 453 cc (1907), 476 cc (1908), and 499 cc (1910), all rated at 3 1/2 horsepower. By 1914, it had evolved into its final 4-horsepower, 550-cc form.

The 1905 engine boasted a number of uncommon features that made it more durable than many competitors, although more costly to produce. Its crankshaft was supported in ball bearings—reportedly an industry first. Both valves were mechanically operated, and the cams were machined into the inner radii of the timing gears. In 1908, Triumph replaced the carburetor it had been purchasing from Brown & Barlow with one of its own manufacture. Triumph stands among a handful of motorcycle companies that have produced their own carburetors through the years, and the Triumph carburetor was one of the period's best. It used separate, parallel barrels for its throttle and air slides, giving smoother response than most competitors.

This detail of the 1921 Type H shows V-belt rim that doubled as a friction surface for the bicycle-type rear wheel brake. These brakes continued on Triumphs through 1925, even after the company changed to chain drive and internal expanding front brakes. Note the engine lube pump on center frame tube—the rider gave it a few pumps before starting, and every 10 to 20 miles while on the road. *Jeff Hackett*

Right
Greg Bidou's 1921 Type H is the last of Triumph's belt-drive singles. It preceded the chain-drive Type SD, basically an upgraded H with a Triumph-made gearbox that debuted in 1922. This almost original Type H runs well and is a crowd pleaser at U.S. Triumph Club rallies. *Jeff Hackett*

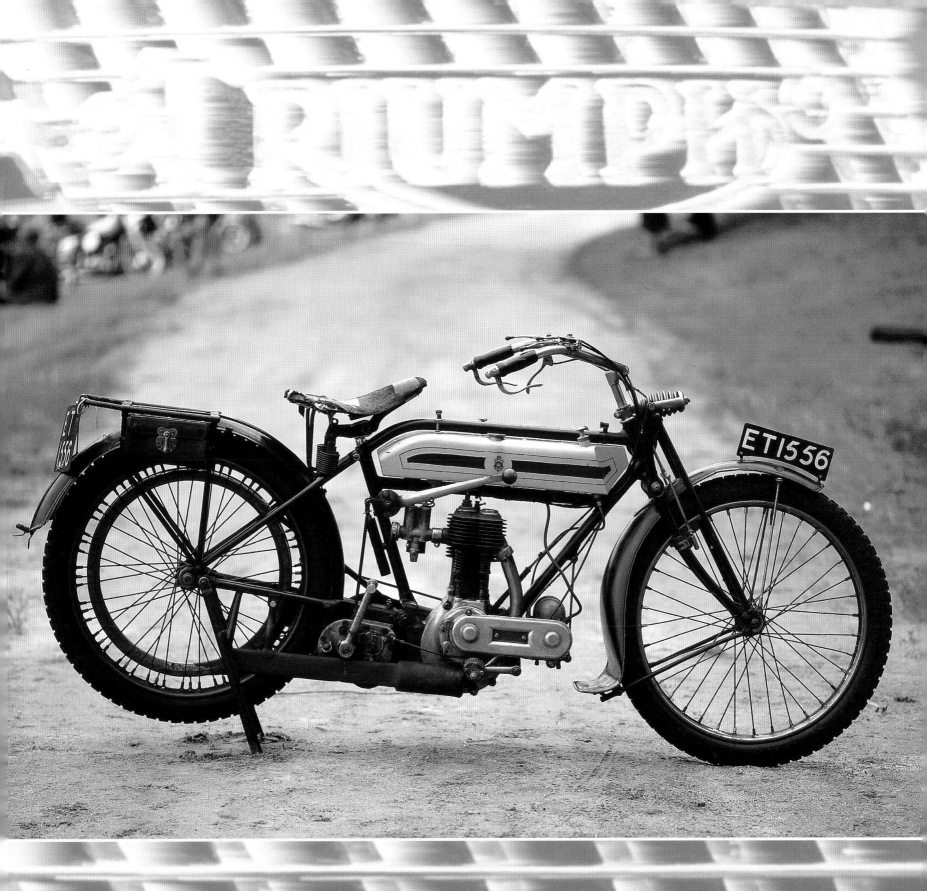

Triumph's Type R racer featured four overhead valves per cylinder. It was developed in conjunction with combustion wizard Harry Ricardo and engineer/racer Frank Halford. Following a disappointing debut in 1921, when only one of the Triumph factory team finished the Isle of Man Senior TT (16th place), the Type R soon recorded a string of successes, including Walter Brandish's second-place at the 1922 Senior TT. Brandish (shown here after the race) was the son of a Coventry Triumph dealer. He was killed the next year at the TT, giving his name to the famous circuit's Brandish Corner.
Mick Woollett archive

Overall, the Triumph powerplant was "well designed and beautifully made," observed the great engineer and combustion scientist Sir Harry Ricardo in his 1968 autobiography, *Memories and Machines*. Some historians view the 3 1/2-horsepower Triumph as the world's first truly reliable motorcycle. It was so highly regarded that when BSA built its first motorcycle in 1912, the company openly copied the industry's benchmark—Triumph.

Running a Triumph in the period before World War I was far more daunting than the push-button convenience of today's Daytona. While traffic was sparse (perhaps the only advantage of being a motorcyclist in those early days), road conditions were abysmal. The unpaved byways were dusty when dry, muddy bogs when wet, and often smeared with various animal droppings.

And then there was the matter of starting and operating the machine, a feat that required the constant juggling of four control levers—the throttle, ignition advance/retard, air, and compression release—just to keep the engine running and the bike moving forward. Saddling up and riding a horse was a far simpler means of travel.

The Triumph's levers were mounted on the fuel tank until 1908, when they were relocated to the handlebars. While this was definitely a big improvement in ergonomics, the early model's rigid frame definitely gave a stiff ride. Even when equipped with Triumph's rocking-action spring fork, which debuted in 1906, all but the smoothest road surfaces would constantly upset the engine's mixture setting, requiring frequent adjustments of the air lever while under way. The drive belt would slip and stretch, frames would crack and break, and the crude ignition systems regularly failed to supply spark. To ensure the engine didn't self-destruct, the rider had to reach behind the center frame tube and work the hand-operated oil pump every 15 to 20 miles—more or less proportional to engine rpm—or every 10 miles with a sidecar attached.

Triumph's 1914 Type A owner's handbook offered advice on descending hills. To supplement the bike's anemic brakes (the foot-operated rear brake scrubbed against the drive belt pulley), engine braking was recommended. To do this, the Triumph rider quickly had to fiddle with the forest of control levers and retard the spark, back off the throttle, and leave the air open. On models equipped with Triumph's own three-speed rear hub (introduced in 1913 and much like the gear-hubs on classic English touring bicycles), second or third gear was suggested. All changes were best made at slow speed, "otherwise a very great strain is placed upon the gears and frame, and breakages may occur," as stated in the 1914 owner's handbook.

Building Bigger, Badder, and Better Triumphs

Increasing demand for his products led Bettmann to expand his factory. To better concentrate on the motorcycle side of the business, he purchased another plant complex on Priory Street in Coventry. In November 1940, a 77-year-old Bettmann was to see this famous Triumph factory bombed into rubble by his former countrymen during the Luftwaffe's blitz on England.

Schulte continued to improve the motorcycles between 1910 and 1915. He and Bettmann were determined to keep quality and reliability high and cost reasonable. "Triumph made survival in business an art form," observed journalist Val Ward in *Classic Bike* magazine. "Penny pinching was emphasized in the old Coventry works, where clerks knew better than to ask for fresh pencils before they had worn out awkward stubs. A Scroogelike economy drive was pursued for years, always with one aim—to enable the factory to tempt new-machine buyers with bikes offering excellent value for money."

WHAT'S IN A NAME?

At the start of World War I, four different motorcycle companies had used the name "Triumph" on their products. Bettmann's original marque was followed by Triumph-Nuremburg. The German subsidiary built the Nipper and the 550-cc SD four-stroke single until 1929. These British and German Triumph concerns separated when Bettmann refused to supply engines for a new, larger model of German design. The two companies remained amicable, though, and struck an import deal, but losing the subsidiary designation meant that the German company could no longer use the name "Triumph" on their motorcycles in export markets. Its new name: TWN—Triumph Werke Nuremburg. The company built motorcycles until 1957, when it was taken over by television and radio giant Grundig.

The United States was home to two Triumph companies. The first model to wear a Triumph tank emblem in America was made by Excelsior in 1907. It was powered by a 2 1/2-horsepower 300-cc Thor single, and it was designed by Hendee (makers of Indian) and made by the Aurora Automatic Machinery Co. Five years later, an investment group in Detroit bought the rights to the Triumph name from Excelsior and started the Triumph Manufacturing Co. This Detroit company built three different models of 5 1/2 horsepower, 550-cc machines. Upward of 1,500 bikes were produced during the obscure company's two-year existence.

Like the other manufacturers during this period, Triumph concentrated on upgrading its clutch and gear-changing technology. In 1908 came a variable-pulley belt drive, which offered a selection of gear ratios. In 1911, a simple clutch in the rear hub was offered. In 1913 the company introduced its three-speed rear hub, plus a new 225-cc two-stroke Junior model. Dubbed the "baby Triumph," it weighed just 129 pounds and was designed as an inexpensive go-to-work hack and lady's bike. Such machines were in big demand in Britain—over 30 different models were on the market by 1915.

With its two-speed gearbox and clutchless operation, the Junior provided a lot of quality for the price (£42 (about $200) in 1913). It was a solid seller for Triumph, which kept it in production until 1926. The German Triumph company built a close cousin called the *Knirps* (Nipper), and the Junior's shadow even extended across the Atlantic. Ignaz Schwinn, who owned the Henderson and Excelsior motorcycle companies in Chicago, licensed the Junior's design for a 269-cc U.S. version, the L18, built by Excelsior. Because of the Schwinn connection, the Junior's rocking-action fork, with its trademark horizontal coil spring, appeared in 1938 on Schwinn bicycles. It achieved its greatest fame in the late 1960s, fitted to the famous "Krate" series of chopper-style Stingray bikes, all of which wear a close copy of Triumph's very first motorcycle spring fork.

World War I and the "Trusty Triumph"

When World War I erupted in August 1914, Siegfried Bettmann had achieved the immigrant's dream. His company was the largest-volume motorcycle maker in Britain. Production at the Priory Street plant was vertically integrated, with Triumph itself manufacturing nearly the entire motorcycle (except for tires, ignition system, saddles, drive belts and the like). The company also produced its own sidecars in an adjacent shop. Triumph exported to every corner of the empire as well as to the Far East and North America. And Bettmann had become lord mayor of the city of Coventry.

Looking beyond the Type A, which had served in various forms for nearly ten years, the company was preparing a much improved machine for a 1915 introduction, the 550-cc Type H. Basically an evolution of the Type A tourer, the Type H produced 4 horsepower and was fitted with the Sturmey-Archer three-speed countershaft gearbox that was intended for the stillborn vertical twin. In addition, the Type H was the first Triumph designed without the supplemental pedals that were still fitted on many motorcycles of the day. With the new gearbox came chain primary drive, although final drive was still by belt. (Triumph lagged behind other makers in adopting chain final drive, a modern feature pioneered by Indian many years before.) But at least Triumph had moved beyond the ancient variable pulley and "free clutch" era.

When the British Army came calling for dispatch (messenger) motorcycles for battlefield use, Triumph first provided a batch of one hundred standard Type A tourers. However, the factory's wartime production soon changed over to the new Type Hs. Between 1915 and the Armistice in 1918, Priory Street built some thirty-thousand Type Hs for military use. The bike proved itself highly reliable and durable in every theater and became the dispatch riders' most popular mount. Reliable army use gave rise to the nickname, "Trusty Triumph," a term that helped boost the company's reputation even further after the war. "Trusty Triumph" was also adopted as the factory's cablegram address.

Postwar, Post Schulte

Following the close of the war, Siegfried Bettmann and Mauritz Schulte parted company. The relationship that had launched Triumph had become strained, Bettmann admitted later. Schulte wanted to sell off the bicycle side of the business and get into automaking.

At this point in time, Bettmann had his mind on other things, too, including his libel case against a London newspaper that had described him as a German spy during the war—typical treatment for anyone with a German surname in that era. Although the courts sided with Bettmann, the damage was done, and he was driven from the office of mayor.

In 1919, Bettmann bought out his old colleague for the then-princely sum of £15,000 (about $75,000). In Schulte's place as Triumph's top manager and company board member, Bettmann hired Colonel Claude Holbrook, the Army officer who had given Triumph its lucrative military contract during the war.

Holbrook took over where Schulte left off, and in 1921 thrust Triumph into automobile production. The company's first car, launched in 1923, featured an engine designed by Harry Ricardo, who had recently designed Triumph's latest and most exciting motorcycle engine.

Triumph's Roaring Twenties

The 1920s did indeed roar for Triumph, although not entirely in a positive way. Becoming an automaker was a hugely expensive proposition, as Bettmann quickly learned. The motorcycle side of the company employed three thousand people at a time when postwar inflation had caused a recession in the motorcycle industry. A price war erupted among manufacturers. Besides continuing production of the economic Junior, Triumph offered two new models aimed at the new market: the LS and the Type P.

The LS was an innovative 350-cc sidevalve commuter machine. Its engine featured a gear-driven primary and a three-speed gearbox cast integrally with the engine—Triumph's first unit-construction powerplant and the first with pressure-fed lubrication. But advanced specification did not equal sales, however, and the LS only lasted through 1927.

The Type P was, simply put, the company's first disaster. Launched in 1924, the Type P was a 500-cc sidevalve single sold at the cut-rate price of £42. It cost the same as the little ring-ding Junior had when the Junior was launched a decade earlier!

Triumph's aim with the new Type P was to buy market share. At first, the strategy worked. Demand for the Type P strained the factory's capacity to produce it. Soon Triumph was cranking out one thousand Type Ps each week, enormous output for a motorcycle plant in the mid-1920s. But the machine had been designed without Mauritz Schulte's high-quality standards. It was a cheaply made product, and it showed. To cut cost, Triumph omitted the engine's valve guides. The lower end was fragile. The front brake consisted of a length of asbestos rope that contracted against the wheel rim!

The bikes broke and blew up in alarming numbers. Priory Street found itself facing angry customers, many of them bringing their machines right back to the factory for rebuilds. It was a debacle that cost Triumph plenty, in both money and reputation. Nearly twenty thousand Type Ps were sold before a "fixed" version, the Mark II, was on the assembly line.

THE FOUR-VALVE RICARDO

Not the first motorcycle engine with four valves per cylinder, Triumph's 1922 four-valve 500-cc Model R single was nonetheless an advanced design for its time. Basically a standard model SD below the cylinder barrel, its top end was designed by Harry Ricardo, one of the world's leading experts on piston-engine combustion. Soon dubbed the "Riccy," the Triumph-Ricardo became the company's sports model and production racer. Almost immediately it rocketed to fame.

Built in small numbers from 1922 through 1927, the Riccy set three motorcycle world speed records, including the 500-cc one-hour record of 76.74 miles per hour and the British flying-mile record at nearly 88 miles per hour. And it saw its greatest glory when Walter Brandish placed second on a Riccy at the 1922 Senior TT.

Harry Ricardo's research had helped boost the output of aircraft, race car, and army tank engines. In 1919, he had proved the causes of combustion "knock" (detonation) and the value of creating turbulence in the chamber to reduce it. This had led to the first "squish-band" cylinder head and thus, higher compression ratios.

In 1921, while studying the effects of fuel octane on engine performance for Shell Oil, he met Frank Halford at the Brooklands speed circuit. Halford was a noted pilot and engineer who had helped Ricardo design an

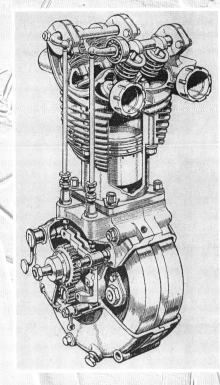

The "Riccy," Triumph's four-valve 550-cc single, powered racers and roadsters in the 1920s. Note ball-bearing rocker shafts. Mick Woollett archive

aircraft engine during World War I. He also loved motorcycles and raced a Triumph. He'd been running his bike on alcohol fuel, and its enhanced performance inspired Ricardo. Already impressed by the Triumph's stout basic design, Ricardo asked Halford permission to build a totally new top end for the engine.

The result was a bronze-alloy cylinder head with a pentroof combustion chamber and four overhead valves—two pairs of intake and exhaust. The spark plug was centrally located, for improved flame travel. Within the machined-steel cylinder barrel was a domed, slipper-skirt piston that gave an 8.0:1 compression ratio, much higher than the 6.0:1 engines then setting the pace at Brooklands.

Halford's four-valve Ricardo-Triumph immediately became a sensation on the British racing scene. In early 1922 he entered it in Open Class events and frequently won against twin-cylinder machines of much larger displacement.

According to Ricardo in his 1968 autobiography, *Memories and Machine*, the Triumph's four-valve layout, when compared with the standard two-valve, gave "the maximum possible valve area" for improved volumetric efficiency. The lighter-weight valves also enabled Halford to rev his long-stroke (80.5x98-mm) engine beyond 5,000 rpm without risk of valvetrain damage. It also resulted in a contract for Ricardo to redesign the Triumph's engines based on those same features, the differences being a lower compression ratio and a cast-iron cylinder head. Triumph applied Ricardo's combustion principles to its new sidevalve Model P single, introduced in 1924.

A cast-iron cylinder barrel distinguished the production model Type R from the factory race version, which used a machined steel barrel. A stronger Druid-type girder fork replaced the old Triumph rocking-spring fork, but otherwise the Type R was based on the SD roadster. Note the special lightweight primary cover (with footpeg cut-out) and dual straight exhausts on this brand-new 1923 Type R, photographed at the Priory Street factory. A Type R ridden by Frank Halford set the world one-hour 500-cc speed record, 76.74 miles per hour, in late 1921. It also set the British flying-mile record at 87.8 miles per hour. And still with a bicycle-type rear brake! Mick Woollett archive

In 1925, Triumph stunned the motorcycle industry by introducing the Type P, a 500-cc single that sold for just £43—far cheaper than competitive 500s. Demand boomed, and Triumph raised its weekly output to 1,000 bikes to meet it. Unfortunately, the low price came from a cheap product—the Type P had no valve guides and the front brake was just an asbestos rope looped around the hub! Owners fumed, but an upgraded Mark II model was not introduced until 20,000 problem-prone Type Ps had been built. *Mick Woollett archive*

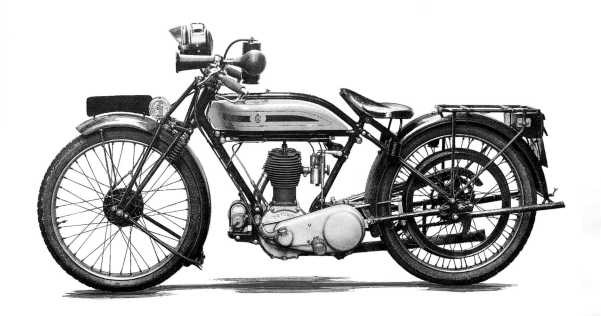

Triumph was fortunate in that, despite all the company's other problems, its model range was led by the stellar four-valve Ricardo tourer and anchored by the still-trusty Type SD. The SD was basically an upgraded Type H with a multiplate wet clutch, chain final drive, and a driveline shock absorber (dubbed Spring Drive, or SD) fitted to the end of the gearbox mainshaft. Because of their all-chain drivelines, both bikes were a major leap forward in refinement, durability, and rideability. They also spearheaded Triumph's use of the stronger and more compliant Druid front fork, an advance that put the old rocking-action fork to pasture. The SD (along with the Ricardo and LS) also enjoyed the company's first application of internal-expanding drum brakes.

These stalwarts carried Triumph through the late 1920s. For the 1928 show season, Holbrook's designers prepared an eight-model range. At the low end was the little Type WS, a 278-cc sidevalve single that weighed less than 200 pounds, a combination that qualified it for a tax break. In Britain during this time, motorcycles that weighed less than 220 pounds dry enjoyed a reduced purchase tax. Triumph figured the WS delivered as much engine as possible under the weight-tax limit. At the top of the line up was the Type ST, one of two new, twin-port, overhead-valve singles. The 500-cc ST was a two-valve production racer based on the 1927 Type TT racer used by the factory team. It was designed by Victor Horsman, a Triumph dealer from Liverpool who was a famous breaker of speed records.

The Type CO was a 350, a "premium" 350 that was ranked just below the ST, its engine developed in-house by Triumph. It was a motorcycle built to last and loaded with high-level quality. Roller bearings were everywhere—on the wheel axles, rocker arms, and in the gearbox. The paintwork was typically Triumph, thick and glossy. Grease fittings were at every pivot point.

At the middle of the model range was a modernized sidevalve 500, the Type CN, along with two other sidevalvers—the NSD (a reframed SD) and the NL, basically an improved Type P Mk. II.

Every model enjoyed all-new cradle frames, improved running gear, and modernized sheet metal. Much of this was made common across the range to boost production efficiencies. Saddle-type fuel tanks were introduced; brakes were enlarged; and pressurized, dry-sump, and semi-dry-sump lubrication was adopted. Amal carburetors replaced the Triumph-made mixers. Stylish fishtail silencers graced many models, and chrome plating became an option.

In its hunt for customers during the hard times of the early 1930s, Triumph joined the slant-cylinder trend popularized by BSA's "Sloper" singles. One result was the 1931 Model WO, an inexpensive 250-cc overhead-valve single. A streamlined crankcase/gearbox cover helped reduce mechanical noise and saved Triumph the cost of polishing the cases underneath. *Mick Woollett archive*

The 1930s: On the Horizon of Change

Triumph was profitable when the 1920s came to a close, and Bettmann pressed forward with the development of the two-wheeled portfolio into the new decade. For the 1930 model year, the company joined the trend toward forward-inclined single-cylinder engines, popularized by BSA's famous "Sloper" models. It was only for style, but newly revised, overhead-valve engines powered the 1.47-horsepower 150-cc Type XO, the 2.49-horsepower 250-cc Type WO, the 350-cc Type NM, and the sports 500-cc Type CD. Besides their cylinder cant, these engines are recognized by their large aluminum crankcases with integral oil tanks (they remained dry-sump systems) and the sweeping-R Triumph logo embossed on each side.

These models continued through the 1933 season, the larger models becoming Silent Scout models with stamped-steel enclosures around their crankcases and gearboxes (for a cleaner appearance) and special cam forms for quieter operation. But the Great Depression had arrived, and Triumph's answer for the economy-minded rider was two Villiers-engined two-stroke cheapies. Named "Gloria," they were designed to meet vehicle tax laws with their 98-cc and 150-cc displacements.

While there were no overhead camshafts or foot-change gearboxes, as were then debuting on AJS, Norton, Velocette, and other machines, Triumph was still widely regarded as a maker of solidly built motorcycles that offered great value to the customer. Nothing fancy or world-beating came from Priory Street.

That was, at least, the popular perception of the day. However, during the next few years, Triumph enlisted the services of two of motorcycling's most brilliant designers. Their bikes were about to change in a big way.

SPEED TWIN AND TIGER 100

By the late 1920s, Triumph's business focus had swung dramatically from two wheels to four. Claude Holbrook had convinced his boss, Siegfried Bettmann, that Triumph could compete with Ford's revolutionary Model T and its British imitator, the Austin Seven. To separate cars and bikes, they formed the Triumph Motor Car Co. to join the existing Triumph Cycle Co.

Triumph's first automobile in 1923 was a success, mainly due to its sub-£200 (about $1,000) price and its frugal Ricardo-designed 1.4-liter engine. Holbrook quickly expanded the car range. In 1927 he launched the 832-cc Triumph Super Seven, the first British light car with hydraulic brakes. Other models with larger engines followed, but car development costs quickly gobbled up Triumph's profits.

At the same time, motorcycle sales were booming. The company's bike output had risen to 30,000 machines per year, and Triumph's reputation for solid engineering continued to grow. Triumph's motorcycle profile was boosted by Tom Simister's third place in the 1927 Isle of Man Senior TT, on an ohv TT-model production racer prepped by the factory.

In 1929, British motorcycle registrations set a record that wouldn't be surpassed for two decades, but the stock market crash that October changed everything. Suddenly, Triumph found itself struggling to hold on. The increasingly dire situation prompted Lloyd's Bank, a major Triumph creditor, to take charge of its investment. With the support of Triumph's board of directors, the bank moved forcefully. First it demoted Triumph founder Siegfried Bettmann, who was now 71 years old, from managing director to vice chairman. The bank then assumed operational control of the company and promoted Holbrook to assistant managing director.

Now it was time to cut costs. Holbrook sold off Triumph's bicycle plant to Downes, another Coventry firm that was later absorbed by Raleigh. In 1932, Holbrook decided to recruit a new chief motorcycle designer to replace A.A. Sykes, who had created the company's range of "sloper" singles as well as some of its car models. Holbrook's choice was Valentine Page, one of Britain's leading motorcycle engineers.

THE SPEED TWIN'S FOREFATHER

Triumph's landmark 1937 parallel twin was spawned from the Ariel Square Four, another famous engine designed by Edward Turner. In late 1928, Turner worked as development engineer in the drawing office of Jack Sangster's Ariel factory in Birmingham. Turner sketched a drawing of an ingenious four-cylinder engine and proposed it to Sangster, who readily approved. Soon, Turner began developing the four-cylinder unit with chief designer Val Page and draftsman Bert Hopwood, two men who would play key roles in the development of Triumph's twins and those of BSA and Norton.

The Square Four featured two crankshafts set in tandem and situated transversely in the motorcycle's frame. The cranks were coupled together by large, straight-cut gears located between the crankpins. All four cylinder barrels were set in a monobloc iron casting and capped by a detachable iron cylinder head featuring hemispherical combustion chambers. Effectively, it was like two parallel twin-cylinder engines mated together. A horizontally split crankcase also carried the engine's oil supply.

The Square Four began life at 500-cc, with a chain-driven single overhead camshaft and roller-bearing big ends on the connecting rods. It was so compact that it slotted into the frame of Ariel's big single! Best of all, the Square Four was torquey and smooth. Its power pulses were smaller and less frequent than those of a twin or

single. The two 180-degree crankshafts (their crankpins spaced 180 degrees apart, so one piston is at top dead center while the other is at bottom dead center) effectively canceled out primary piston inertia forces. Magazine road testers loved it, noting that the engine's secondary vibrations were about the same as a typical four-cylinder car engine.

The Square Four debuted as the star of the 1930 Olympia Motorcycle Show in London. One year after the stock market crash was hardly the right time to launch a big, expensive touring bike, but once its overheating problems were cured, the Square Four quickly became a status machine and a premier sidecar hauler for members of the public who could actually afford one.

The Square Four was steadily evolved. It was stretched to 600-cc then redesigned more along the lines of Triumph's twin, with vertically split crankcases, pushrod valvegear, plain rod bearings, and dry-sump lubrication. It grew to 1,000 cc in the late 1930s and gained an aluminum cylinder block and head after World War II.

Quiet, comfortable, heavy, and exclusive, the big Ariel that started the vertical-twin revolution remained in production through 1958. About 16,000 Square Fours were built, and the engine design was resurrected in the late 1970s by Suzuki, which used it in two-stroke form to win (with rider Barry Sheene) a pair of 500-cc Grand Prix World Championships.

Turner began designing his smooth, compact Ariel Square Four in 1928, spurred by increasing demand for sophisticated, high-performance machines. It was built from 1931 to 1958 in three different engine sizes (500-cc, 600-cc and 1,000-cc) and with sohc and pushrod valve gear. Shown is a 1,000-cc ohv engine from 1940. Note geared crankshafts. Lindsay Brooke archive

Page was a tremendous hire for Triumph. In the early 1920s, while head of design at engine maker J.A.P., he had developed an overhead-cam 350 that set many records at Brooklands. He also had designed a desmodromic valve-gear setup that never entered production. From 1925 until his hire by Triumph, Page had worked at Ariel, where he thoroughly revamped that company's entire model range, added a four-valve single, and prepared the radical 1930 Square Four for production.

Holbrook's aim in landing Page was to modernize Triumph's motorcycle range, which Page did swiftly. Of the previous-generation machines, Page kept only one—the 150-cc Type XO. Everything else was replaced with a new lineup of singles that applied the same engineering principles that Page had proven successful at Ariel. The 18 new-for-1934 models were simple, reliable products that were easily maintained. Their engines, both overhead-valve and sidevalve types, used gears on the timing side to drive the magdyno and double-plunger oil pumps, which became a Triumph feature for decades; their cast-iron cylinder heads were Triumph's first with fully enclosed valve gear.

The iron cylinder barrels were a new type that Triumph highlighted in its advertising. The jugs were specially hardened and oil-tempered to give a better frictional surface, better ring sealing, and an longer life. The bikes' rugged frames featured large, machined lugs and massive tubes.

Page designed the new 500-cc "Mark 5" ohv singles as a range that could satisfy the requirements and pocketbooks of many customers, with minimal changes to the production line. (In this regard, Page pioneered the modular concept of design used by Triumph today.) The 5/2 was the standard no-frills model. One step up from it in price was the 5/4, basically a deluxe version of the 5/2 with a chrome tank and headlight. Then came the 5/5 sports version. The /5 option designated high-compression pistons, a hot cam, and polished ports, and was available on all 250-cc, 350-cc, and 500-cc singles. Topping the range was the 5/10, a twin-port production racer. All of the 1934 Triumphs were still behind the times with their standard hand-shifted gearboxes, though a foot-shift option was available at the cost of £1 (about $5).

Solid and durable, if not exciting performers, the Page 250-cc, 350-cc, 500-cc, and 550-cc machines helped stabilize the motorcycle division's finances. To keep costs down, they shared many common parts among model lines. Thus, the 350-cc and 500-cc overhead-valve singles were essentially the same motorcycle, except for their engines.

Page, however, was only beginning. The 41-year-old had a surprise up his sleeve—a new, large-capacity twin whose inspiration would come from his work at Ariel.

The First 650-cc Twin

Page's brain must have been swimming in calculations the day he witnessed the prototype Square Four on the dynamometer. Immediately after joining Triumph and starting on the new single-cylinder range, he began drawing up a 650-cc vertical twin.

The Model 6/1 was designed specifically for sidecar duty. It was built like a Clydesdale rather than a racehorse. Everything about the bike was large—from its vertically split crankcase containing a 7-pint oil tank to its cast-iron top-end with separate left and right cylinder heads. Even the helical-geared primary drive and nine-plate clutch were oversized. Unlike Page's new Triumph singles, the 6/1 used a single-plunger oil pump. It did, however, have a unitized gearbox—an advanced feature for the period.

When the 6/1 was introduced in August 1933, most machines were 500-cc or smaller. Page was twenty years ahead of his time with his new 650 twin, but he probably sized it as a more economical alternative for sidecarists than the 1,000-cc fours and V-twins of the period.

The bike itself worked well. In 1981, journalist Peter Watson sampled a 1935 restored solo model, one of the very few 6/1s in existence, for a *Classic Bike* magazine road test:

The 6/1 certainly packs a punch. On smooth roads the vertical twin feels superbly comfortable and has brakes quite powerful enough to restrain its 412 pounds. A fair amount of vibration comes through the handlebar, but once you're up to 60 miles per hour that really smoothes out . . . an abundance of low-down torque, and the one-down, three-up gearbox feels fine if you take your time.

Watson also noted the engine's valve clatter due to its exposed rocker gear, which was an unusual oversight of Page's, who generally made certain Triumph's singles had enclosed valves. Watson's overall impression was of a motorcycle with delightful power characteristics.

The 6/1 earned a reputation as a solidly built sidecar tug. It won a gold medal in the 1933 International Six Days Trials sidecar class, the year all eleven Triumph entries finished with gold or silver medals. The same year, a 6/1 sidecar rig won the coveted Maudes Trophy, covering 500 miles in less than 500 minutes at Brooklands. It also was victorious in the sidecar class of Italy's epic Milan-Rome-Naples Road Race, averaging 50.4 miles per hour over 500 miles. A modified 6/1, sleeved down to 500-cc and fitted with a Zoller rotary-vane supercharger, lapped Brooklands at more than 105 miles per hour.

This is the bike that designer Val Page envisioned in 1932 when he left Ariel to join Triumph. The Model 6/1, a 650-cc vertical twin, was introduced at a time when most big-bore bikes were either V-twins or fours. Designed as a sidecar hauler, the 412-pound machine was a commercial failure. It was expensive to produce, and fewer than 500 examples were built between August 1933 and late 1936. Model 6/1 features included linked brakes with hefty 8-inch drums and a ratcheted "parking brake" for the rear wheel. The four-speed gearbox gained a foot-shift mechanism in 1935, the year this restored example was built. In 1933, a 6/1 with sidecar won a silver medal at the ISDT. It then covered 500 miles in 500 minutes at Brooklands, netting Triumph the Maudes Trophy. *EMAP archive*

The 6/1 engine's bore and stroke measured 70x84 mm. It was a massive unit, with a huge crankcase containing a 7-pint oil tank. Among the few similarities with Turner's later Speed Twin were a 360-degree crankshaft and vertically split crankcases. The large flywheel runs on the outside of the left-hand case, and the single camshaft sat behind the cylinders, like postwar BSA and Norton twins. Primary drive was by double-helical gears—the engine ran "backward."
Mick Woollett archive

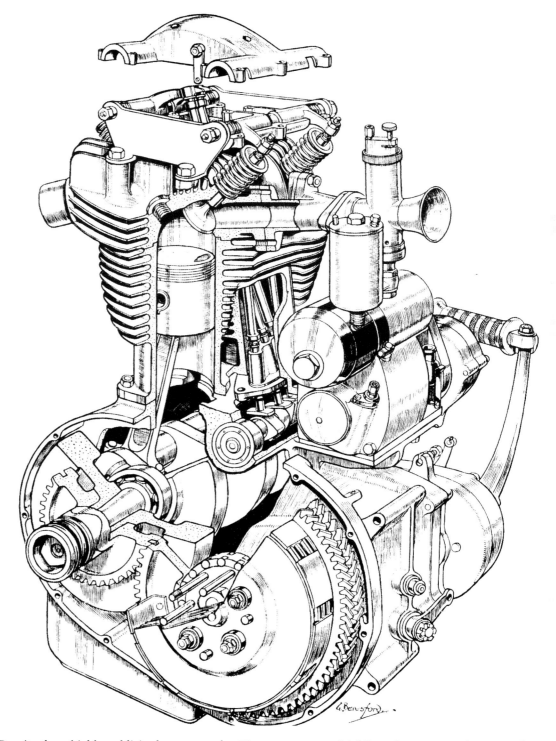

Despite these highly publicized successes, the 6/1 was a commercial failure. It was expensive to produce, because it did not share its chassis and running gear with other models. The price was £76 (roughly $400) in 1934, the same as Turner's Speed Twin four years later. Exactly how many 6/1s were built during the model's three-year production run is debated today. Depending on whose research is used, totals range from less than 100 to about 600, making the 6/1 among the rarest of Triumphs.

Besides bringing workmanlike, if not beautiful, designs to Triumph, Page brought higher standards to the company's design office. From his years at Ariel, Page learned the importance of making highly detailed original drawings, ones so comprehensive that they required far less cleaning up before being passed to the production department. This saved time on any new motorcycle project, and it also laid the groundwork for Edward Turner's arrival a few years later.

When judging Triumph's Val Page-era motorcycles today, it is easy to conclude that Page's one real weakness was that he lacked the artist's flair. His quiet, scholarly demeanor may have been manifest in the bikes he created. They were all about reliability and value-for-money, not style.

What Page lacked in aesthetics, Turner soon made up for on the Tiger singles and Speed Twin. "It was often left to others to make the best of Page's motorcycles, but his basic designs sold in the hundreds of thousands," observed Ariel historian Jim Lee in a 1983 *Classic Bike* magazine feature. Among those designs was the immortal postwar BSA Gold Star.

Two Model 6/1 twins, one with a Triumph-made "chair," heading for adventure in this June 20, 1934, magazine cover. For years, Britain's weekly motorcycle magazines "sold" their covers to the motorcycle companies as advertising. The companies vied for the coveted magazine covers, in particular those big-selling issues reporting the Isle of Man TT and major motorcycle shows like Olympia and Earls Court.

The Model 2/1 was a 250-cc twin-port single designed by Val Page as an affordable commuter bike. It produced a claimed 13 horsepower at 5,200 rpm, offered 100-mile per gallon fuel economy at a steady 40 miles per hour, and had a top speed of about 65 miles per hour. This unmolested 1936 example, owned by U.S. Triumph restoration expert Mike Benolken, is an early foot-shift version. The 250 was also available as the Model 2/5, with chromed fuel tank and headlamp. In 1937, Edward Turner transformed them into the jewel-like Tiger 70. *Jeff Hackett*

Company Woes

If the lackluster Model 6/1 twin did nothing else in 1934 and 1935, it briefly thrust Triumph out of its single-cylinder shackles. But even as Page's new offerings kept the motorcycle side of the company profitable, they couldn't protect Triumph from mistakes on the car side. Bettmann and Holbrook were preparing to cease production of small, family cars and move into larger, more powerful models. For 1934, the year Triumph cars won the International Alpine Rally, they planned a bona fide sports car, the Gloria Dolomite, which was basically a copy of Alfa Romeo's fabulous 8C roadster and was powered by a 2.3L straight-eight engine. In exchange for rights to the 8C's design, the deal called for Triumph to provide Alfa with license to produce the 6/1 twin in Italy.

At least that was what Holbrook hoped for. Fewer than six of the supersport Glorias were built before the bottom fell out of Triumph. The company was gushing red ink, mainly from losses on the car side. The Dolomite project merely quickened the flow.

The 1936 Model 5/10 was Triumph's 500-cc single-cylinder road racer built for the clubman. It was a continuation of the factory-team racers the company had entered in the disastrous 1934 Isle of Man TT—all three bikes failed to finish. The 5/10 featured 8-inch brakes from the 6/1 twin, lightened and polished engine internals, a machined steel con-rod, and 7:1 compression. The bike could be ordered with a choice of gearing and either 3- or 4-gallon gas tanks. *Mick Woollett archive*

The Lloyd's Bank overseers decided to end Triumph motorcycle production, sell the Priory Street factory, and focus the company's resources on automobile production at another plant in Coventry. That operation would be run by Holbrook, who had completely lost interest in motorcycles. Just before all of that happened, however, a savior entered the picture—a dynamic businessman named Jack Sangster.

The Triumph Engineering Co., Ltd.

In 1932, Sangster had taken over Ariel when the Birmingham-based motorcycle and car manufacturer run by his family for over 30 years was in equally grim financial straits. When he heard that Triumph was for sale, Sangster immediately broke the news to Ariel's chief designer, Edward Turner. Together they discussed a takeover plan.

Turner later claimed in an interview that it was he who suggested purchasing the ailing company to his boss. He also claimed to have insisted that Sangster get the Triumph name along with the rest of the motorcycle assets. Holbrook initially did not want the company name included in the deal, because he didn't want a Triumph badge on any product other than his cars.

Sangster made a bid, and in January 1936 he acquired Triumph's motorcycle operation for a reported £41,000—at the time about $220,000. Holbrook would remain with Triumph's car business, which became a totally separate company. Digging up a name that Siegfried Bettmann had first registered in 1906, Sangster immediately christened his new company The Triumph Engineering Co., Ltd., in order to differentiate it from Holbrook's carmaking firm. Then Sangster made two brilliant personnel moves.

First, he asked the elderly Bettmann to become chairman over a brief transition period. Having the man who forty-nine years earlier founded Triumph serve as its figurehead helped give the revived company credibility with its suppliers and dealers. Sangster's second important move was to appoint Edward Turner director, general manager, and chief designer. In addition to a salary, his contract gave him 5 percent of the company's net profits and 4.9 percent of its share equity—slices of the pie that would grow over the next decades and make Turner a very wealthy man.

Buying Triumph was no easy undertaking. Despite his assets and background, Sangster needed heavy financial backing by Lloyd's Bank to pull it off. "We leased the factory, and the plant," recalled Turner years later. "We didn't buy any spares; we agreed to sell them on commission. In other words, the capital venture was reduced to an absolute minimum. And I found myself sitting in the chair, gathering all the pieces together to see what I was going to do with it."

Among the most important pieces were the men who would play influential roles in the British motorcycle industry for the next four decades. One was Jack Wickes, a 21-year-old who worked in the blueprint department. Wickes had taken college engineering classes and was a natural artist. He was preparing to leave the reformed company when Turner convinced him to stay and become his personal assistant. It was one of the best moves the Triumph chief ever made.

"Jack's role was to transform Edward's sketches into finished artwork and contribute styling ideas of his own—for which he never received credit," explained Turner biographer Jeff Clew, in a 1999 *Classic Motorcycle* feature. Turner often referred to Wickes as "my pencil"—high praise from such a difficult boss. Wickes stayed at Triumph as chief stylist until the mid-1970s. He is credited with many of the details that made the bikes so enduringly beautiful, including the classic headlamp nacelle, various tank badges, and trim and paint schemes.

The other key person was Bert Hopwood, the skilled engineer who had followed Turner from Ariel to Triumph. It was up to Hopwood to take Turner's initial designs and rationalize them for production within very tight cost confines.

Turner, of course, would head the design department as well as manage the company, with Val Page having left Triumph for BSA four months earlier. To meet the first week's payroll, Turner had to overdraw the company's bank account. Even then, workers were asked to accept reduced wages.

"That," he said plainly, "was the beginning of the new Triumph, The Triumph Engineering Co., Ltd."

Ripe for a New Model

Triumph's brush with death, and its rescue by Sangster, happened during an alarming period for Britain's motorcycle industry. The use of its products was rapidly declining. From a peak of about 730,000 machines registered for use in 1930, five years later the total number had dropped to 516,000, according to records of the British Cycle and Motorcycle Manufacturers and Traders Union. As well, motorcycle use continued to fall. By 1938, just over 462,000 bikes were on the road.

Meanwhile, car ownership was rising steadily. As the Great Depression began to ease in 1935, jobs and money slowly returned. But motorcycle sales didn't. The Depression had created a glut of cheap secondhand cars in England, just as it did in the United States. Inexpensive Austins and Morrises cost little more to purchase and operate than all but the smallest motorcycles. Many people who had commuted by motorcycle or sidecar rig were not motorcycle enthusiasts. They realized there was far more value in a vehicle that carried four people and also kept them warm and dry in the bleak British weather.

To make matters worse for the industry, motorcycle exports outside the British Empire were also in a tailspin. They'd hit a wall of tariffs erected by countries frightened by the economic slump. In those markets that remained open, German "dumping" of small-displacement bikes was forcing British makers to slash prices. Led by DKW, NSU, and Zündapp and driven by Nazi ambitions, the Germans boosted their exports nearly sixfold between 1935 and 1937.

Britain's motorcycle industry was hurting, but not for lack of creativity. Eleven different four-cylinder bikes were displayed at the 1935 Olympia Motorcycle Show in London, including Matchless' V-4 Silver Hawk, which featured futuristic cantilever rear suspension and linked brakes. Brough Superior's SS100 V-twin was already the

Polished cases, Silver Sheen paint lined in blue pinstriping, chrome fuel tanks, single-downtube frames, rounded oil tanks, and enclosed valvegear—Triumph's luscious Tiger 70, 80, and 90 singles wowed the public in 1937. All were available in either high- or low-pipe versions. This 1938 factory ad artwork shows the 350-cc Tiger 80. *David Gaylin archive*

TRIUMPH TIGER "80"

350 c.c. O.H.V.

PRICE: £60

Fully equipped with Lucas Magdyno Lighting and Electric Horn.

A Smith illuminated Chronometric Trip Speedometer (80 m.p.h.) will be supplied unless otherwise ordered, £2-10-0 extra.

superbike of the era, though it was soon to be challenged by Philip Vincent's mighty Series A 1,000-cc HRD Rapide. And Triumph's experimental shop was playing with overhead cams and hydraulically actuated valvegear.

Innovation was thriving on the racetrack too. Though Triumph had quietly exited the racing scene after its dismal showing at the 1934 Isle of Man TT, when all three team bikes failed to finish, British firms AJS, Norton, and Velocette were locked in an escalating war of speed and technology with their German and Italian rivals. Sophisticated designs that were built to win Continental Grands Prix sported double overhead camshafts, liquid cooling, and superchargers. BMW's racers pioneered the hydraulically damped telescopic front fork, its clean design influenced by aircraft landing gear struts. Gilera's transverse, dohc four-cylinder rocketships made 65 horsepower and revved to nearly 9,000 rpm.

It was all exciting stuff, and it riveted motorcyclists who stayed informed with the two leading magazines of the day, Britain's *Motor Cycling* and *The Motor Cycle*. Yet for all but the wealthiest riders, the majority of new bikes rolling out of the factories were slogging sidevalve or overhead-valve singles, or nasty little two-strokes. The British consumer, barely out of economic peril, remained tightfisted with his motoring cash. If he couldn't swing a used car, then an old-fashioned, workaday 250-cc to 500-cc single seemed to best fit his needs. Indeed, the thumper was so established as the body and soul of English motorcycling that many riders were suspicious of alternative designs.

EDWARD TURNER, GENIUS

It may have been preordained that Edward Turner would become synonymous with a motorcycle company recognized as a twentieth century styling leader, as his maternal grandparents were London coachbuilders. As a young boy visiting their workplace one day in 1908, he was fascinated by the graceful curves of the carriages he saw in the shop. Three decades later, his innate creativity made Triumphs the most coveted mass-produced motorcycles in the world.

At 17, Turner lied about his age and joined the British merchant marine, shipping out as a radioman during World War I. After the war, he tried being a theater singer. But his interests changed abruptly when his brother bought a Harley-Davidson twin. Motorcycles became the centerpoint of his life. Turner became a regular at the Brooklands speed circuit in the 1920s, and developed into a skilled rider. Savings from his sailor's pay were used to open a South London motorcycle shop. Known alternatively as Chepstow Motors or The Turner Equipment Company, it was there that he designed and built his first motorcycle, a 350-cc ohc single. Turner made all of the drawings and machined his own components. At least three complete Turner bikes were produced, and one of them was mentioned in a 1925 article in *The Motor Cycle*.

By 1927, Turner had become a Velocette dealer and was racing one of the company's singles. Soon after he married, he moved to the industrial Midlands and pitched his design talents to Jack Sangster at Ariel. A decade later, his Speed Twin turned the motorcycle world on its ear.

Turner was an enigma. He could be utterly charming one moment, tyrannical the next. He was inherently defensive, which caused him to browbeat subordinates, including his top engineers. "This was despite (or perhaps because of) the fact that he actually relied on them heavily, in a field where engineering flaws put lives at risk," reckoned Steve Wilson, author of the comprehensive *British Motorcycles Since 1950* book series. Turner often jealously referred to his graduate engineers as "you academics," and although he loved to show junior draftsmen his ability to read a micrometer, he would frequently overrule men who knew the real solutions.

As Soichiro Honda did years later at his company, Turner brought a design dictatorship to Triumph that lasted until his retirement in 1964. Turner specified everything, from each model's paint colors to the design of Triumph's annual Earls Court show stand. Also like Honda and a few other industry giants, his mercurial mood struck fear into his employees.

Triumph's former adveritsing manager, Ivor Davies, wrote in a 1978 *Classic Bike* profile of Turner:

Whenever Turner's secretary phoned down to the Triumph experimental shop to announce that the great man wanted to test ride a particular model,

Triumph managing director and chief designer Edward Turner was a tyrannical genius. He ran Triumph for 26 years and built a legend. He's shown here in the early 1950s with American Bobby Turner (no relation), who'd just set U.S. speed records at over 135 miles per hour on a modified Thunderbird. David Gaylin archive

the effect was like an electric charge jolting the department. Section head Frank Baker would rush to alert the fitters: "Edward's coming down!," and the appropirate machine would be placed ready for Turner's arrival, which would be broadcast by the slamming of doors as he strode down the corridor toward the shop. Often hatless, he would then hurtle off on the bike at breakneck speed along the road leading to the village of Meriden 2 miles away.

And if Turner was dissatisfied with the machine, and there was no one to take the bike from his hands on his return to the factory, it was not unknown for him to simply step off the motorcycle, wantonly allowing it to crash to the ground.

Don Brown, the dynamic American who headed Triumpn's western U.S. sales in the late 1950s and early 1960s, knew Turner well. He recalls that in the head office at the factory, the boss's desk sat on a raised platform. "That way, when you walked in to see him, it seemed like he was peering down on you," Brown laughs. "It was imposing whe you walked in there."

The Triumph boss's lack of formal engineering training was very obvious to the real engineers who worked with him, including Bert Hopwood an later, Doug Hele. They considered most of his engine designs to be overstressed, in part because of his twin obsessions: light weight and low cost. Many of his "low-cost" designs, such as the infamous Sprung Hub, would end up costing Triumph more in the long run, through warranty claims, than if the costlier alternative had been selected in the first place.

Turner's guiding principle was "making the minimum amount of metal perform the maximum amount of duty," noted Mike Estall in his definitive *Triumph Tiger Club Bible*. Certainly this dogma served Triumph well in many areas, but sometimes it also came back to haunt both the customer and the company. Those who worked with him over the years admitted that Turner's talents were multifaceted. He certainly was a master stylist, salesman, and businessman. With few mechanical changes to Page's single-cylinder models and keen eye for line, color balance, and overall form, Turner accomplished one of the most important facelifts of an entire model range in motorcycle history.

Perhaps most important for Triumph, Turner's vision in the late 1930s to gain a beachhead in the lucrative American market led to his close friendship with Bill Johnson, founder of Trimph's western U.S. distributorship.

Edward Turner's brilliance was best described by Bert Hopwood in his book, *Whatever Happened To The British Motorcycle Industry?*. "He had a flair for pleasing shapes, and the ability to 'smell out' what the buying public would accept," wrote his former colleague.

One long look at a classic Triumph twin on its sidestand proves the enduring strengh of Turner's talent.

Progress, as seen on the show room floor in mid-1930s Britain, was measured incrementally. None of the high-profile premium and exotic machines was a commercial success. Clearly the industry was ripe for a fresh sort of motorcycle, one that would fill a huge gap in the market, attract new buyers, and invigorate the business.

Turner boldly turned Triumph around almost overnight. First, he axed unprofitable models, including the short-lived 6/1 650-cc twin. Second, he restyled Val Page's range of singles. These reliable performers already looked outdated. Revamping the lineup, Turner found many places to slash costs, through even more use of common components. He settled on just two types of frames, two types of front fork, and one basic gearbox for the entire range. Finally, and most importantly, he began to develop an all-new motorcycle.

Throwing himself into the job, Turner worked 18- and 19-hour days in a small design office set up near the factory's assembly area. "I never stopped working before midnight," he told interviewer Jim Lee in 1973. "My poor first wife used to come in and see me over the drawing board, because I was running the business during the day, supervising the drawing office over stuff that was coming along, then going back and making my sketches at night. It was quite a business and very enjoyable."

He pushed engineer Bert Hopwood and a trio of draftsmen as hard as he pushed himself. When they were finished for the 1936 model year, the company's overhead-valve singles—the humdrum 250-cc Model 2/1, 350-cc

The 1939 Tiger 80 on test for *Classic Bike* magazine. Turner's styling magic still draws crowds whenever these prewar Tigers are ridden today. *EMAP archive*

Model 3/2, and 500-cc Model 5/5 (all of which had won gold medals in that year's International Six-Days Trials)—were transformed into the 2H, 3H, and 5H and their sporting counterparts, the Tiger 70, 80, and 90.

Turner had made the entire range look lithe and handsome by replacing the old sheet metal with more rakish forms. His masterpiece, and the bikes' focal point, was a new teardrop fuel tank, nicely rounded in front and tapering sensuously back to the saddle. The tank's proportions were perfect, blending with the glamorous buffed primary and timing-gear covers. The voluptuous tank helped establish the often imitated, but never duplicated, Triumph look.

The Tiger models were stunners. Their tanks were chrome plated, and their side panels painted in lustrous silver sheen enamel and outlined with twin blue coach lines. Just the name, Triumph Tiger, was a big boost for the company's dealers and image.

"Let out the clutch, crack open the throttle and the 20-horsepower engine pulls impressively," wrote Sean Hawker, who tested a restored Tiger 80 for *Classic Bike* magazine in 1995. The test Tiger reached about 75 miles per hour and Hawker was impressed by the bike's agility—a combination of its 330-pound mass and 52.5-inch wheelbase. He also commented favorably on the 7-inch brakes' performance. Period magazine tests on the new Tiger quoted a stopping distance of 36 feet from 30 miles per hour, using only the front brake on wet concrete.

The differences among members of the Tiger family were minor. The same basic chassis carried three different fuel tanks: 2.75 gallons on the Tiger 70, 3.0 gallons on the Tiger 80, and 3.25 gallons on the Tiger 90. Both the T80 and T90 came with a tank-top mounted instrument panel, a feature the little Tiger 70 was initially without. All wore 3.0x20-inch tires in front, and 3.50x19-inch tires in the rear. Buyers had a choice of single- or twin-port cylinder heads, high-level or low exhaust pipes, and either street tread or knobby tires.

In his *Classic Bike* test, Hawker made a critical observation that probably jived with the popular conception of Triumph's sporting singles during their heyday. "The 350 is arguably the Tiger to go for," he noted. "The 250 is on the slow side, and the 500 has a longer wheelbase, 45 extra pounds, and a half-inch less ground clearance." It also cost more and offered only 8 more horsepower, not enough to make up for its extra heft.

Triumph still produced both sidevalve and ohv "cooking" singles, for those looking for simple, practical transportation without the Tigers' flash and added cost. Perhaps the most popular was the 3H—the T80's plain-clothed brother. Unlike the Tiger, the 3H's fuel tank was painted silver with cherry red panels, rather than chromed. It had unpolished ports, ran a modest 6:1 compression ratio instead of 7.5:1, and was available with either magneto or coil ignition. The machine was sold through 1940, when it donned olive drab paintwork and became the 3HW (the W for War Department), a favorite of British Army dispatch riders.

But it was the dazzling Tiger range, particularly the T80 and T90, that became the industry's most talked-about models in 1936 and 1937. Thanks to Turner's styling magic, Triumph production had jumped to over 6,000 bikes per year, more than double the output for 1933. These, though, were really only stopgaps, a temporary step for Turner while he prepared his bombshell.

Turner's Strokes of Genius: The 1938 Speed Twin

The project that preoccupied Turner during 1936 and 1937 was aimed at replacing the Tiger singles and their many competitors as motorcycling's most popular type. Indeed, the classic overhead-valve, long-stroke single was still the engine to beat. It was simple, compact, tractable, inexpensive to make and operate, and relatively light in weight. It had stood the test of time. Yet in Turner's eyes, it was the same old thing.

The 1938 Speed Twin, also known as the 5T, proved that Turner could do better. Stylish, light, responsive, smooth, and refined, the Speed Twin changed the direction of motorcycle design and dominated it for 30 years. Until the advent of Honda's CB750 Four in 1969, Triumph's twin and its many progeny owned motorcycling.

The Triumph "was a perfect example of the right design at the right time," noted motorcycle historian Edward Tragatsch in his 1977 book, *The Illustrated Encyclopedia Of Motorcycles.* "It was the first commercially successful vertical twin." Added Ivor Davies, who worked at Triumph for over 30 years, "The genius of (Turner) was that from the side, the Speed Twin looked just like a twin-port single, which were ten a penny in those days. Motorcyclists don't like fancy designs, so the clean way he designed the Speed Twin got over any suggestions of it being unconventional. It looked just like what they'd always been buying. But it went so much better than the singles that it was an instant success."

A 500-cc parallel twin has firing impulses that are half as strong, and arrive twice as often, as those of a 500-cc single. It also offers a shorter stroke. Both characteristics benefit smoothness, particularly at low and mid rpm. "To make a more powerful single, you have to make the displacement bigger, and firing impulses become more obvious and less comfortable," reasons motorcycle engineering writer Kevin Cameron. In a 1999 article in *Vintage Bike,* the Triumph International Owners' Club magazine, Cameron explained that a twin also offers greater overall valve area than a comparable one-lunger—and with the shorter stroke, that means more airflow and higher rpm potential.

Turner's drawings showed that a parallel twin with vertical cylinders could slot right into the existing Tiger 90 single-cylinder frame. Not having to tool-up a new chassis for the new engine would save Triumph money—something Turner liked very much. He also chose a 360-degree firing order for his new twin. In this layout, which Val Page had employed in the 6/1, both crankpins are side by side, so both pistons rise and fall together. The cylinders fire alternately, their impulses evenly spaced at 360 degrees of crankshaft rotation.

The new engine's crankshaft was a three-piece unit, with forged web/crankpins bolted to a large central flywheel. The crank was supported in the vertically split cases by hefty 2 3/4-inch ball bearings on each side.

"It is interesting to note that the new attempts at vertical twins are meeting with success and, in my opinion, they cannot fail to be better than the single," commented veteran British motorcycle engineer Granville Bradshaw in a 1938 issue of *The Motor Cycle*. "It is a bit sad, of course, that they have to retain the balance of the single cylinder by the two pistons rising and falling together, but this appears to be better than one up and one down, with irregular firing impulses."

Why Turner rejected a 180-degree firing order for his new twin was never recorded. A 180-degree parallel-twin crank has its crankpins on opposite planes—one piston is up while the other is down. Each cylinder's firing impulses are spaced unevenly, at 180 degrees and 540 degrees of crankshaft rotation. This layout tends to give greater low-speed shakes than the 360-degree type, making the motorcycle buzzier around town.

Both configurations have their drawbacks. Given similar displacements, neither holds a clear edge in overall smoothness. Anyone who has ridden a 1970s Triumph Daytona with 360-degree crank and a Honda CB450 (which used the 180-degree system) back-to-back can attest to this.

Perhaps to Turner's ears, the 360-degree twin's throaty exhaust note was superior to a 180-degree twin's staccato tone. Its intake timing worked well with a single carburetor. But with its pistons pumping up and down together, Turner's 500 twin was far from silky as the revs increased. To minimize the vibration, Turner knew he had to keep reciprocating mass (the weight of the parts moving up and down) as low as possible. So he chose a solution that is still considered radical today: forged aluminum connecting rods.

The accepted material for con-rods used in most car, motorcycle, and aircraft engines is steel. Among its many properties, steel features a threshold of stress resistance known as its fatigue limit. Cameron explains that if stresses applied to the steel part are kept below the fatigue limit, the part will not break in operation. Aluminum, being softer and more ductile, has no fatigue limit, which is why most engine designers don't trust it for highly stressed reciprocating parts like con-rods. The risk of the component failing in operation, particularly at high revs, is greater with aluminum.

Turner thought differently. He may have been influenced by Frank Halford, the same man who helped Harry Ricardo develop the four-valve Triumph single. In 1922 Halford pioneered forged aluminum con-rods and pistons in a 1.5-liter six-cylinder car engine. Halford raced the engine in an Aston Martin at Brooklands during the years Turner frequented the circuit. By 1930, Turner had specified aluminum for the rods of the Ariel Square Four.

For his new parallel twin's con-rods, Turner selected the same alloy used on the Square Four—Hiduminium R.R.56—which was forged to a Rolls-Royce specification (hence the R.R. prefix). Besides saving weight, R.R.56 allowed him to run the big-end directly on the steel crankpin without using a bearing insert. Only the steel bearing cap contained a white-metal Babbitt lining. The heat dissipation properties were excellent, and penny-pinching Turner saved money by eliminating two rod bearings per engine. (The company eventually switched over to replaceable shell-type bearing inserts for all of its engines.)

Ultimately, fatigue was not an issue in Triumph's choice of forged aluminum rods. Virtually every British parallel twin that followed the Speed Twin also featured them, and most held up superbly. Many of those engines have survived a half-century of use and abuse, including racing, and are still going strong.

The Triumph's 498-cc displacement came from a 63x80-mm bore and stroke. Unlike Val Page's earlier 6/1 twin, the Speed Twin featured a one-piece cast-iron cylinder block instead of the 6/1's two-piece affair. It also had separate intake and exhaust camshafts, fitted ahead of and behind the cylinders, rather than a single cam

The 1938 5T Speed Twin, restored by U.S. Triumph experts David Gaylin and Mike Benolken. This early model has the "six-stud" cylinder bolt arrangement that soon proved unreliable—the cylinder blocks tended to lift under sustained high throttle. Two extra studs were added in 1939. Triumph's Amaranth Red paint color (actually a deep brownish red) was a Speed Twin hallmark into the 1950s. It was also used on the 150-cc Terrier single. *Jeff Hackett*

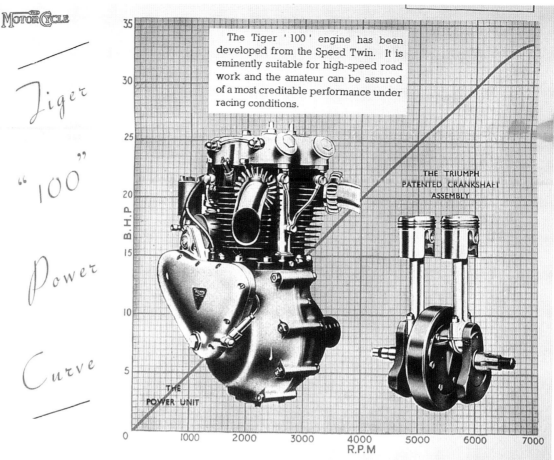

THE MOTOR CYCLE

Tiger "100" Power Curve

The Tiger '100' engine has been developed from the Speed Twin. It is eminently suitable for high-speed road work and the amateur can be assured of a most creditable performance under racing conditions.

THE TRIUMPH PATENTED CRANKSHAFT ASSEMBLY

THE POWER UNIT

like the 6/1. Its iron cylinder head boasted deep hemispherical combustion chambers and was clamped to the cylinder block with six bolts. The earliest examples of the Speed Twin are thus known as "six stud" engines. Flat-top pistons gave a 7.2:1 compression ratio and breathed through a pair of widely splayed overhead valves per cylinder and a slightly downdraft 15/16-inch Amal Type 6 carburetor.

Other equipment included a Lucas magneto, gear driven off the intake camshaft and mounted behind the cylinders; a dry-sump lubrication system, another difference from the 6/1, with a plunger-type oil pump designed by Turner for Ariel's 1929 singles; and a separate four-speed gearbox and wet, multiplate clutch. It also carried over the ratcheting twist-grip from the Tiger singles, which helped ease pressure on the throttle wrist—an early form of cruise control.

To make sure his new engine would stand up in customers' hands, Turner had preproduction versions subjected to a series of four-hour dynamometer runs at 5,800 rpm. He also had a complete motorcycle attached to a loaded sidecar rack up 10,000 miles of durability testing before the still-secret machine was announced to the public in July 1937.

It all added up to a winner. Claimed output was 28 horsepower at 6,000 rpm—four horses more than the 500-cc Tiger 90 single—in a slim package that weighed 5 pounds less overall. Turner's shrewd design and common-parts strategy allowed Triumph to price its landmark twin at only £5 (about $25) more than the single. The payoff was a nimble machine, tractable in all conditions and smooth by the standards of the day. It also achieved a 93.75-mile per hour top speed in a 1937 road test by *The Motor Cycle.* Who could refuse such a blend of style, performance, and value?

"If the general run of production models is around the standard of the machine submitted for test, this new vertical twin will cause a furor," wrote columnist "Torrens" in *The Motor Cycle,* about the Speed Twin he'd tested. The day after the magazine's test bike was returned to Coventry, Torrens received a telephone call from Edward Turner. The designer "wanted to chat the model over." Could the magazine suggest improvements, Turner asked. Only two occurred to Torrens: a brighter bulb in the oil pressure gauge for night riding, and a redirected oil bleed for the drive chain, which had coated the rear of the test bike with Castrol's finest.

Motor Cycling called the Speed Twin one of the two most outstanding new machines of 1938. The other was the 350-cc New Imperial, with its cantilever rear suspension. The writer called the Triumph engine "a delightful and really glorious thing to drive. Its smoothness is fascinating; so is its responsiveness." He went on to praise many other aspects of the Speed Twin, in particular the quieter running and easier starting than most singles offered.

Over a half-century later, motojournalists tested restored examples of the 1938 Speed Twin, and their opinions were also favorable, even with the quantum leaps in motorcycle design, technology, and refinement. "I nervously dropped the clutch and wound open the throttle, expecting the early six-stud engine to either hesitate or blow up," noted *Classic Bike's* Sean Hawker, on his 1993 road test. "Neither happened. Power came in crisp and strong." He was impressed by the bike's predictable handling on smooth surfaces, but panned the puny 7-inch brakes' anemic bite.

Mike Benolken's exquisitely restored 1940 Speed Twin, showing a large 8-inch headlamp and "pedestrian slicer" fender-mounted front license plate. Outer "check" springs on the front fork were new for 1940. *Jeff Hackett*

In a 1999 *Classic Bike Guide* sampling of a freshly restored 5T, Jim Reynolds noted the bike's smoothness up to 60 miles per hour as "a revelation." Reynolds confirmed what numerous testers have said about the early 5T, which he dubbed the "British Standard Twin Cylinder Motorcycle."

Sales of the first Speed Twin in Britain were so brisk that Triumph shut down Tiger 90 production in early 1938 to facilitate production of the new twin, but kept building the smaller sports singles up until the start of World War II. Almost immediately, the model's attributes caught the attention of London's Metropolitan Police, which had a large motorcycle fleet. The cops bought 24 of the early Speed Twins, the first of many thousands of Triumph twins they'd purchase over three decades.

The Speed Twin with separate engine and gearbox—referred to as the "pre-unit" engine—was produced through the end of 1958, when its unit-construction successor (engine and transmission as part of the same casting), the 5TA, was launched. Major engine changes during the pre-unit Speed Twin's 15-year production run (it wasn't built from 1941 to 1945, due to the war) include the addition of two extra cylinder studs in 1939; stronger rods and a new crankshaft in 1951; coil ignition and alternator in 1953; larger crankshaft main journals and con-rod big ends in 1955; and a wider cylinder base flange and crankcase joint in 1956. It never gained an aluminum cylinder head, unlike other Triumph twins. Major chassis changes were the adoption of telescopic forks in 1946, the headlamp nacelle in 1949, and swinging arm rear suspension in 1955.

Triumph's new twin was as slender as the twin-port singles then in vogue. Tank-top instrument panel includes dash light, ammeter, oil pressure gauge, and main switch. Weight with a gallon of oil and no fuel is 370 pounds. *Jeff Hackett*

Two features remained unchanged—the Amaranth Red paint, a deep maroon enamel that was the Speed Twin's signature through 1960, and the overall pleasant demeanor of the bike. While quickly overshadowed by much sportier Triumph models, the Speed Twin always stood for reliable, high-value performance. It was Triumph to a T.

Twin-Cylinder Revolution

The success of the flashy Tiger singles and the new twin's introduction caused Triumph's profits to rebound. The company that had been on its back in 1935 produced a £7,000 (about $35,000) profit in 1937. It earned five times that in 1939, due mainly to the twin's popularity and to Britain's improved economy. The latter was sparked by the drastic rise in defense industry jobs, as Britain prepared for the inevitable war with fascist Germany and Italy.

Output at Triumph's Priory Street factory rose by 75 percent. To accommodate the growth, Jack Sangster expanded the machine shop and office area. Triumph was healthy again, a force to be reckoned with. It proved that there is no substitute for the right product at the right time.

The turnaround fit perfectly into Sangster's grand plan: to build a broad product range that would allow him to challenge industry giant BSA. By 1938, he was on his way. For the lightweight and economy markets he had New Imperial, a marque he'd just saved from bankruptcy. He intended to revamp it, Triumph style. Ariel served as his meat-and-potatoes brand, ranging from commuter bikes up to the flagship 1,000-cc Square Four. And Triumph, while it overlapped some of Ariel's displacement range, would be aimed at sporting riders.

He also had a new market with boundless potential—North America. In the United States, mammoth and crude 750-cc to 1,300-cc Harley-Davidson and Indian V-twins ruled unopposed, save for a handful of British or European models imported by a few scattered dealers or the ultraexclusive Indian Four favored by some police forces. While Triumph already exported to over 25 countries, the huge North American market held the most promise by far.

The United States was ripe for a middleweight, sporting motorcycle. That fact became plain to a few visionary dealers during the 1930s. In New York City, Reggie Pink had been importing AJS, Ariel, BSA, and numerous other British marques since 1926. When Jack Sangster bought Triumph in 1936, Pink's long association with Ariel helped add Triumph to his show room. In 1938, he sold the 250 DeLuxe, the Tiger 80 and 90 singles, and the Speed Twin—the latter priced at $446.46. A year later, Pink offered Triumph's entire 13-model range. Although he was not sanctioned by Triumph as an official distributor, Pink even franchised a few dealers in the eastern states. In the five years prior to World War II, he imported roughly 100 new Triumphs.

In Canada, two main Triumph dealers emerged during the same period. These were Nicholson Brothers in the western provinces and Sammett and Blair in the east. Both had formal ties to the factory. But it was in Pasadena, California, that Triumph really took off in America. Two business partners—Bill Johnson, an attorney, and his friend Wilbur Cedar, an accountant—jumped into the motorcycle business in 1936 when they purchased a tiny shop called British and American Motors, an Ariel-BSA-Indian dealer.

Johnson had been a motorcycle enthusiast ever since he first saw a new Ariel Square Four on the street in Los Angeles. He was so captivated by the big machine that he wrote a letter to Edward Turner in England. It began an everlasting friendship and key business link between the two men.

Which one's prettier—a restored 1940 Tiger 100 or Don Gordon's 1941 Boeing Stearman biplane? The Tiger's "cocktail-shaker" mufflers had removable end-caps to easily convert them into racing megaphones. Every Tiger 100 engine featured hand-polished ports and was dyno tested before leaving the factory. *Jeff Hackett*

Turner had been scouting for a factory distributor in the United States for both Triumph and Ariel, and he sensed Johnson to be a good candidate. The two agreed to do business. After a shaky start, Johnson Motors, Inc., was launched in 1937. First, the shop sold Tiger singles, in addition to Ariels and Indians. Later, in 1938, Johnson and Cedar received their first new Speed Twin, and one of America's most famous vehicle importers—known by its cablegram "JoMo"—was on its way.

Back in England, Turner didn't rest on the Speed Twin's laurels. Even before the bike's debut he had planned his second stroke of genius. Introduced as a 1939 model, the Tiger 100 was a sports version of the 5T. It boasted a higher compression ratio (8.0:1) and forged pistons, polished inlet ports, and a slightly larger (1.0-inch) carburetor. Special exhaust silencers featured removable end caps—a few minutes spent with a screwdriver gave you open megaphones for racing! All of this added up to 8 more horsepower than the Speed Twin and allowed the Tiger to achieve an honest 100-miles per hour top speed with the rider lying flat on the tank.

The T100 cost about $50 more than its softer-tuned brother. And to boost its allure, Turner included a dyno sheet with each bike. This custom touch showed the Tiger's owner how his individual bike's engine had performed on the factory dynamometer. An optional bronze cylinder head, for improved cooling, was available for an additional $31.50.

Aside from its speed equipment, the Tiger 100 was even prettier than the 5T. Its fuel tank panels and fenders were painted in Silver Sheen enamel, outlined in blue pinstriping. The silver color made Turner's twin look even lighter, leaner and more purposeful. Actually, it was the finish of the

Tiger attack! Dave Gaylin (left) and Mike Benolken take their 1940 T100s for a fast ride over rural New Jersey roads. Lucas candlepower is pitiful day or night. *Jeff Hackett*

prototype 5T before Turner finally chose red for the Speed Twin. And the Tiger's performance matched its looks. Modified T100s began scoring competition wins in Britain, Australia, and the United States.

In 1940, the Tiger earned its greatest success, in California, where Johnson Motors-sponsored Bruce "Boo Boo" Pearson won 32 out of 36 half-mile dirt-track and TT races, stunning his Harley- and Indian-mounted competitors. That same year, Canadian racer Chuck Stockey stuffed his new bronze-headed Tiger in the back seat of a Dodge coupe and drove to the Daytona Beach races. He placed second in the amateur 100-mile race, after starting in the eighty-seventh position.

Triumph's twins were the new stars of Britain's motorcycle industry, but many riders remained convinced that single-cylinder machines were more rugged. So to prove the durability of his new products, Turner staged one of the many publicity feats of his career. In March 1939, he pulled a new Speed Twin and Tiger 100 from dealers' stocks and gave the bikes to the Auto-Cycle Union, which sanctioned time trials and competition events. The ACU then subjected the two machines to a thorough flogging on road and track.

The comprehensive endurance run included a 1,912-mile road test through England and Scotland plus a stop at the Brooklands circuit for a sustained six-hour top-speed blast. The bikes survived the punishment with flying colors, their only problems being a flat tire on the T100 and a broken oil line on the Speed Twin. Turner had struck a deal with *Motor Cycling* to cover the test, and he used the magazine's positive report in subsequent factory sales literature.

The success of Triumph's new twins provoked industry giant BSA to react. Soon after the T100 was on sale, BSA began testing a prototype 500-cc parallel twin of its own. It was designed by Val Page and included two features he'd used on Triumph's ill-fated 6/1 twin—a single camshaft set behind the cylinders, and a semi-unit gearbox. But the BSA A7 twin would not reach production until 1946, due to Germany's invasion of Poland in September 1939.

When World War II began, Triumph was riding high. The company held the 350-cc, 500-cc, and 750-cc speed records at the Brooklands circuit. A Triumph single ridden by Allan Jefferies had won both the highly publicized Scottish Six-Days Trials and British Experts Trial, and demand for the new twins was outpacing the Coventry factory's capacity. Triumph had a nine-model product range, but the war temporarily halted the parallel-twin revolution. Like the rest of the British industry, Sangster's businesses joined in military production. An all-new 350-cc vertical twin, planned for 1940 in standard (3T) and sports (Tiger 85) guise, was canceled.

The War Ministry immediately began requisitioning civilian vehicles for military use. Across the British Isles, motorcycles were scooped up for army use, even new machines sitting in show room windows. Among them were more than one thousand new Triumphs awaiting dispatch at the factory. Remarkably, while civilian production for the home market ended with Britain's entry into the war, Triumph continued to build 1940 model Speed Twins and Tiger 100s for its distributors in North America. The two Canadian outlets sold probably at least 200 new Triumphs, most of them twins, before the war. Johnson Motors equaled that number. Indeed, Bill Johnson was selling every Triumph twin he could get.

"We shall be permitted to send to the U.S.A. and Canada, supplies of our twin-cylinder types, which have made so many friends amongst sporting American riders," wrote Edward Turner in a stirring 1940 magazine advertisement. "By this means, we hope to continue our contribution to private motorcycling—the finest of all open-air sports."

The close relationship he'd built with Johnson meant that Johnson was receiving bikes and parts well after the battles in Europe began. However, the supply was cut off on the night of November 14, 1940. That night, a massive 400-plane air attack on Coventry—history's first saturation bombing raid—destroyed or damaged nearly 45,000 homes and much of the city's industry. German Heinkel and Dornier twin-engined bombers turned Triumph's Priory Street works into a grotesque pile of rubble. While the city suffered more than 550 casualties and over 900 were wounded, Triumph's night shift miraculously escaped without casualties. Some of the plant's machine tools were salvaged, and many critical blueprints also survived.

These remnants were taken to a vacant, tin-roofed foundry in the nearby town of Warwick. There a makeshift factory was established. Not even Hitler's Luftwaffe could kill Triumph! Unfortunately, it did succeed in killing the 3TW, a lightweight 350-cc ohv twin that Triumph had just begun producing for the army. The 3TW boasted unit construction, and it was the world's first motorcycle with alternator electrics. When the bombs fell, the initial batch of 50 bikes and the 3TW assembly line were destroyed. The stillborn model (it was to be called the 3T, had the war not intervened) was not continued.

An old joke, probably started at BSA, goes that the night of the air raid, Edward Turner went to the roof of his plant and painted a big white bull's-eye for the German bombardiers. Turner and Sangster certainly knew that British factories destroyed during wartime would be rebuilt with financial help from the government's Ministry of Supply. Though his company did not have the large-scale military contracts of rivals AMC, BSA, and Norton, Sangster still convinced the Ministry that Triumph justified a brand-new plant to continue military output.

So in early 1941, a greenfield site just outside of Coventry, between the hamlets of Meriden and Allesley, was cleared for construction. A year later, Triumph production resumed at the plant, which would later be known as Meriden. In one fell swoop, with help from the Luftwaffe, Jack Sangster and Edward Turner had the most modern motorcycle factory in the world. The plant began making the army-spec 3HW single. Between late 1939 and the war's end, Triumph built nearly 50,000 motorcycles. About 40,000 of them were 3HWs, and most went to the Royal Navy.

The new factory also churned out components for a variety of military vehicles and aircraft. One product was a portable electrical-generator set, powered by a detuned version of the 500-cc Speed Twin engine. The generator unit was designed to be carried by Lancaster bombers for in-flight battery charging. Known in Royal Air Force jargon as the Airborne Auxiliary Power Plant—"A-squared P-squared" to Triumph workers—its cylinder head and block were cast in aluminum alloy. Both castings featured square-sided cooling fins to mount the generator unit's sheet-metal shroud. The lightweight head and block were later used with modification on the factory's first postwar road racer, the 500-cc Grand Prix, as well as the first TR5 Trophy.

Military production had hardly begun again at Meriden when Edward Turner abruptly left Triumph to join BSA's design office. This defection, though never fully explained, reportedly infuriated his boss, Sangster. In his landmark 1981 retrospective, *Whatever Happened to the British Motorcycle Industry?,* Bert Hopwood called the

split "inevitable." Turner had become hostile to Sangster and regarded him as a faceless boss who profited immensely from Turner's talent—even though Turner himself was profiting greatly from Triumph.

At the time, Turner had not recovered emotionally from the death of his first wife, Edith, who was killed in a 1939 car crash. Some who knew him believed this devastating personal tragedy, along with diabetes, was a cause of his irascible behavior. "It may be fair to comment that Turner before 1939 was a different, more dynamic, less cantankerous man than Turner after 1945," notes British university professor Barbara Smith, profiling Turner in the *Dictionary of Business Biography*.

Others disagreed, including Frank Griffiths, who was Turner's chauffeur for more than 20 years. "He never was any different," claimed Griffiths in an interview with journalist Peter Dobson in the 1980s. "(Turner) knew what he wanted and nobody, but nobody, got in his way. He was always impatient and couldn't sit still."

Turner's BSA hiatus lasted only 14 months, long enough to design a military sidevalve 500-cc twin, which was never produced. He also continued design work on the prototype ohv twin that eventually became the BSA A7. When Turner returned to Triumph in 1943, he saw what Hopwood had been designing with an eye to the postwar market. It was a 700-cc four-cylinder machine, with its engine mounted transversely in the frame and a projected 50 horsepower at 6,500 rpm.

In his book, Hopwood claimed that the "handsome and awe-inspiring" bike that preceded Honda's world-beating four by 25 years was even mocked up for Sangster's review. But Turner would have nothing of it, and the project was abandoned. Soon the war would be over. It was time for Triumph's parallel twins to lead the motorcycling world.

Far Left
Two prewar Tiger 100s together is a rare sight today. Mike Benolken restored these bikes as a pair in 1998. While the silver-painted fenders with black center stripe are the correct paint scheme, Dave Gaylin prefers the reversed silver-on-black scheme that Triumph used on its Tiger singles. The Tiger 100 set the standard for every sporting vertical twin to come. *Jeff Hackett*

Based on the prewar Model 3H 350-cc ohv single, the 3HW was Triumph's World War II army bike. A reliable slogger, it weighed 340 pounds and produced about 17 horsepower at 5,200 rpm. Over 40,000 were built in the new Meriden factory between 1942 and 1945. *EMAP archive*

TRIUMPH IN THE 1950s: THE THUNDERBIRD

Armed with the motorcycle industry's most modern factory, its hottest product and its most influential designer, Jack Sangster, made another bold move in late 1944. As Allied armies began their final push into Hitler's Germany, Sangster began meetings with BSA executives for the purpose of selling Ariel Motors and New Imperial. Five years earlier, Sangster had viewed Ariel as his cornerstone for competing with BSA in high volume. Now he put all his faith in the resurgent Triumph.

Ever the dealmaker, Sangster worked the Beeza boys to his advantage. BSA initially offered him £80,000 (nearly $500,000) for the two marques and all their assets, according to historian Steve Koerner, writing in *The Classic Motorcycle.* By the time the deal was inked, Sangster had jacked up the price to £376,000 (almost $2 million) —and he got it. Now he and Turner could focus all their attention on Triumph, which was already gearing up for postwar production. Indeed, Turner announced his company's 1945 civilian model range even before the Allies were within howitzer range of Berlin! In doing so, he got the jump on his British competitors.

"Sangster was particularly interested in expanding sales in the North American market," notes Koerner, "and ensured that Triumph became the spearhead of the motorcycle industry's export drive." In 1945, he sent Turner to visit Bill Johnson in California to get the U.S. ball rolling in earnest.

Triumph charged into 1946 with an entirely twin-cylinder model range. The Speed Twin and Tiger 100 were essentially the same as in 1940 but fitted with the company's new telescopic front fork. They also sported new electrical systems with separate magneto and dynamo. New, too, was a 350-cc vertical twin. The model 3T was styled to look like its larger brothers but was designed for lower-cost production. The cast-iron cylinder head featured integral rocker boxes, and the con-rods were steel, not forged aluminum.

Triumph positioned the 3T as a starter twin and was readying a Tiger 85 sports version. But the 350's sales in all markets were far outpaced by the more powerful and costly Speed Twin, and by 1951 it was gone. The Tiger 85 never entered production.

Also making its appearance in 1946 was the Sprung Hub. Designed by Turner in 1938, it was a full-width rear wheel hub that incorporated its own rudimentary internal suspension. Triumph had prepared to introduce the Sprung Hub in 1940 to counter the growing popularity of the plunger-type rear suspension of other makers, but World War II delayed its debut. According to veteran Triumph service manager John Nelson, Turner's hub design was influenced by the fixed landing gear of the Gloster Gladiator biplane fighter, which used a pair of 16-inch Dowty sprung hubs.

The Triumph hub gave 2 inches of vertical wheel travel. It slotted right into the rear axle dropouts in the existing rigid frame, adding 17 pounds to the weight of the motorcycle but negating the cost of developing a proper swinging-arm rear suspension. That the hub continued as the company's sole means of rear suspension through 1955 (aside from the plunger setup on the Terrier and early Cub singles) was more a testament to Turner's penny-pinching than affirmation of a sound design. Indeed, Triumph lagged behind most of the industry in moving to swinging-arm frames.

British motorcycling writer Peter Dobson quipped that the infamous Sprung Hub "has passed into folklore as a pain at the rear end." In his 1990 *Classic Bike* test of a Hub-equipped 1952 Speed Twin, Dobson found that

The Tiger 100 Grand Prix production racer debuted in 1947, a year after Ernie Lyons won the Manx Grand Prix on a factory-built version. The GP was based on the Tiger 100 bottom end, but used the aluminum square-barrel top end of the lightweight generator engine Triumph produced during wartime. Fewer than 200 GPs were made through 1950, the year American Rod Coates won the Daytona 100-mile amateur race on one. Features on the 310-pound racer included open primary drive, twin carburetors, 4-inch megaphones, 8-inch brakes, sprung rear hub, and aluminum fenders. The tuned 500 was rated at 46 horsepower at 7,200 rpm—good for about 120 miles per hour. *Mick Woollett archive*

Period snapshot of a 1948 Tiger 100 shows Triumph's new telescopic fork—the primary difference between the 1946 to 1948 5T and T100 models and their prewar predecessors. The author's father purchased this bike new from Rod Coates, an independent dealer who later became service manager and racing director in Triumph's eastern U.S. headquarters. Note the convex headlamp lens—some models had flat lenses. *John L. Brooke*

at a normal cruising speed, the bike's rear end felt composed. It gave as decent handling as any Triumph of that era can give and was most comfortable with the added preload of a pillion passenger.

"But if you try to chuck the bike around a bumpy bend, it will yaw and wallow," Dobson reported. In truth, the Sprung Hub was no worse a component than the new Turner-designed fork. Though it was attractive and provided 6 inches of travel, the fork was inferior in performance to virtually every major British telescopic fork of the period, particularly Norton's. Together with the hub, it earned late-1940s and early-1950s Triumphs a reputation for uncertain handling at high speed.

"The postwar Triumphs handled badly, but Turner did not want to know," admitted former Experimental Department head Frank Baker, in a 1993 *Classic Bike* interview. In an effort to convince his boss that they could be dangerous, Ivor Davies, the company's head of advertising and press relations, filmed Baker on a Tiger 100 at high speed. "It was frightening to watch," recalled Baker, "but Turner still would not believe it."

Even with the advent of a proper swinging-arm chassis in 1954 and a few fork upgrades, Triumphs were not considered good handlers, at least when compared with anything other than the poor-handling Harley-Davidsons, until major frame and fork improvements were made in the 1960s.

The Grand Prix Racer

With the rebirth of motorcycle sports after World War II came new opportunities for Triumph's all twin-cylinder model range. The exotic supercharged racers that had ruled European road racing in 1939 were now banned, and high-octane gasoline was scarce. The many forms of motorcycle competition in America and Australia were ripe for light, well-balanced, easily modified, and affordable machines.

The world's first true "dual-purpose" twin was Triumph's TR5 Trophy, a model that was equally at home on-road or off. The original introduced in 1949 (shown) used the same basic square-finned cylinder head casting of the GP, but with a single carb. The 500-cc Trophy remained in Triumph's range until 1971, and was reprised in 1973 as the TR5T. *EMAP archive*

Even if the emergent racing scene held promise for Triumph, Edward Turner seemed to have little of it. His assertion from before the war that his company would not get into "works" road racing for Europe and the Isle of Man still held. No stranger to the paddock himself, Turner knew that to win at the international Grand Prix level required far more costly, purpose-built machines than he was willing to offer. Indeed, Triumph hadn't fielded a full works road-race team since its 1934 Senior TT debacle. "Let Nortons lose their shirt racing," Turner allegedly sniffed.

Motorsports are irresistible to the British, however, and Turner conceded that winning races helps sell the marque in the show room. Immediately he gave off-road trials and scrambles his official blessing. He rehired Allan Jefferies, his prewar jack-of-all-trades rider (and a Triumph dealer), who was fresh out of the army, and in early 1946, the factory built a trials bike from a standard 3T twin. This was a radical departure because singles dominated trials. The trials 3T was assembled in Meriden's Repair Shop, which preceded the factory's race shop. With rookie rider Jim Alves aboard, the lightweight twin decisively won the first event entered.

Thus began Meriden's postwar competition era. From the late 1940s through the 1960s, Triumph fielded medal-winning factory teams in prestigious events such as the International Six-Days Trials (ISDT) and Scottish

53

5th Annual Catalina Grand Prix
MAP OF RACE COURSE

CATALINA GRAND PRIX
TO AIRPORT
PITS
AVALON BAY
GOLF COURSE

TRIUMPH TROPHY
Patent Nos. 529443, 475860, 469635.

AFRICA

The yet u on s all with rrain is in arily.

Built to incorporate every refinement required by the competition rider the Triumph "Trophy" model has a long string of successes to its credit from every corner of the world. Easy and accurate to handle, thanks to its light weight (295 lb.) and a steering geometry evolved as a result of experience gained in fiercely contested competitive events. The engine, using the same unique die-cast alloy head and barrel as the "Tiger 100," is designed to provide a high power output at low revolutions, yet give adequate top end performance when required. Riding standard "Trophy" models the Triumph team completed the 1950 International Six Days Trial without loss of marks, winning a Manufacturer's Team Award—the third to be won in succession (1948-49-50).

O.H.V. vertical twin. Bore 63 mm., stroke 80 mm., 498 c.c. Dry sump lubrication. Air cleaner. Manual control magneto. Two-in-one exhaust. 6¼" ground clearance. 70° lock. Telescopic forks. Wide ratio four-speed gearbox. 2½ gall. tank. Folding kickstarter. Pillion seat. Quick release headlamp. Tyres 400—19 rear 300—20 front. Finished silver sheen and black. (For complete technical data see back pages.)

SPECIFICATION

PAGE 7

In 1951, the TR5 gained Triumph's new die-cast, round-barrel cylinder and head, with their lovely close-pitch cooling fins. Trophy 500s won countless enduro and trials events all over the world until the two-strokes took over in the late 1960s. *Brooke and Gaylin archives; Jeff Hackett photo*

Six-Days. Works' riders also won many British scrambles events. Over the next three decades, Triumph built competition models from 200-cc to 650-cc that were designed specifically for winning in the dirt, including American track and desert racing. But until the mid-1960s, Meriden's involvement in road racing mainly consisted of supporting the privateer, usually through its dealers worldwide.

Occasionally, though, it produced a few batches of racing twins to serve select purposes. The first of these was a winner right from the start. In early 1946, Freddie Clarke and his Experimental Department colleagues Frank Baker and Ernie Nott secretly built a tuned version of the 500-cc AAPP twin that they'd developed during the war for RAF portable generators. Its aluminum cylinder head and barrels (both with squared-off cooling fins) made the engine much lighter than the standard Tiger 100, with which it shared its lower end. Clarke began testing the new engine on Meriden's dynamometer without Turner's knowledge. The results were promising: more than 40 horsepower at 7,200 rpm. The engine, with an 8.3:1 compression ratio, twin Amal 1.0-inch carburetors, and megaphone exhaust, was fitted to a Sprung Hub-equipped T100 chassis. The bike had numerous racing modifications including rearset pegs, dropped handlebars, a 4.5-gallon steel fuel tank, and aluminum wheel rims.

Turner eventually discovered the clandestine project. He gave it his reluctant support because the investment was low. But he demanded that there be no hoopla surrounding its debut. If it failed or was uncompetitive, the project would be killed. Triumph entered the bike in the 1946 Ulster Road Race, held over public roads in Ireland.

Many race goers were surprised to see the new machine listed as an official factory entry in the race program. They weren't as surprised to see one of their native sons, Ernie Lyons, in the saddle. Lyons was a tough motorcycle-racing farmer from County Kildare. He is credited as the first person to race a Speed Twin, nearly scoring a leaderboard finish in the 1938 Manx Grand Prix before crashing near the end. He also rode Triumphs in grass track and scrambles events, campaigning a prewar Tiger 80 single and T100.

While Lyons and his Triumph achieved no success in the Ulster, they were victorious in the next race—the Manx Grand Prix, held on the iconic Isle of Man TT course. Winning the Senior (500-cc) Manx carried great prestige for rider and machine, and in 1946 it was the first postwar event held on the TT circuit. In abysmal conditions—it poured rain all day—Lyons and his Triumph led the Senior Manx GP from start to finish. He crossed the finish line 43 seconds ahead of the second-place Norton, having averaged 77.24 miles per hour—quite impressive in such nasty weather. At the end of the six-lap, 226-mile race, Lyons' leathers were soaked through, and his goggles were half-full of water! It was Triumph's first Isle of Man win since Jack Marshall's 1908 victory.

Lyons' bike performed flawlessly, averaging 40 miles per gallon and showing good speed potential. Its frame suffered a fractured front down tube, which, combined with the squirrelly handling of the Sprung Hub chassis affirmed Lyons' skill and forever linked his name with Triumph. More important, it delighted Edward Turner. At a post-race dinner honoring Lyons, Triumph's jubilant boss indicated to the press that he just might support road racing on certain levels. Turner already knew that Lyons' Manx GP win had garnered Triumph much attention in overseas markets, in particular in the United States.

The logical result was a production-racer version of Lyons' winning twin. Catalogued as the Grand Prix model, it went on sale in late 1947. Less than 200 examples were produced through early 1950. The 120-mile per hour Grand Prix enjoyed decent success during its brief lifespan. Besides Lyons' gritty win, other successes included a 1947 win and record lap at Belgium's Circuit de la Chambre by factory-sponsored David Whitworth, who also placed third at the Dutch TT that year; a 1948 Senior Manx GP win by Don Crossley; fifth place at the 1949 Isle of Man Senior TT by Sid Jensen; first by C.B. Groves at the 1949 Port Elizabeth 200 in South Africa; and American Rod Coates' 1950 win in the Daytona 100-mile amateur race.

At 310 pounds, the Grand Prix was nearly 50 pounds lighter than a plunger-framed Manx Norton with the same power. But unlike the Manx, the production-based, pushrod Triumph engine was not designed for the stresses of 200-plus-mile racing. That fact was clear when all of the nine Triumphs entered in the 1948 Isle of Man Senior TT failed to finish the race.

Americans and Canadians loved the Speed Twin and Tiger 100, buying as many as Triumph could provide to Johnson Motors in the United States, and to Canadian distributors Sammett & Blair and Nicholson Bros. Many of the early twins were raced, as shown by this 1947 photo of Al Evans' T100 taking the inside groove at Corona Speedway against an Ariel single. *Lindsay Brooke archive*

TRIUMPH FEATURES

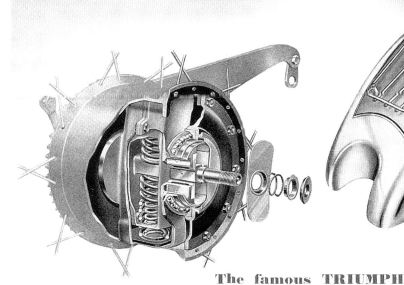

The Triumph TELESCOPIC FORK

With six inches of hydraulically damped movement these forks set a high standard of controllability and comfort. The sectioned drawing shows the internal arrangement. Note how long supple fork springs are enclosed inside the stanchions which enables these latter vital components to be of maximum possible diameter and strength. No adjustments of any kind have to be made by the rider and maintenance is reduced to checking the oil level every 10,000 miles.

PARCEL GRID
(above).

A useful tank-top fitting available as an extra on all models. Chromium plated grid to which small parcels may be attached—particularly valuable to the long distance solo rider.

The famous TRIUMPH SPRING WHEEL

(Patent No. 524885)

This remarkable springing system has achieved great popularity in all parts of the world. It is essentially simple, efficient and reliable. The massive aluminium alloy hub shell totally encloses all the moving parts and attached to this is a powerful eight-inch brake. The Spring Wheel is mounted in the frame in exactly the same way as a normal wheel and adds a mere three per cent to the total weight of the machine.

HOW IT OPERATES. The spindle remains stationary bolted into the frame as usual while the wheel and hub move on a curved path taken from the centre of the gearbox sprocket which ensures that chain tension remains constant at all times. This movement is controlled by springs, two below the spindle and one above. Lubrication is by a single grease nipple.

OTHER TRIUMPH FEATURES

The detachable rear mudguard fitted to the "Tiger 100" and "Speed Twin" is illustrated and described on Page Four.

The Triumph instrument "Nacelle" is fully described and illustrated on Page Seven.

PROP STAND (on left).

Available as an extra on all models. Attaches to the nearside cradle member of the frame. A spring retains the stand out as a prop or in the folded back position. Can be fitted to all Triumph models from 1937, state whether over or under 350 c.c. when ordering.

AIR CLEANER (on right).

Triumph design patented Vokes air cleaner. By means of a "transparent" oil tank the illustration shows how neatly this piece of equipment is fitted between the oil tank and battery. Very efficient oil-wetted muslin filament readily detachable for cleaning.

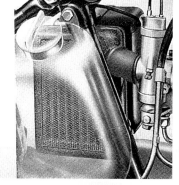

Page Eight

Telescopic forks and a streamlined headlamp nacelle shouted "modern" in this 1949 sales brochure, though Americans preferred the separate headlight-and-speedometer look of the Trophy models. Triumph's internally sprung rear hub was already obsolete, compared with the swinging-arm rear suspensions of 1949 AJS, Matchless, Royal Enfield, and Vincent models.

During the same period, standard Tiger 100 models became one of the most popular rides in the Clubman's TT, a new Isle of Man race for street-legal production bikes. In the event's nine-year history, starting in 1947, T100s scored one first-place (Bernard Hargreaves, 1952), five second-place, and three third-place finishes, proving the inherent flexibility of the early Triumph twin.

Triumph also developed a second model around the "square barrel" 500-cc engine, this one aimed at off-road riders. Its influence in the motorcycle world and importance to the company far exceeded the Grand Prix's. The bike was patterned on Jim Alves' 3T-based trials machine, with a host of further refinements. The all-aluminum twin had 6.0:1 compression and "soft" cams and made a tractable 25 horsepower. It was fitted to a rigid frame with a 20-inch front wheel, Dunlop trials tires, a slender 2 1/2-gallon fuel tank, and Siamesed raised exhaust. It weighed just 304 pounds without lights.

Alves developed the machine with Henry Vale, the first manager of Meriden's newly created Competition Shop. Established soon after Lyons' Manx GP win, the Comp Shop proved that Edward Turner had started to take motosports seriously. The prototype was given to Allan Jefferies to ride in the 1948 ISDT, held in San Remo, Italy. Jefferies was part of Triumph's three-man team (the others were aboard modified Tiger 100s) that earned gold medals and the overall Manufacturer's Prize that year. The prototype trials twin performed so well in the ISDT that a production version—the TR5 Trophy—was quickly approved for the 1949 catalog.

The 500-cc Trophy twin was a lithe, agile little bike. It was the first postwar "dual purpose" motorcycle, setting the pattern for many imitators during the next three decades and beginning a 25-year string of famous high-piped Triumph Trophy models that were equally capable on- or off-road.

Enter the 650

The worldwide sales success of Triumph's vertical twins in the immediate postwar period was stunning, and competitors swarmed in to grab their slice of the pie. "The alacrity with which other manufacturers rushed parallel twins off their drawing boards in the 1940s, as the market swung slowly back to normality was probably the greatest compliment ever paid to Edward Turner," observed journalist Jim Reynolds in a 1999 issue of *Classic Bike Guide.*

BSA finally introduced its 500-cc A7 Star twin in 1946. Royal Enfield followed with a 500 twin in 1948; Norton and Ariel added their entries a year later. The era of the UBM—the overhead-valve, parallel twin Universal British Motorcycle—had begun. It was the engine to beat for over two decades, until four-cylinder Japanese bikes (the UJM) took over in the 1970s.

By late 1948, increasing demand for new Triumphs drove Meriden to add a night shift to keep pace. The factory was building 250 bikes a week, roughly 65 percent of which were exported. Company profits reached £195,000 ($1 million) —nearly eight times that of 1946. The motorcycle revolution that Edward Turner and Jack Sangster had started with their 500-cc parallel twin was now 10 years old. It was time to step up in size and offer customers something more powerful.

Turner's timing couldn't have been better, because in 1949 the British government devalued its currency. This was part of a national strategy to earn hard currency, particularly U.S. dollars, after World War II. The war had virtually bankrupted Britain, and the government was desperate to pay down its debt. So it pressured auto and motorcycle makers to export their products.

At the request of U.S. Triumph dealers, the factory added a black paint option for the 1953 Thunderbird. Resplendent with gold striping on the fenders and wheel centers, these "Black Birds" were an immediate hit and quickly caused sales of blue T-birds to plummet. Note the rear "sprung hub" on this restored example. *Jeff Hackett*

Typical of 1950s Triumphs, the Thunderbird's nacelle shows a 120-mile per hour Smiths speedometer with shift points and kilometer speeds marked on its face. The ammeter is on the left and the high-beam button is in the center. Steering damper was standard. This restored model wears a period TriCor leather tank bag (original price: $9.00), which mounts to the standard tank-top parcel grid. *Jeff Hackett*

The sterling devaluation allowed Triumph and the other British bike makers to sharply lower their prices in overseas markets. The interventionist policy dictated that those firms not earning their fair share of foreign cash would lose access to important raw materials like steel. The currency swing and its lower prices made the easy handling British machines, with their hand clutches and foot shift gearboxes, even more alluring to American buyers.

It was a different story in the home market, however. Britain remained mired in a postwar austerity ruled by government-mandated rationing. Licensed private vehicles were limited to only enough fuel for 100 miles of travel per month. And British motorcyclists were unable to buy many new models destined for export markets that would earn the country hard currency.

Besides adding the new TR5 Trophy to its 1949 range, Triumph also gave the popular Speed Twin and Tiger 100 a distinctive new look. Gone was the tank-top instrument panel, its threaded mounting inserts now used to fit an optional chrome parcel rack. The speedometer, ammeter, horn, and switchgear were now nestled inside a streamlined headlamp nacelle. This stylish design, cleanly integrated into the top of the fork assembly, was penned by Jack Wickes. Triumph's gifted chief stylist may have been influenced by a similar nacelle on Jawa's first postwar 250, which debuted in 1946. Wickes also had an eye toward automotive styling, which was beginning to take its cues from jet aircraft.

Triumph's nacelle became one of the company's design hallmarks, remaining in production on various street models through 1966. But Turner had even more up his sleeve, and in September 1949 he unleashed it to the world with typical flair. The 650-cc 6T Thunderbird was developed specifically for Triumph's major export markets— particularly North America, where Johnson Motors and many other dealers wanted a bike with more power than the 500s and the ability to sustain higher cruising speeds over longer distances. British riders would also welcome such performance, particularly those who pulled a sidecar. Indeed, a few months earlier *The Motor Cycle* had run a major feature story which strongly encouraged Britain's bike makers to build larger-displacement, multicylinder machines to better meet the unique needs of the huge American market. The magazine favored 750-cc parallel twins; did its editors have a crystal ball?

Creating Triumph's first 650 since the prewar model 6/1 was as simple and cost effective as fitting a bigger engine into an existing chassis. Meriden's Experimental Department, led by veteran development men and former TT racers H.G. Tyrell-Smith and Ernie Nott, stretched the Speed Twin's cylinder bore from 63 mm to 71 mm and stroked its crankshaft 2 mm, to 82 mm. The additional 150-cc displacement gave the new engine great flexibility. It delivered the same power at 4,000 rpm as the Speed Twin produced at 6,000 rpm. Its flatter, deeper torque curve enabled the bike, which weighed about the same as the 500, to pull higher gearing at a more relaxed

Far left
Primary side of the 1953 T-bird shows its automotive-type SU constant-vacuum MC2 carburetor, first offered for 1952. In 1954, Ford Motor Co. asked Triumph's permission to use the already world-famous Thunderbird name on its new two-seat sporty car. *Jeff Hackett*

A 1950 magazine ad trumpets Thunderbird records set by three factory riders at Montlhery, France. The 385-pound twin was capable of about 105 miles per hour in standard trim.

gait. Gentle cams and a low 7:1 compression ratio made starting and trolling through traffic a breeze. These were strong selling points for riders on both sides of the Atlantic.

The larger engine warranted more robust internals, a beefed-up gearbox, and a five-plate clutch. But the new 6T, officially catalogued as a 1950 model, shared most of its running gear (including the optional Sprung Hub) with its smaller brothers. It cost the same to produce, but sold for £10 (about $28, after the 1949 devaluation) more.

Turner came upon the Thunderbird name in early 1949 while driving from New York to the Daytona Beach races with American Triumph dealer/racer Rod Coates and his wife, Marge. Passing through South Carolina, they spotted a giant totem pole in front of the ubiquitously named Thunderbird Motel. Sitting atop the pole was the eagle-like thunderbird of Native American mythology. Turner was impressed, and the name stuck with him. Five years later, Triumph would grant the Ford Motor Co. permission to use the evocative name for its new two-seat roadster.

To prove the durability and performance of his new flagship, Turner staged what today would be called a "media event"—a 500-mile, high-speed torture test to launch the machine. Four early-production Thunderbirds were taken off the Meriden assembly line, fitted with pannier bags packed with tools and spares, and ridden to Montlhéry, a 1.6-mile speed bowl near Paris. There, three of the bikes (one was kept in reserve) were run at over 90 miles per gallon for 5 1/2 hours, only stopping for fuel. England's two weekly motorcycle magazines, *The Motor Cycle* and *Motor Cycling*, were invited to report the results, and a timekeeper from the Auto-Cycle Union certified the proceedings. A coterie of Meriden staff were on hand for support, including off-road aces Allan Jefferies and Jim Alves, tech wizards Tyrell-Smith and Nott, publicity chief Ivor Davies, and sales supremo Neal Shilton.

The machines were piloted by Triumph factory testers Alex Scobie, Bob Manns, and Len Bayliss. Their 500-mile runs completed, each rider then wound open his twistgrip and put in a final flying lap on the banked circuit at just over 100 miles per hour. The bikes were then loaded up and ridden back to Meriden, to be prepared for their world debut at the Earls Court motorcycle show.

The test bikes were fueled with the 72-octane "pool" gasoline then available in Britain. They were indeed standard, apart from minor modifications aimed at increasing the riders' safety—Dunlop racing tires, KLG competition sparkplugs, smaller Trophy saddles, and rear-set pegs. The only mechanical fault that occurred was a split fuel tank; it was swapped for the backup bike's tank. In the post-test inspection, *The Motor Cycle* reported that the engines showed no oil leaks and valve clearances were still within spec. A chain guard was cracked and one bike's headlamp and ammeter were inoperable.

What wasn't reported at the time was, two months earlier Turner had taken two late-prototype T-birds to Montlhéry for dress rehearsals of the test. Years later, Alex Scobie revealed that in the first attempt the bike threw a connecting rod after 25 laps. A few weeks later, the second bike cooked its clutch and shredded its rear tire after 375 miles. These failures forced the necessary engineering changes to be made in time for the September speedfest.

At Earls Court, the T-bird was a star of the show. At Johnson Motors in California, however, first impressions were quite different.

JoMo parts manager E.W. "Pete" Colman quickly uncrated the first Thunderbird to arrive in the United States. He carefully set up the bike, made all adjustments, donned his goggles, and set off on a test ride into the hills outside of Pasadena. But Colman, a nationally ranked speedway racer before the war and a skilled tuner, had barely left the city limits before disappointment struck.

"The bike felt no quicker than a 500 through the gears," Colman told the author in 1991. "And once we had it carefully broken in, it would barely touch 90 miles per hour. We played with various jetting combinations, but clearly the first 6T was undercarbureted. We jokingly called it 'the Cast-Iron Snail.' I cabled Tyrell-Smith with requests for a larger carburetor."

The 650 Thunderbird set numerous speed records in the United States in the early 1950s. This unknown tattooed rider, shown warming up his modified T-bird at the Bonneville Salt Flats, prepares to make his run wearing only swim trunks and a helmet. In doing so he emulates Rollie Free, who set a world record of 150 miles per hour on a Vincent Black Lightning in 1948. Free believed he could be more aerodynamic (and thus go faster) without clothing, lying on the bike with his legs outstretched behind him. Many aspiring speed-heroes copied Free, and the bare-skin trend lasted at the Salt Flats until 1952. That's when swimsuit-clad Tommy Smith, who was coated with graphite grease to make him more "slippery," crashed his tuned Thunderbird at nearly 140 miles per hour. Smith lost much of his skin, requiring agonizing skin grafts. Full leathers were required thereafter at Bonneville. *Lindsay Brooke archive*

As would happen many times during the next three decades, technical input from its American distributors helped Triumph make a better motorcycle. Halfway through the 1950 season, the Thunderbird's 1.0-inch Amal carburetor (the same as the 500's) bore was enlarged to 1 1/16 inches. What the 650's bigger intake manifold, ports, and valves needed was the larger bore, never mind that Edward Turner had told the British press that the extra power afforded by a larger carb would be *undesirable*!

Given its proper breathing, the T-bird became a favorite all-rounder for the solo rider, two-up tourers, sidecarists, and police forces. In a letter to the editor of *Motorcyclist* in June 1951, Herschel Hensley of Elkton, Virginia, echoed the T-bird's effect on many young riders—and the brand allegiance it was creating.

"Three weeks ago, I was trying out the first Thunderbird to be bought by anyone here in the Shenandoah Valley," Hensley wrote. "It was my first ride on one, and I was trying it out for acceleration

Left
Triumph "Tigerized" the Thunderbird in 1954, creating the T110. The sports 650 introduced Triumph's new swinging arm frame, years behind many competitors. Also new was the wide-base twinseat. Living up to its name, the Tiger 110 was capable of 110 miles per hour. This is a restored 1955 model in Shell Blue livery. *Jeff Hackett*

The last year for the T110's cast-iron cylinder head was 1955; it was replaced the following year by the new aluminum head. Triumph's hottest 650 featured a stouter crankshaft and bearing assembly as well as a higher (8.5:1) compression ratio and polished ports. It utilized the company's E3134 racing camshaft on the intake side, and Amal's new Monobloc carburetor. Claimed power was 42 horsepower at 6,500 rpm. *Jeff Hackett*

Below
The 1954 T110 was the first Triumph to feature the company's upgraded 8-inch front brake, with ventilated backing plate. Very effective in operation, it was quickly adopted to the Tiger 100 and TR6. *Jeff Hackett*

TR5 Trophy models did not receive the new swinging arm frame until 1955, a year before this example was built. High-level, two-into-one exhaust is a trademark feature of the early Trophies. This lovely Shell Blue machine was restored from very rough condition by Canadian pre-unit Triumph specialist Bob Buchanan. *Lindsay Brooke*

in all gears when a deputy sheriff pulled a siren on me and gave me an earned lecture on speeding. Then he started to lecture me on riding the 'wrong' machine. Said I should be on an H-D and quite frankly called me a liar when I told him the 40-inch Triumph would stay with a Harley twice its displacement, on average roads in a day's run. Although I am about as loyal an American as any, I still feel it is my privilege to choose the machine I want to ride."

Speed tuners around the world also took advantage of the new 650's potential. Johnson Motors transformed its first anemic example into *Wonderbird*, utilizing twin carburetors, Grand Prix cams, and other tricks. Running on aviation gas, rider Blackie Bullock set the first of what would be hundreds of Triumph speed records at the Bonneville Salt Flats. Bullock went over 132 miles per hour (without a fairing) on *Wonderbird* in 1951, nailing a new AMA record that stood for seven years.

The same year, Thunderbird-mounted Walt Fulton won the inaugural 100-mile Grand Prix on California's scenic Catalina Island, storming into the lead after starting in 103rd position. Across the globe in Italy, Triumph factory rider Jim Alves copped a gold medal at the 1951 ISDT. He rode a hybrid built by the Comp Shop—a TR5 Trophy powered by a 650-cc 6T engine. This prototype "Trophybird" foreshadowed the TR6 Trophy introduced five years later.

The Thunderbird ushered in more styling changes for the 1950 range. One was the all-painted fuel tank, handsomely trimmed with four horizontal chrome strips surrounding the Triumph badge. The enamel finish replaced the chrome-plated tanks that were rusting on export machines, causing warranty problems. At first the TR5 Trophy was the sole model to keep its chromed tank, but within one year it too would be painted, a victim of Korean War metals rationing. The other new feature welcomed by riders and passengers was Triumph's optional Twinseat, which replaced the old bicycle-style solo saddle and pillion pad setup.

When 1950 ended, Triumph had produced slightly over 14,000 machines—two-thirds of them for export. From this point on, the United States became the company's most profitable market.

Unlike the Speed Twin's debut, Triumph's move into the 650-cc class did not go unchallenged. In fact, Turner was almost beaten to the punch by his old protégé. Design engineer Bert Hopwood had jumped from Norton to BSA in early 1949. He'd heard rumors that his former Triumph colleagues were developing a 650-cc twin, and he began a crash program to match it. BSA's first 650, the A10 Golden Flash, was designed in 10 days, and prototypes were tested three months later. The A10 also was unveiled at the 1949 Earls Court show, wearing a larger (8-inch) front brake than the Thunderbird's 7-incher, but otherwise very close in specification and performance.

Thus began the British industry's evolution of the 500-cc parallel twin. Over the next two decades, the major manufacturers followed Triumph by sticking with vertically split crankcases, pushrod-actuated valvegear, and 360-degree crankshafts. They bored and stroked their way to 600-cc, 650-cc, 700-cc and finally, 750-cc displacements and added twin-carb cylinder heads. Turner himself believed that 650-cc was the practical limit of the design, where performance and vibration coexisted in relative harmony. More cubes meant more reciprocating mass and, as engine speed increased, more teeth-rattling, metal-fatiguing vibes. The lust for higher performance also spurred higher compression ratios and radical cam forms, neither of which improved smoothness or reliability.

In 1956 a single-engined Triumph streamliner built in Texas set the world motorcycle speed record of 214 miles per hour, at the Bonneville Salt Flats. Ridden by flat-track star Johnny Allen, with an engine built by Triumph tuner Jack Wilson, the bullet-shaped bike helped coin the name "Bonneville" for Triumph's hottest 650 twin. Triumph held the ultimate motorcycle record for the next 14 years. Commemorative tape-measure at top was a U.S. dealer trinket in the late 1950s. *Brooke and Gaylin archives; Jeff Hackett photo*

But in the 1950s, the 650-cc parallel twin as defined by the Thunderbird was motorcycling's ideal package. The world couldn't get enough of them.

Sangster Sells Out to BSA

The 1950s began a new era for motorcycle makers. The "seller's market" that, since 1945, had put transportation-starved nations back on wheels was gone. Many countries had erected import-tariff barriers to protect their newly rebuilt home industries. The Cold War had begun. Britain was slowly pulling out of its postwar bleakness, which eased availability of new machines for the lads at home.

Triumph now had to compete more aggressively for global sales. Sangster and Turner met the challenge by building on Triumph's lead in the American market. The two commissioned a market-research study and concluded that the immense U.S. market could gobble up many times more machines than the one thousand per year they were shipping to Johnson Motors. The answer was a two-pronged distribution strategy: In January 1951 Triumph established a wholly owned distributor on the eastern coast of the United States. Based near the port of Baltimore, Maryland, The Triumph Corporation—"TriCor" as it was soon dubbed—was headed by Denis McCormack, a respected British expatriate executive. To manage the company's service department and racing efforts, he hired Rod Coates, the 1950 Daytona winner and a zealous Triumph dealer.

Restored 1956 TR5/R, found as a rusty frame and matching engine cases by U.S. Triumph restorer Jaye Strait. Built for the American distributors as a production road racer, the TR5/R combined the best Tiger and Trophy components, with straight-port T100C twin-carb cylinder head and 8-inch TR6 front brake. Engines were hand-assembled and bench tested at the factory. TR5/Rs were built in 1956 only; all 112 examples were shipped to the United States. *Lindsay Brooke*

The establishment of TriCor ended Johnson's sales monopoly and split the United States into eastern and western sales regions. TriCor ended up with the larger potential customer base, handling everything east of Texas. JoMo's western states territory had fewer people but it included California—motorcycling's Promised Land. The sales potential was enormous; only one person out of six hundred in America rode a motorcycle, while the ratio in Britain was one out of one hundred.

Bill Johnson and McCormack became friends and were equally respected by Turner and his managers. TriCor and JoMo, however, were separate, sometimes rival organizations. Their competitive energy, a steadily growing dealer base, and a strong product range gave Triumph the best position of any "foreign" motorcycle maker for U.S. growth.

Turner's contract with Jack Sangster permitted him six months per year away from Meriden, and he loved coming to America to visit the American distributors. His frequent attendance at U.S. dealer meetings, as well as at the Daytona races and other high-profile events, helped boost Meriden's influence in a market still under the political fist of Harley-Davidson.

Harley and the floundering Indian were under serious assault by the British motorcycle invasion. As if the wave of powerful new 650-cc twins and the pair of well-financed Triumph distributors weren't enough to frighten Milwaukee, in March 1951 came more ominous news. Jack Sangster sold the Triumph Engineering Co. to the giant Birmingham Small Arms Co. When he'd sold Ariel seven years earlier, he'd given BSA first right of refusal if ever came the time to sell Triumph. Some historians speculate he sold out to BSA because of concern over Britain's massive inheritance tax, which literally would have cost Sangster's family a fortune upon his death.

No matter why the sale occurred, Triumph's acquisition by BSA helped seal the marque's fate 20 years later. Sangster later called it the biggest mistake of his career, although it financially set up Turner and him for life.

The £2.5 million (about $7 million) deal came at a time when Triumph had more than £1.0 million cash ($2.8 million) in the bank. It had also tripled its U.S. exports to 2,800 bikes within the past year. Now the surging Triumph was part of BSA, an industrial goliath that produced nearly 50,000 machines in 1950 and was the world's largest maker

From 1957 to 1959, the T100/RS superseded the TR5/R as Triumph's production racer for the American market. It used the 5-gallon Thunderbird gas tank and a special 1-gallon oil tank. The 4-inch megaphones are the open pattern first fitted to the Grand Prix model. In 1957, the factory built 132 of these racers, plus seven spare engines. Retail price was $947. *Lindsay Brooke*

of motorcycles over 200-cc. Press releases promised the two marques would continue to operate independently with no policy changes. Sangster remained as Triumph's chairman and gained a seat on BSA's board of directors; Turner kept the title of managing director and his open dislike for all things BSA.

Neither of the American distributors was immediately affected by the acquisition. But the prospect of this mighty empire conquering more American motorcycle sales prodded an ever-defensive Harley-Davidson into court. In June 1951 H-D filed a "dumping" charge with the U.S. Federal Trade Commission against all of the British bike importers.

Harley hoped the government would slam the "Limey" invaders with a crippling 40 percent import tax, but its complaint was quickly denied. The FTC correctly ruled that the British makers were simply creating a new middleweight market that the domestics were ignoring, at their peril.

All-Alloy Tigers

Judged by its major model introductions, the decade of the 1950s was the most important in Triumph's one hundred year history. Besides the Thunderbird, the big launches during this remarkable period included the Tiger 110, TR6, Terrier and Cub singles, 3TA and 5TA unit-construction twins, Tigress scooter, and the immortal Bonneville. Sometimes overlooked but no less significant were the new Tiger 100 and TR5 Trophy models introduced for 1951.

The big news on these bikes was their engines' new top ends. Their cylinder heads and barrels were die-cast aluminum, a first for a Triumph production road bike engine. The closely pitched cooling fins gave the engines an exquisite, aircraft-engine look. The Tiger had higher compression and racier camshafts; the off-road Trophy had a "softer" tune. The alloy components reduced overall weight, which was a major sales hook for sports-oriented riders. The engines weren't without teething problems, however; on early examples, the head-joint spigots of the iron cylinder liners would break. A redesigned liner with a shorter spigot ended the problem. The alloy head and barrels also amplified the valve-gear clatter compared with the Speed Twin, which retained its cast-iron engine.

The alloy 500s rank among the most beautiful of all Triumph models and became the company's workhorse in every type of competition event around the world, taking countless wins and championships on pavement and in the dirt. Like most Triumphs, the bikes were extremely popular with tuners and equipment suppliers. They remained in the catalogue through 1959, even after the unit-construction 500 was introduced.

Not to be outdone by the aftermarket, Triumph itself offered a Speed Kit for the T100 from 1951 through 1954. It was Turner's low-cost way of replacing the Grand Prix production racer and boosting the standard Tiger's output to 42 horsepower—a 10 horsepower gain. For your $154, the Speed Kit bought over $300 worth of goodies: a megaphone exhaust, twin racing carburetors, high-compression pistons, hot camshafts, a larger oil tank, dropped handlebars, rearset pegs, tachometer, and a number plate. It was a clubman's racer in a box—just bolt it on, tune it up, and go racing!

"This policy is to prevent our Works being called upon to produce racing machines," explained Edward Turner at the Speed Kit's introduction, "and it should be understood we must refuse to take orders for machines in racing condition." Turner's words didn't quite ring true, however. In 1953 came the T100c, a Tiger outfitted with the Speed Kit right off the production line. It was Triumph's answer to the BSA Gold Star and was only offered for one year; 560 examples were built. The T100c was the first of a few batches of factory-assembled 500-cc racers mostly aimed at the U.S. market and sold in both road race and dirt-track configurations through 1959.

The all-alloy 500s were a glimpse at the 1960s, when die-cast aluminum became the standard material for Japanese and European motorcycle engines. No official explanation has been recorded as to why Triumph reverted to sand-cast iron for succeeding twin-cylinder engine barrels. The probable reason was lower cost and quieter operation.

Little Dogs and Cats

As the first 650-cc Thunderbirds were rolling out of the factory in late 1949, the first drawings for a very different Triumph were appearing on the drafting tables upstairs in Meriden's design office. Having set the pace in the middleweight market with his twin-cylinder models, Edward Turner now set his sights on the customer looking for lightweight, frugal two-wheeled transport.

The T15 Terrier, introduced at the Earls Court show for the 1953 season, became the sixth model in Triumph's range. It was the company's first true lightweight since the 1933 XO and its first single-cylinder

Rare T100/RS showing the engine's splayed-port Delta head and flexibly mounted Amal GP carburetors. Incorrect Allen-head case bolts spoil an otherwise superb restoration, seen here at Daytona in 1997. *Lindsay Brooke*

Introduced for the 1954 model year, the T20 Tiger Cub brought many new customers into the Triumph family. In typical Triumph style, it also was easily modified for competition and won countless events in Britain and the United States. Compared with the crude two-strokes that were its competitors in the 1950s, Triumph's 199-cc four-stroke ohv single offered a "big-bike" feel, high fuel economy, and no messy gasoline premixing. The Cub was sold alongside its 149-cc Terrier predecessor through 1957 and was given many upgrades through its 14-year production run. *David Gaylin archive; Jeff Hackett photo*

model since the military 3HW. In its Earls Court report, *Motor Cycling* called it "the outstanding machine of the show."

The Terrier shocked the commuter bike world, long dominated by crude, smoky two-strokes that required messy premixing of their fuel. Here was a 150-cc overhead-valve four-stroke with die-cast aluminum cylinder head, alternator electrics, a four-speed gearbox unitized with the engine, and plunger rear suspension. With its shapely tank, headlamp nacelle, and deep Amaranth Red paint, the 175-pound T15 was styled to resemble a baby Speed Twin. Even the smallest components seemed to be part of a unified styling theme, giving the little bike that raffish charm inherent in every Triumph. It was another brilliant stroke by Turner and Jack Wickes.

The advertising shouted "A Real Triumph in Miniature!" and the price was about £20 (about $50) more than the two-stroke BSA Bantam. But the new kitten suffered endless electrical problems during its rapid six-week development. This prompted concerns about the production bikes and sparked yet another of Turner's public relations stunts. Soon after the T15 entered production, he had three machines plucked off the line for a tour across the length of England.

With a carload of support staff in tow, Turner, Works Manager Bob Fearon, and Service Manager Alec Masters rode their new Terriers from Land's End to John O'Groats—1,008 miles in a total running time of just 27 1/2

A restored American-market 1959 T20, the standard road model complete with 16-inch wheels and headlamp nacelle. In the UK market, it wore an almost enclosed middle section. *Lindsay Brooke*

hours. Average speed over the narrow English roads was 37 miles per hour, fuel consumption exceeded 107 miles per gallon, and the entire trip was reported in the press.

The Terrier was produced through early 1957. It directly sired every unit-construction single built by BSA through 1974—from the 50-cc Ariel Pixie to the 500-cc TR5MX Avenger scrambler. But its most loved offspring was a true Triumph—the T20 Tiger Cub. Announced in October 1953, three months after Terrier production began, the 200-cc Cub was one of the world's best-loved lightweight motorcycles. Nearly 113,000 Cubs of all flavors—from standard road-going models with valenced fenders, to high-piped trials and scrambles versions and even military-spec Cubs—were produced at Meriden and in the final years (1965 through 1969) at BSA's Small Heath factory. The model was exported to over 140 countries.

The Cub could do everything. In mild-mannered T20J (Junior) spec with a teeny Zenith carburetor, it taught youngsters the basics of riding. Wrapped in a streamlined shell, it set an AMA speed record of nearly 140 miles per hour at the Bonneville Salt Flats in 1959. The same year, with Triumph factory trials ace Roy Peplow aboard, a Cub became the first motorcycle under 250-cc to win the famous Scottish Six-Days Trials. Cubs won 1/4-mile American short-track races and the punishing 500-mile Jack Pine Enduro. They took travelers across continents and handled daily police work with agility and 100-mile per gallon thrift.

The Cub's engine design evolved from the earlier 149-cc Terrier and shared the smaller bike's 25-degree-inclined cylinder and four-speed unitized gearbox. Bore and stroke measured 63x64mm. Points for the coil-ignition system on this 1959 model resided in the distributor behind the cylinder, and the little engine breathes through an Amal 13/16-inch Type 332 carburetor. All Cubs left the factory with aluminum paint on their cast-iron cylinder barrels, a detail missed on this restored machine. *Lindsay Brooke*

There was even the T20SL, the Sports Cub with the heart of a café racer. Meriden service wizard Hughie Hancox recalled the 1960 version to be "a cracking little Cub," with 9:1 compression, a remote-float Amal Monobloc carb, and high-lift "R" camshaft. The Sports Cub wooed the lads with its big-bike styling and the same blue and white paint scheme as the '60 Bonneville.

With the twistgrip cranked wide open and the rider lying prone, the Sports Cub's mighty 15 horsepower could propel it to over 75 mph. "It was called the 'baby Bonnie' because it went so well," Hancox enthused.

Tiger 110 and TR6

In 1953 Edward Turner promoted John Nelson, who had been working as a quality inspector, to chief of development, replacing H.G. Tyrell-Smith. When Nelson took over, Turner had him modernize the factory's development department. He wanted it to "look like a laboratory," recalled Nelson in a *Classic Bike* profile. The department's centerpiece was a modern, soundproofed engine test chamber with a state-of-the-art Heenan and Froude dynamometer and control console. There, production and race-kitted motors sang their songs for hours and sometimes days on end. And as in every other department in the plant, workers always knew they should be prepared for an unannounced visit by The Man himself.

ET, as the workers called Turner, "used to appear on the shop floor, going walkabout to see how things were," noted Hancox. "You hoped and prayed that this little man, with his piercing piggy eyes and Saville Row suits, didn't stop and look over your shoulder, for it was no good trying to fluff it if you couldn't do the job—because he could."

Turner had his draftsmen and engineers busier than ever in 1953. Besides launching the two lightweight singles, they were developing a 650-cc sports machine that would boast Triumph's first swinging-arm rear suspension and 8-inch front brake. This was the 1954 Tiger 110, or "Ton-Ten" as it was soon nicknamed by Britain's street racers. Unveiled at the 1953 Paris show in its dramatic polychromatic Shell Blue paint, the T110 was Triumph's fastest product yet, capable of 105 miles per hour in street trim and a true 110 miles per hour without mufflers.

"Combining a superb road potential with light handling and smooth, powerful braking, the T110 is a machine that cannot fail to impress the sporting rider," crowed *The Motor Cycle*. "Few road burners, in truth, would ask for a higher cruising speed than the Triumph eagerly provides." The rival *Motor Cycling* clocked 117 miles per hour during its initial testing, although the test bike may have been "breathed on" by Meriden's Comp Shop before being handed over to the magazine. This was a common ploy in the British industry in those days, aimed at getting the most favorable test numbers.

The new 42-horsepower 650 was the logical evolution of the Thunderbird, and another direct response to the American distributors' request for more "ooomph"—in this case eight horses up on the T-bird. The engine retained an iron cylinder head but added an extra cooling fin. Inside were larger inlet valves operated by a E3325 sports camshaft, 8.5:1 compression pistons, and larger crankshaft journals with ball bearings now on the timing and primary sides. The Tiger also featured a Lucas generator and magneto with manually adjustable ignition timing. A "mag" was still a must for sports machines in the 1950s, even though Triumph was changing over to alternator electrics.

The new frame had been developed from the prototype swing arm chassis used by factory trials rider Jim Alves since 1953. Finally, Turner admitted that his Sprung Hub was obsolete, though it remained in the lineup another year as the swing-arm frame was introduced across the model range. The new frame allowed the oil tank, air filter, and battery box to be blended neatly into the space under the twinseat. By squeezing the engine and gearbox more closely together and using a new, shorter primary chaincase, the bike's wheelbase grew less than 1 inch compared with the rigid-framed models. The downside of the swinging arm and twin shock absorbers was an additional 45 pounds of weight.

"Through the 1950s, the T110 set a standard for combining speed and reliability with up-to-date looks," wrote Mick Duckworth in a *Classic Bike* retrospective. While no match for Norton's Featherbed-framed Dominator in terms of steering precision and overall handling, the big Tiger "bridged the gap between the usual 650s and the 1,000-cc Vincent V-twin, which cost nearly 50 percent more and was nearing the end of production when the T110 appeared," Duckworth noted. Even as it gained fame in the hands of Mike Hailwood and Dan Shorey by winning the 1958 Thruxton 500-mile production-bike race, Triumph's new pavement-ripper also became known for its comfort and flexibility.

The atmosphere at Meriden and its employee morale was sky-high in the 1950s, and it was reflected in their workmanship—and in the company's minimal warranty claims during the decade. "They were proud of the company's success and very conscious of its reputation," noted John Nelson, who became Triumph's international service manager in the 1960s. Entire families had worked at "Triumphs," as many called it, for generations. Some of the most experienced toolmakers and assembly workers had been with the company for over 40 years. Many of them were lifelong motorcyclists, using solo and sidecar machines for daily transportation just as we use automobiles today.

Inspection at Meriden was very rigorous, recalled Nelson in a *Classic Bike* interview. Fred Willis, the man in charge, was a stickler for maintaining drawing standards. Left-handed crankcases exactly matched the right-handed ones. Components fit properly. That may sound quaint today, but much of the machinery used at Meriden was ancient equipment that had been transferred from the old Priory Street factory after it was bombed in 1940. While Triumph enjoyed the British industry's most modern plant, many of the tools it used to cut the metal, bore the holes, and drive the screws were powered by nineteenth century lineshaft-and-pulley technology.

There was no pressure to change, however. The company's benchmarks were its British contemporaries—young Honda was still toddling in the Japanese market. Worldwide demand for Triumphs was growing every year, and the plant could easily satisfy all markets. Turner preferred to keep Meriden's weekly production at or below his "ideal" level of about 400 machines. In 1949, the factory's output was nearly 12,000 bikes; through the 1950s it never exceeded 25,000 per year. Demand stayed high and so did quality. How drastically that would change in the following decade!

Downstream of the assembly lines were other areas charged with keeping Triumph quality and customer satisfaction high. A team of road testers braved the worst British weather to wring out eight bikes per day, covering over 200 miles on public roads. Quite a few of the testers, including the legendary Percy Tait, were racers and trials riders on the weekend. Equally critical was the Service Department, which, along with its adjacent parts warehouse, was Triumph's direct link to its distributors, dealers, and owners in over 140 markets worldwide.

The T20C was the first of many high-piped Cub models for off-road use. Launched in 1957, it wore the road model's nacelle through 1959, when it gained a separate headlamp and speedometer. The C-model also ran on 19-inch front and 18-inch rear wheels. Fork gaiters were a new T20C feature when this 1958 example was built, but were flexible plastic rather than the later rubber-type shown here. *Lindsay Brooke*

The department handled all repair and maintenance of the company's products, observed Hughie Hancox, world-respected Triumph restorer who joined Service in 1953 and worked there for 20 years. Within it were over 30 experienced mechanics, parts specialists, and technical correspondence clerks who answered letters from Triumph owners and dealers. The mechanics worked at 15 service benches, so numbered because that's how many customer motorcycles were taken in by appointment each day. Most of the bikes brought in had problems that Triumph dealers couldn't solve. But on slow days, the factory would accept repair jobs directly from bike owners—including globetrotters arriving midjourney for a rebuild, on their way to the next continent.

Turner's "little factory in England" (as he whimsically described Meriden to U.S. Triumph dealers) and its products had become a cash cow for parent BSA. In 1956 Jack Sangster, now BSA's chairman, appointed his old partner to head Beeza's huge motorcycle division. A year later Sangster added the struggling Automotive Group, including Daimler cars and Lanchester buses, to Turner's responsibilities. Historians regard these promotions as a major mistake. The BSA empire was bleeding red ink and, although Turner helped Sangster return it to profitability by selling off weak firms, it stretched Turner beyond the level of his own competency and clearly burned him out.

Across the U.S.A. on a Tiger 110

In June 1957, Mike Whitney hopped aboard his 1955 T110 in Massachusetts, met up with his pal Howard Foster on a '49 Harley, and set off for a ride around the United States. The first leg of their journey took them to California, where they met Bob Utz, another friend from New England with a 1957 BSA. Their odyssey—10,000 miles in 32 days—was an experience that is remembered vividly by Whitney, who's still an avid Triumph rider and collector today.

"Motorcyclists then were a minor culture, but we weren't seen as Brando wannabes. Harleys were Tradition; Triumphs represented The New, and my Tiger always drew interest wherever we went. It was the Eisenhower era, a simpler time. We had Jack Kerouac, the Beats, and rock n ' roll. But sex, drugs, and Vietnam were way off.

"Heading west on our bikes seemed to all of us like an American thing to do. Other than possible road accidents, we felt secure. It definitely was not the *Easy Rider* scene. Everywhere we went on our trip, folks we met were generally great, and police usually didn't hassle. But some cops took us for migrant fruit pickers!

"My unfaired Triumph and Howard's rigid Harley averaged 55 miles per hour, and we considered up to 500 miles to be a good day's travel. My three years' experience riding Triumphs had taught me lessons on vibration and Lucas electrics. But on two all-night rides (one across the Mohave Desert) there were no problems. The iron-head T110 was remarkably reliable, a swift runner with real suspension, OK brakes, and easily fixed mechanicals. Triumph had a great dealer network, and most cycle shops were friendly, small places.

"The Tiger suffered only two problems in 10,000 miles of hard riding: a split gas tank and blown primary chain. The typical Triumph maintenance drill was change three oils (engine, gearbox, and primary case); check the tappets, points, all nuts and lighting; adjust two chains—and worry. For Howard, it was change the Harley's engine oil. The T110 was at its best in sporting country, and I had zero spills.

"Our 'dress code' was Langlitz Leather jacket, dungarees or khakis, engineer boots, goggles, and an aluminum helmet. We camped roadside — on Lookout Point in Yosemite, next to lion cages at the San Francisco Zoo, and in a big roadside ditch in South Dakota. Or we just sponged off friends who happened to live near our wayward route. It was safe out there! Three nights out of 32 were spent in roadside cabins.

"The $250 in cash I brought along — no credit cards then — covered my expenses for the entire trip. At 19 cents per gallon of high-octane premium, my gasoline tab came to just $48 for 10,000 miles. We ate light, buying breakfast and supper when we could.

"Like any journey the trip took on a life of its own, with the land and weather dictating our pace. Traveling, particularly against the wind on the T110, was often tough going. The Midwest was a blur of bugs, smeary goggles, thunderstorms, and flat, straight, boring roads. Fabled Route 66 through Texas threatened us with flash floods, and gave the Triumph two flat tires. We droned on into relentless headwinds through New Mexico and

Mike Whitney and his long-distance 1955 T-110. This bike wears small 3.25-gallon TR5 Trophy gas tank. Note the "air dam" front license plate mounting. Robert Whitney collection

Arizona. On the long desert stretch from Las Vegas to San Diego, we were cold and sleepless.

"But the pain didn't compare to the countless high points. Sequoia and Yosemite. The California and Oregon countrysides. Idaho and Wyoming. And the classic California beaches. Best of all were the Big Horn Mountains with their sweeping roads, blue skies, upland meadows, clear streams, and snow-capped peaks. While in the Big Horns, we camped among the Lodgepole pine forests. What a fantastic scent!"

And the vignettes: "The northern Texas lady asking if it was true that there were trees in Connecticut . . . the cop in smoggy L.A. bull-horning us at 10 a.m. to speed up, screaming that we were blocking traffic by only doing 55 miles per hour . . . and the three bears we nearly hit in Yellowstone. Notable side trips were Tijuana, Mexico, (we couldn't leave fast enough); Webco Inc., the famous maker of Triumph accessories; a new place called Disneyland, and Crater Lake, which had plenty of snow.

"Our longest day in the saddle was 750 miles to Milwaukee. The greatest anticlimax was passing through all-night rain, poor vision, slick roads, on empty stomachs — and finally hitting a glorious day in the Berkshire Mountains. From there we raced home across western Massachusetts, some 5,150 miles from San Diego."

The following winter, Whitney's Triumph received a minor hot-rodding. With it, he says, "the fun went way up but reliability went down." Eventually a friend of his took the trusty Tiger to Europe for yet another long vacation. After crossing two continents, visiting eight countries, and clocking up over 45,000 miles, the T110 had served its riders well. And it rewarded Mike Whitney with an affection for Triumphs that's lasted nearly 50 years.

Through it all his allegiance was unshakably with Meriden, where he remained the tyrannical boss as the company leapt from strength to strength. The marque was glorified in 1955 when an American-built Triumph 650-powered streamliner piloted by Texan Johnny Allen set the world motorcycle speed record at 193 miles per hour at the Bonneville Salt Flats. The following year Allen and the same machine raised the mark to 214 miles per hour. The coveted "World's Fastest Motorcycle" crown belonged to Triumph.

Less known to enthusiasts outside the United States was Triumph's 1-2-3 finish at the Big Bear Run in California. There the big news was the trio of TR6 Trophy models that led the tortuous desert race from start to finish. Another new Triumph 650 had arrived and it proved fast, strong, and reliable right out of the box. The concept of a 650-cc Trophy model had been bubbling up through Meriden's Comp Shop for years. With the advent of the swinging arm frame and T110 engine, now fitted with Triumph's new "Delta" aluminum cylinder head, the concept was put into production for 1956.

Here was a big-motored Triumph designed for any duty. The TR6 could be converted into a 105-mile per hour competition mount simply by removing its quick-detachable headlamp and stands. The first versions targeted off-road riders in the western U.S. states, hence the slender 3.25-gallon fuel tank, 20-inch front wheel, and Lucas K2FC waterproof magneto. The TR6 model range was soon offered in high- and low-piped models, with a choice of street or off-road tires and gearing, quick-detachable rear wheels, and optional skid plates and tachometer.

With gobs of torque spread over a mile-wide power band, the TR6 was equally pleasant to ride in town, on the highway, or across the open desert. In the latter venue it became immortalized as the "desert sled," dominating America's great cross-country races for over a decade. Although it was launched for export only (and unavailable in Britain for nearly two years), works-prepared 650 Trophies ridden by Triumph off-road ace John Giles scored gold medals in the 1956 and 1958 International Six-Days Trials.

Far left
Introduced in 1956, the TR6 Trophy twin married the T110 650-cc engine with the TR5 Trophy chassis. To many Triumph fans it was the company's best all-around product. The early models came in two basic variants: TR6/A (low-piped roadster) and TR6/B (high-piped street scrambler). This restored 1959 B-model, in two-tone Aztec Red and Ivory paint scheme, is owned by Mike Whitney. *Jeff Hackett*

The TR6/B engine was a torquey performer, capable of winning major cross-country races with very little preparation. Standard features in 1959 included alloy cylinder head with 1 1/16-inch Monobloc carburetor, 8.5:1 compression, racing E3134 intake cam and valve springs, Lucas K2FC competition magneto with auto-advance, and a wide-ratio four-speed gearbox. Like all of Triumph's 650 twins that year, the TR6 gained the new one-piece forged steel crankshaft designed for the Bonneville. The oil tank incorporated a froth tower, which ensured steady lubrication under continuous high-speed running. *Jeff Hackett*

As a street machine, the TR6 pulled new buyers into the Triumph fold. Its lean, purposeful styling eschewed the T110's headlamp nacelle and metal-shrouded forks for a separate chromed headlamp, gaitered forks, sports fenders, and iron cylinder barrels painted silver to resemble bare aluminum. It was the sports-utility bike of its day and kicked off the street-scrambler craze of the 1960s and early 1970s.

"In the degree to which it combines tractability and unobtrusiveness with sheer zip and stamina, the Trophy reaches a very high standard indeed," lauded *The Motor Cycle*. But with the praise came hints of unsociability yet to come. Magazine road tests in Britain and the United States began noting a greater degree of vibration in the TR6 (and in the T110) than in the softer-tune Thunderbird. Testers also reported an appetite for only the highest-octane fuel, otherwise "pinking" would occur. The push to squeeze more performance out of Turner's parallel twin was beginning to show its ugly side.

Close-up of the TR6/B's quick-disconnect headlamp plug, also used on TR5 Trophy models. Ride your Triumph to the race, remove the lights for racing, and then refit them for the ride home. *Jeff Hackett*

Right
The 1958 Model Twenty-One (3TA) was Triumph's first unit-construction (engine and transmission in same assembly) twin to enter production since the model 6/1 of the 1930s. It also was the first to suffer Edward Turner's controversial "bathtub" rear enclosure. Styled by Jack Wickes, the two-piece tub was intended to keep the motorcycle clean in Britain's wet climate. Turner wrapped the 22-gauge sheet metal around other 500-cc and 650-cc models; Americans usually stripped it off. The 350-cc twin was easy to ride, thanks to 17-inch wheels and a low 28.5-inch seat height. Note the car-type ignition distributor behind the cylinder, driven by skew gears off the intake cam. Horn is an aftermarket item. *Jeff Hackett*

Triumph Takes a Bath

By the late 1950s motorcyclists found themselves sharing European roads with motorscooters in ever increasing numbers. Scooters were often viewed with equal parts amusement and condescension, but their impact during the 1950s was profound. Born in the late 1940s in war-torn Italy, the modern scooter brought a new clientele to two-wheeled motoring. Their small size made them economical, maneuverable, and easy to park. Their colorful body enclosures offered riders protection from road spray while cloaking the nasty parts exposed on a motorcycle. This made them attractive to women and non-gearhead men alike.

Scooters personified youthful freedom and European *joie de vivre*. They also represented a major source of export revenue. By 1957, over half of all British two-wheeled imports were mopeds and scooters, mostly from Vespa and other Italian makers. But Britain's manufacturers so far had missed the boom.

None of this was lost on Edward Turner. His endless quest to draw new customers to motorcycling and Triumph inspired user-friendly contraptions such as the Slickshift gearbox. It also plunged Triumph into the scooter craze and led the company toward semi-enclosed motorcycle styling.

In 1956, Turner completed designs for BSA's first scooter. Two models were quickly developed—a 175-cc single-cylinder two-stroke and a 250-cc ohv twin-cylinder four-stroke with optional electric starter. When the machines were announced in late 1958, the press was surprised by the marketing plan. Both models would be built by BSA and sold under two brands—Sunbeam (the B1 and B2) and Triumph (the TS1 and TS2). This was the first time a Triumph production model was badge-engineered from another company's product. It would only happen once again, when the 1968–1970 BSA Starfire became Triumph's TR25W Trophy 250.

The Tigress was an ill-timed venture. It hit show rooms just as Britain's scooter boom was fading. Vespa and Lambretta firmly held the market, and the Tigress had not the value nor verve to unseat the Italians. Remarkably, Triumph would dabble in scooters again from 1963 to 1969 with the 100-cc automatic Tina and T10. Like the underwhelming Tigresses, they barely made a mark in scooterdom and are comparatively rare today on the classic-bike scene.

GOING CLUTCHLESS
The Slickshift Gearbox

In 1958 Triumph attempted to expand motorcycling's appeal, and its own sales, by introducing the Slickshift gearbox. The simple system was hoped to lure novices who were daunted by a motorcycle's hand clutch and foot shift operation.

In effect the Slickshift was a clutchless transmission — there was no need to use the handlebar lever to change gears. Foot pressure on the shift lever in either direction disengaged the clutch before engaging the new gear. As long as pressure on the foot lever was maintained, the gearbox remained between gears. Gradual release meant a gradual engagement of the drive again, just as with a clutch.

Triumph offered the Slickshift on all B-range (pre-unit 500-and 650-cc) twins except the Bonneville from 1958 through 1960. In 1961 and 1962, it was available on just the Thunderbird and T110. Though it was easy to learn and worked well, the Slickshift was a sales flop. Even newcomers to the sport preferred to shift gears conventionally. Many Slickshift-equipped Triumphs ended up being converted back to a conventional clutch system—a simple job, because the mechanism was part of the gearbox outer cover.

But Triumph's eastern U.S. distributor didn't give up. TriCor briefly tried to market the Slickshift on its own, by offering it in the accessory catalog as a retrofit to all 1954 through 1957 twins—and with slight modification to pre-1954 bikes, too. "Bring your machine up to date by adding Triumph's latest exclusive feature," crowed the 1958 TriCor catalog about item number CD113, the "Slick Shift Auto-Clutch Control Kit." The $25.74 kit could be installed in 30 minutes, with "no need to dismantle the gearbox."

Some riders kept their Slick Shifts, however, and a few even won races with them. Howard "Shotgun" Winchester of Corpus Christi, Texas, raced a 650 twin from 1958 through 1960 in Class-A scrambles, and he quickly realized that the Slick Shift was a benefit in getting off the start line quickly, and sliding through the corners.

"When the flag dropped, you had to grab the clutch, put the machine in gear and go," Winchester recalled in *Classic Bike*. "Now (with the Slick Shift) I could sit on the line with the Triumph in gear — the pedal held by

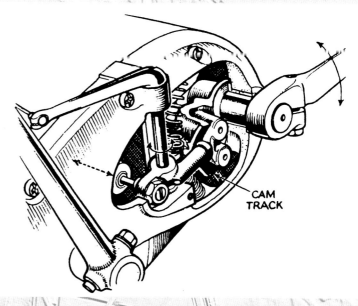

CAM TRACK

my toe — and when the flag dropped, I was gone! I was never beaten off the line because I was the only Triumph rider racing with the Slick Shift."

"Shotgun" explained that most Triumph racers of the period removed the Slick Shift mechanism without bothering to use it to advantage. When he sold his 1958 racer, Winchester kept the Slick Shift gearbox and swapped it onto a new 1960 Triumph. He also kept winning races.

"In my opinion, Triumph and Edward Turner were way ahead of the competition," he reckoned. He was right. In the 1970s Honda and Moto Guzzi both launched motorcycles with automatic transmissions, for the same reason as Triumph. They flopped, too.

While BSA was tooling up for Triumph-badged scooters, Meriden was preparing to launch its first all-new twin since 1938. The 350-cc model Twenty-One that debuted in 1957 was a milestone for Triumph. It ushered in the "unit construction" era of powerplants with integral four-speed gearboxes, to be followed by a range of similarly designed 500-cc models in 1959. The bike's name celebrated 21 years of The Triumph Engineering Company and its 21-ci engine displacement. The latter hook didn't capture American interest as intended, because 350 twins were not marketable stateside until Honda blew the segment wide open in the early 1970s.

But Turner believed there was opportunity in late-1950s Britain for an economical, style-setting middleweight. The Twenty-One (soon designated the 3TA) was born with a deeply valanced front fender rather like those that adorn chubby Harley-Davidsons. The rear of the bike wore a two-piece stamped-steel enclosure that shrouded the oil tank and upper half of the shock absorbers. It looked like an inverted bathtub. Seat height was just 28.5 inches off the ground, thanks to 17-inch wheels. And the seat tilted up to reveal a neat tool tray, with each spanner on display like flatware in a kitchen drawer.

The bodywork, which included the trademark headlamp nacelle "was done to make a device that you could hose down, as well as keep its rider clean," Wickes recalled in 1988. The low seat height made it easy for shorter riders and novices to maneuver. It was the antithesis of the macho TR6 Trophy or BSA Road Rocket—and that's exactly what Turner and his design "pencil" Jack Wickes wanted. To their credit, the Twenty-One targeted a new clientele, which might be put off by a traditional "naked" motorcycle.

The concept of a semienclosed machine was not new. Vincent had tried it in 1955 and Honda would reprise the theme in the 1980s with its ill-fated Pacific Coast. But despite its functionality, the sheet-metal acreage made the Triumph look portly, scooterish, and somewhat effeminate. It also was a hassle to remove for maintenance. But that didn't stop Meriden from "bathtubbing" the 500-cc 5TA, the Thunderbird, and even the Tiger 110.

Americans would have little of it, however. The enclosed models usually went unsold across the United States forcing dealers to strip off the metal panels by the dumptruck load. Wickes finally realized his company's folly during a California visit in 1960. At Bud Ekins' Triumph dealership near Hollywood, he was taken into the back shop by the master desert racer.

"Look at this," scowled Ekins, pointing to a mountain of discarded bathtubs and valenced fenders. "Why do you put them on? We don't need them."

If the 1950s didn't prove that Triumph was all about sporting motorcycles, the next decade's sales certainly would.

The long-stroke 3TA was designed as a low-cost engine, with stamped-steel con-rods (instead of forged aluminum) and lacking a primary chain tensioner. Output was 18.5 horsepower at 6,500 rpm, capable of about 80 miles per hour and 70 miles per gallon fuel economy. Cast-iron cylinder barrels were sprayed silver to look like aluminum, a trait shared by all Triumph 350-cc and 500-cc unit twins through the 1971 model year. *Jeff Hackett*

FOUR

KING OF THE 1960s

"Triumph's successes weren't the result of its motorcycles being particularly better than or especially different from all the other British bikes of the 1950s and 1960s, because they weren't," wrote *Cycle Guide* editor Steve Thompson in 1976. "But somehow the marque, with its lean, classic styling, legendary performance, nimble handling, and total commitment to racing, became a symbol of everything motorcycling stood for, and the embodiment of the sport itself.

"A Triumph looked, ran and sounded the way a motorcycle was supposed to look, run and sound," Thompson opined. "And no matter how many other motorcycles a rider owned, he ultimately longed for a Triumph."

It was truer than ever in late-1950s Britain, where motorcycle longing exploded into a sales boom. The decade began with severe austerity in the wake of World War II and Korea and a shortage of the 650-cc twins that were earning vital export dollars. It ended with a robust national economy and more of the big roadburners available on the home market.

Full employment (under 2.5 percent unemployment), minimal inflation, and higher wages for a shorter work week had turned the Midlands automobile industry into a mecca for high-paying jobs. Triumph's Meriden factory was smack-dab in the middle of it. British working blokes "never had it so good," as Prime Minister Harold Macmillan boasted in a speech.

For election year 1959, Macmillan lit a fire under consumer spending. He relaxed credit rates and lowered the purchase tax. Suddenly, that Tiger Cub, Speed Twin, or Thunderbird became much more attainable for the working man. With juicy incentives to buy a new bike combined with the UK's driest weather in 200 years, nearly 332,000 new machines were sold. It was an all-time record, although half of them were scooters and mopeds from Vespa, Lambretta, NSU, and Zundapp.

Mighty Triumph and BSA captured the lion's share of sales of the 250-cc and larger bikes. It was a blockbuster year that set the stage for unimaginable growth in the 1960s. But for the British makers, the tables were turning. "By 1963 imports (led by Honda) had begun to outnumber the home-produced models," recalled *Classic Bike Magazine* writer Peter Watson in 1986.

Close-up of '59 Bonneville cylinder head shows the stuff that created a legend. The two 1 1/16-inch "chopped" Amal Monobloc carbs lacked the integral float bowls of the regular Monobloc and instead used an Amal GP central mixing chamber, mounted on the frame's seat post. Not the easiest setup to keep in sharp tune, particularly for low-speed running, as many early-Bonneville owners discovered. *Jeff Hackett*

Left
The original 1959 T120 Bonneville was basically a Tiger 110 fitted with Triumph's twin-carb Delta cylinder head. Why Edward Turner chose to clothe his new supersports model in a headlamp nacelle and deeply valenced fenders, instead of styling it as a twin-carb Trophy 650, is one of the great mysteries in Triumph history. Tangerine and Pearl Grey paintwork were also unpopular. The black battery box and oil tank distinguished British and Canadian market T120s from the U.S. models, whose midriffs were Pearl Grey. *Jeff Hackett*

The competitive landscape in the United States was changing fast, too. Honda Motor Co. set up its first office in California and was confident of selling 5,000 of its small-bore machines *per month* at a time when Johnson Motors was selling 2,500 Triumphs per year in the 19 western states. Former JoMo salesman Jack McCormack joined the fledgling Japanese firm as its first national sales manager, and often visited prospective Honda dealers on his TR6.

Triumph's U.S. leadership first viewed Honda's 1959 entry with little more than curiosity. After all, BSA and Harley-Davidson were their main competitors and Honda's bikes were mere tiddlers. But in 1961 came the 305-cc Super Hawk—as quick as a Tiger 100 but with far better brakes, an electric starter, and a lower price tag. Two years later, Honda sold 90,000 motorcycles in the United States and controlled more than 60 percent of the market.

During the next few years it opened scores of franchises at many established Triumph stores. Indeed, Honda executives considered Triumph's two U.S. distributors and its dealer network to be the industry's best, and they welcomed partnering with them.

With nothing smaller than the Tiger Cub to compete for the first-time rider, JoMo and TriCor soon began encouraging their dealers to add a Honda franchise. Having a complete range of lightweight, user-friendly Hondas to complement Triumph's "big bikes" (with their lucrative parts and service work), was like having a license to print money. Triumph-Honda shops were the industry's most coveted, and the dealers prospered. It was a plum for Triumph, as long as the Hondas stayed south of the 500-cc line.

A year after its shaky introduction, the Bonneville was restyled to look like a proper Triumph, with sports fenders, separate headlamp and gauges, and rubber fork gaiters. The move ignited sales, creating one of motorcycling's greatest icons. For the 1960 model year only, U.S.-market Bonnies were officially cataloged as the TR7/A (low pipes) and TR7/B (high pipes), even though their toolbox transfers and engine cases were marked T120. From 1961 through 1965, the high-piped Bonnie was redesignated the T120C. This rare TR7/B Bonneville Scrambler was restored by Cliff Rushworth of London-based Ace Classics. *Mick Duckworth*

Not everyone jumped on the Japanese bandwagon, however. Sam Hawley was a successful Triumph dealer in Saginaw, Michigan, where well-paid autoworkers bought a lot of his motorcycles. In 1994, he recalled a day 33 years earlier when Jack Mercer, TriCor's regional salesman, visited his shop.

"Jack wanted us to take a Honda franchise," Hawley told the author. "He figured that Honda would help us expand our business for Triumphs." Standing with Mercer amidst a row of gleaming Trophy 650s, Hawley imagined his show room full of 50-cc and 90-cc step-throughs. Then he turned to his brother Don (the shop's mechanic) and said, "You know, Donny, sellin' Hondas would be just like sellin' lawnmowers."

Hawley passed up the Honda opportunity and never wavered in his Triumph faith. "I'd probably be a lot richer today if I'd taken Mercer's advice," he recalled with a chuckle. "But I wouldn't be as happy." He was still restoring Triumphs and selling parts in the late 1990s.

Turner Meets Honda

Ironically, the Japanese juggernaut was seen first-hand by Edward Turner. In late 1960 Turner visited the factories of Honda, Suzuki, and Yamaha on a trip sponsored by Mikuni, the carburetor giant which was then Triumph's distributor in Japan. What he saw opened his eyes wide to the looming threat.

"It is essential that our industry in general and the BSA Group in particular should know the facts and what we are up against in the retention of our export markets," Turner wrote in his extensive report of the trip, which he circulated among BSA upper management. At the time Triumph was exporting half of its production; by decade's end, it would be more than 80 percent.

First made public in Ivor Davies' 1980 book, *It's A Triumph*, the report warned that if the British bike makers did not step up to Japan's challenge, "The home market for motorcycles will be assailed and although personally I do not think the Japanese Motor Cycle Industry will eclipse the tractional type of machine that the

The 1960 TR7/B shared Triumph's new twin-downtube duplex frame with the company's other 650-cc models. The new frame was a disaster. It telegraphed more vibration to the rider than the previous frame and was prone to cracking near the steering head. It also caused fuel tank brackets to break. In an attempt to cure the problem, Meriden tried to stiffen the frame by adding a lower fuel tank rail—which merely raised the vibes even more, splitting tanks! The problem continued until the 1963 model year, when a new single downtube frame was introduced. *Mick Duckworth*

British motorcyclist wants and buys, they are bound to make some impact on our home market by virtue of the high quality and low prices."

At the time of Turner's visit, the Japanese were producing over 500,000 motorcycles per year, with output steadily rising. By comparison, the entire British industry built 140,000 machines. Triumph's total output stood around 28,000 units (roughly 10,000 of them Cubs), according to British motojournalist Steve Wilson in his superb book, *Triumph T120/T140 Bonneville.*

Turner was particularly awed by Honda from its vast R&D department to its amazingly efficient assembly lines. The immense Hammamatsu factory produced nearly every part of the motorcycle. "The surface finishes on machined parts and standards of accuracy were, I should think, better than our best work," Turner commented.

He also noted that Honda tested every new machine on automated "rolling road" rigs inside the clean, dry factory. On these devices, the motorcycle was started and remained stationary, while a worker ran it up and down through the gears to check the engine, gearbox, drive chain, lights, and electrical system. The rig gave a readout of each bike's performance. At Meriden, road testing was a literal job. A team of Belstaff-suited riders led by the indomitable Percy Tait braved rain, sleet, and local traffic to evaluate bikes chosen randomly off the assembly line.

It is interesting to note the reception given Turner, the father of the modern middleweight motorcycle, by Soichiro Honda, father of the modern lightweight. Rather than meet the British motorcycle industry icon himself, Mr. Honda instead sent his brother Benjiro, manager of the Hammamatsu plant, to serve as host. The company founder was nowhere to be seen during Turner's well-announced visit. By Turner's own account, Benjiro Honda politely criticized Triumph's 650-cc range as being obsolete, but praised the unit-construction 3TA and 5TA twins as being as up-to-date as any Honda model.

The hidebound BSA board unfortunately did not react to Turner's "Japan Report." The board's shortsightedness helped doom the company 10 years later. It is the author's opinion that the 1960–1964 period marked the last critical "window" through which Triumph-BSA could have turned itself around, given market foresight, the resources to develop new products, and the will to compete. Revenues from both brands were strong and there still was ample cash available to invest in new tooling, which was sorely needed at Triumph.

Peter Starr worked at Meriden in the early 1960s. He recalled the atmosphere of the plant in a 1994 *Rider* magazine feature: "The factory, set in the geographic heart of England, was aging," noted Starr. "Like many engineering firms in the 1960s, the lathes and milling machines were antiquated, driven by belts strung from a common power shaft that spanned the length of the building.

"The machinery ran the gamut from a 1912 bar automatic machine used for making fork top nuts for the World War I war effort, to semiautomated, punch-card-controlled borers. It was a dichotomy that presented quality control problems needing skilled labor to minimize.

"One could walk past rows of milling machines almost obscured by crankcases stacked eight abreast and 10 feet high," he continued. "The machine operators stood on wooden platforms to avoid slipping in the white cutting oil that spilled on the floor. Amid the smell and acrid taste of rusting steel, frame tubes were bent and then brazed to precast steering head lugs by men who were the blacksmiths of the motorcycle industry."

Like the machine shop, Meriden's paint department employed a mixture of men and women, a holdover from World War II. "They created the quality look of Triumph with mixtures of paint bearing exotic names," Starr recalled. "There were men who spent their entire lives hand-striping gas tanks, almost a Triumph trademark."

Most of Triumph's component production was "piecework." Everything was made in batches and the workers were paid for each individual item they made. If they produced their required quota ahead of time, the workers would sometimes sit down for a game of cards next to the pile of finished parts. Piecework was a holdover from the craft guilds of the previous century, when English workmanship was the envy of the industrial world.

By the 1960s, however, it was an inefficient, costly process, kept alive by the many powerful labor unions that controlled Meriden's shop floor. The assemblers had a union. The electricians had a union. The machinists, painters, and shipping department each had a union. And with worldwide demand for new Triumphs far outstripping the factory's production, the unions knew they'd get what they wanted simply by staging wildcat strikes.

Halfway around the world, the Japanese makers that had so impressed Turner were building more bikes per day than Triumph built in a week. And they had superior overall quality, if not yet the style, size, and handling to topple the Brits.

To most motorcyclists, however, what counted was the look, sound, and charisma of the machine and who was in the winner's circle each weekend. By that measurement, Triumph had no peer. In America, the durable TR6 scored victory after victory at the tough cross-country races. The new unit-500 twin also was beginning to beat the BSA Gold Stars and Harleys on West Coast dirt tracks in the hands of Sammy Tanner and Joe Leonard.

In Britain, the Speed Twin carried thousands of owners to work or holiday, while the cast-iron Thunderbird racked up impressive mileages and remained a favorite sidecar tug. And the diminutive Tiger Cub was a lightweight for all purposes.

The Cub's stature had soared in 1959 when Roy Peplow won the Scottish Six-Day Trial on a factory-prepared model. It was a milestone victory for the T20, the first time any machine under 250-cc beat all comers in the world's premier trials event. Peplow's win on the plucky little single instantly made dinosaurs out of the 500-cc heavyweights in observed trials.

While Honda's Super Cub was starting a craze, Triumph's Tiger Cub was already *the* sports lightweight to own on both sides of the Atlantic. Riders who used their frugal Cubs for daily transport could point to a host of high-profile successes—Peplow's Scottish upset; victories at the International Six-Days Trials (ISDT); Catalina GP; Big Bear Run and, in 1962, the overall win at the grueling 538-mile Jack Pine Enduro in Michigan. Cubs also shook the Salt: California Triumph dealer Bill Martin tucked his highly tuned T20 motor inside a modified aircraft belly tank, took it to the Bonneville Salt Flats and averaged 139 miles per hour on gasoline, for a new AMA speed record.

The peppy, easy-handling Cub continued to introduce riders to the Triumph life through 1968, by which time it had become a BSA Bantam-framed mongrel and was outclassed by the more refined lightweights from Japan. During its final years, Cub production was transferred to Beeza's Small Heath works to free up Meriden for more twin-cylinder output.

Despite Honda selling far more bikes, the 1960s was Triumph's decade. And it began with a blockbuster.

The *Monster* Births the Bonnie

Motorcyclists rarely are satisfied with last year's performance. The birth of Triumph's legendary Bonneville is often linked to American cries for more horsepower, particularly from the influential U.S. distributors. Although this is partially true, the lust for more muscle wasn't an American-only thing.

Britain's first superhighway, the London-to-Birmingham M1, opened in late 1959. Suddenly, all but the hottest T110s, Gold Stars, Velocette Venoms, and other sporting tackle (Vincents excluded) seemed barely adequate. The M1 had no speed limit in those early days, and every kid with an untamed throttle hand wanted to show his bike's stuff. Other fast motorways and bypasses were under construction. And the advent of the popular Morris Mini meant more cars and more road traffic.

No rider worth his leathers could deny that a quicker, more powerful 650 Triumph was worth having. Such a machine had been in development since 1955, when Comp Shop manager Henry Vale and his chief tuner, Frank Baker, began converting the new Delta cylinder head to twin carburetors. Their immediate focus was the work's 650-cc scramblers being built for Triumph's off-road ace, John Giles. Fitting a large air cleaner on the single-carb TR6 for dirt work interfered with the bike's center frame tube. But a dual-carb head, with its inlet ports splayed (offset at an angle from center) could package twin Monoblocs with oversize filters.

A few of these special heads were fitted to Giles' race bikes. In 1957, the Comp Shop built its first dual-carb, splayed-port production bikes, a small batch of Tiger 100s. Triumph also offered the head as a dealer-installed option for 500s only. A year later the dual-carb head was featured on the TR5AD Trophy (the "D" stood for Delta). This limited edition "hot" 500 was Triumph's priciest model in the United States, retailing for $18 more than a TR6. In all, only 47 splayed-port 500s were built in 1957–1958, according to Triumph Owners Club records. Their presence helped ignite demand for a similar top-end for the 650-cc models.

One of Triumph's off-road stars, the legendary John Giles, aviates a mud-spattered Trophy 500 at the Experts Grand National scramble in Britain, July 1961. The scrambles and trials ace won a gold medal in the 1958 ISDT on a Trophy 650. He was still winning vintage-class races in 2000. *B.R. Nicholls*

Customers wanted more "umph" and Triumph obliged initially through its service parts operation. A dual-carb Delta head for the 650s appeared as part number CD110 in TriCor's 1958 accessories catalog, the company's mother lode of speed goodies. This $96 kit sold out quickly; most were fitted to TR6s. Demand caused the U.S. distributors to continue pressing the factory for a dual-carb 650-cc production model—a supersports Trophy.

Club racers in Britain wanted the same; their Tiger 110s were having a tough time against the Gold Stars. One exception was the 1958 Thruxton 500-mile endurance race, where T110-mounted Mike Hailwood and "Banbury" Dan Shorey teamed up for the victory.

That year it all came together, as usual, in the factory's Experimental Department. Percy Tait was given a dual-carb T110 "mule" to flog on his daily 300-mile test circuit. Nicknamed the *Monster*, it was equipped with a much stronger bottom-end, necessary if the more powerful engine was to hold together on the street and in competition. For high-rpm durability, a new one-piece forged crankshaft replaced Turner's original two-piece design.

Optimum breathing was achieved with a race-proven E3134 inlet camshaft from the Tiger 100 and a milder E3325 exhaust cam from the Tiger 110, along with revised timing and a pair of 1 1/16-inch Amals, fed by a separate, centrally mounted float bowl. Compression ratio was up a half-point, to 8.5:1. Dropped T100C handlebars allowed Tait to wring every bit of speed out of the bike.

The *Monster* sparked excitement at the factory whenever Tait was aboard. "It wasn't uncommon to see people standing outside just to listen to the music of Percy approaching the factory," recalled service maestro Hughie Hancox in his entertaining book, *Tales of Triumph Motorcycles and the Meriden Factory*. "You could hear him accelerate out of the village, power up the hill and over the top, then start his changing down from over 100 miles per hour to brake for the factory gates. Magic!"

Frank Baker took the *Monster* to the Motor Industry Research Association high-speed track, where Tait circulated the banked oval at 128 miles per hour "and he had a hell of a job to stop" with the marginal single-shoe brakes, Baker noted later in a *Classic Bike* interview.

Baker, Hancox, and their mates were elated when told the dual-carb T110 project was given the green light. Indeed, just prior to the prestigious 1958 Earls Court motorcycle show, Edward Turner ordered the hot 650 to debut as a production model for 1959. For its name he borrowed from the world's most famous speed venue, the site of Johnny Allen's 214-mile per hour record runs: Bonneville.

The bike's official T120 model code hinted at true 120 mile per hour capability. In truth, the sharpest stock Bonnies (including the later 750-cc models) would rarely exceed 112 miles per hour with a tailwind. The dual-carb engine made a claimed 46 horsepower at 6,500 rpm, 4 more horses than the T110. The go-fast gear added 9 pounds, taking the dry weight to 404 pounds.

While Triumph's new flagship had plenty of speed potential, it suffered a serious case of the Sheet Metal Blues. Basing the Bonneville on the 1959 T110 was a grand mistake by Turner. Even with its screaming Aztec Red (bright tangerine) and Pearl Grey two-tone paint scheme, the Bonnie inherited the Tiger's big, black headlamp nacelle with inset instruments, deeply valenced fenders, metal shrouded fork, and wide seat. The look shouted "touring bike" instead of "sports machine."

The logical platform for the Bonnie was the lean, lithe TR6. Why Turner didn't base the first Bonnie on the athletic Trophy is one of the most vexing mysteries of Triumph history. Correspondence between Don Brown, then sales boss at JoMo, and Meriden's export manager A. J. Mathieu confirms that Turner intended to wrap both the TR6 and Bonneville in full bathtub bodywork for the 1960 model year! The T110 styling was already halfway to that makeover.

It's chilling to consider what stamped-steel enclosures would have done to Triumph's racehorses, not to mention their impact on the company's sporting image. Certainly Turner had first-hand knowledge of U.S. motorcyclists' tastes. He knew the Yanks loved the Trophy look. But his thinking on the original Bonnie's styling may have been influenced by his "other" job, heading BSA Group's automotive division. Carlike bodywork gave better weather protection, he believed, and made cleaning the bike much easier.

Bungling the Bonnie's birth caused widespread disappointment and slow sales of the T120 in the U.S. market. First-year Bonnevilles soon piled up in the TriCor and JoMo warehouses, and the backlog wasn't sold off for another 12 months. By that time, Triumph had learned its lesson and gave the Bonnie proper Trophy styling. It was offered in two guises: a low-piped roadster and high-piped street scrambler, the latter sold only in the United States. It was in roadster form that the Bonneville legend took off. The machine quickly became Triumph's most desired model. Soon it was Triumph's best seller in the United States.

American cross-country racing hero Bud Ekins was part of Triumph's factory team in two International Six Days Trials during the 1960s. He's all business here, as usual, splashing his TR6 through Llandrindod Wells during the 1961 event. Ekins also rode a works-prepped TR6 in the 1964 ISDT. *B.R. Nicholls*

Movie idol Steve McQueen was an accomplished motorcyclist, high-ranked amateur racer, and Triumph lover in the 1960s. He's shown here on the set of the World War II film, *The Great Escape*, with the 1961 TR6/A used to make the famous barbed-wire jump in the movie. The Trophybird was modified by McQueen's pal, Bud Ekins, to "resemble" a stolen army BMW. Ekins, an expert stunt rider, did the actual jump for the camera. *David Gaylin archive*

The 1960 range comprised nine models, and with it came an all-new duplex frame for the 650s. Designed to be stiffer and thus improve handling, it featured twin front down tubes, a steeper steering head angle and shorter wheelbase. However, the new frame couldn't stand up to the abuse of American desert racers, whose punishing treatment caused numerous breakages. One of them had a catastrophic result.

Edward Turner, attending the Big Bear Run with Bill Johnson, reportedly witnessed the death of a young racer when the steering head of his 1960 TR6 snapped off. Turner ordered an immediate investigation of the cause. The subsequent redesign incorporated an extra tube running longitudinally underneath the fuel tank. The "fix" improved torsional rigidity. The magazines were quick to sample the revamped product.

"Steering is considerably heavier than previous Triumphs and considerably improved by being more positive," wrote *The Motor Cycle* writer David Dixon of a 1961 Bonneville. "The model is rock-steady at all speeds. There are few machines I would ride hands-off at 80-plus on wet, windy days and on greasy roads, but I had no qualms about doing so on the Bonneville."

Dixon noted the reworked Bonnie required a fair bit of effort to heel over, but once into the corner it remained on line. Only the propstand on the left or the footrest on the right impeded lean angle. The bike earned its first major road race win in July 1961, when John Holder and Tony Godfrey gave Triumph its second Thruxton 500-mile victory in four years.

In sunny California, Joe Parkhurst's new *Cycle World* magazine chose a 1962 Bonnie for its inaugural road test. Triumph's roadburner showed its well-rounded manners. It started easily and idled reliably, if a bit lumpy.

"From about 2,000 rpm in fourth gear, one can just crank it on," wrote the editors, "and as long as too much throttle is not given until the speed builds up, the T120 will pull smoothly away. Not only that, but with even our fairly bulky test rider aboard and sitting bolt-upright, this remarkable machine would easily push past 100 miles per hour and run steadily at that velocity as though it would never tire."

Stiffening the duplex frame had a downside: It telegraphed more engine vibration to the rider. The dilemma was becoming familiar: As it boosted power of the 500-cc and 650-cc parallel twins through higher compression ratios, hairier camshafts, and bigger carbs, Triumph could only chase their vibes further up the rev range by altering crankshaft balance factors, changing final drive ratios, and other minor tricks. It was impossible to rid the evil shakes entirely with the traditional configuration.

Owners got used to blown light bulbs, fractured brackets, and endless time spent tightening nuts and bolts. It was the price of admission if you wanted to ride a Triumph. In the 1960s, only BMW built a truly smooth middleweight Twin.

Triumph upped its reputation as World's Fastest Motorcycle in 1962, when Bill Johnson (no relation to Johnson Motors' founder) piloted this tube-framed streamliner to multiple AMA and FIM world speed records. The 15.6-foot-long projectile was designed and built by Joe Dudek, then chief mechanic at North American Aircraft in California. Dudek modeled the fiberglass shell after the fabulous X-15 rocket plane. With a single 667-cc T120R engine running on gasoline, the bike went 205.76 miles per hour. Then, on nitro fuel, it raised the ultimate AMA Class S-A record to 230.26 miles per hour, followed by an FIM world record at 224 miles per hour. *Lindsay Brooke archive*

A New 650 and Daytona Triumphs

With his parallel twin approaching 25 years old and his company riding high atop its market, Edward Turner began contemplating retirement. In mid-1961 he hired his old colleague, Bert Hopwood, away from Norton, where he'd been managing director. Hopwood was appointed general manager of Triumph Engineering Co. and

TURNER'S V-8 SPORTS CAR

In 1956, BSA management asked Edward Turner to design a V8-powered sedan for its Daimler car division. Turner immediately went to Jack Wickes, Triumph's chief draftsman and a supremely talented stylist in his own right. The two of them started roughing out details of a pushrod ohv 2.5-liter V8. Within eight months a prototype was running on Daimler's factory dynamometer.

It was a gem. Turner loved Cadillacs, and he and Wickes used Cadillac's renowned ohv V-8 as their inspiration for much of the Daimler engine. The main difference was in the cylinder heads, which closely resembled early Chrysler Hemi V-8 heads. However, the Daimler heads were aluminum and their hemispherical combustion chambers and valve geometry were copied from Triumph's 650-cc Thunderbird.

The little V-8 proved to be robust. It also liked to rev and responded willingly to tuning. According to Daimler historian Brian Long, in his book, *Daimler V8 SP250*, a prototype produced 200 horsepower and pulled strongly to 8,000 rpm when fitted with eight Amal Monoblocs—and Triumph E3134 cam forms!

Wickes sketched a four-door sedan for the V-8, but the project was sidelined for a two-seat roadster. British sports cars were winning American customers and BSA Group hoped to cash in on the craze. It was unfortunate that their offering, the SP250, failed to hit the mark, in spite of its excellent engine.

Launched in 1959, the SP was unique in many ways. Besides V-8 power (when most competitors had four cylinders) and 120 mile per hour potential, the flashy roadster also featured a fiberglass body, Dunlop disc brakes on all four wheels, and an optional automatic transmission. Auto writers loved the SP250's acceleration and high level of equipment, but they criticized the car's excessive chassis flex during hard cornering

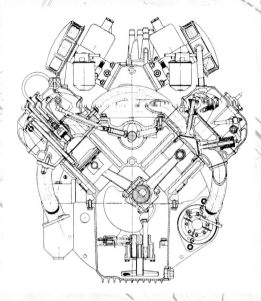

The valvegear layout and some basic geometries of Edward Turner's 2.5L Hemi-head Daimler V-8 were influenced by the Triumph Speed Twin. Bore and stroke measured 3.0 x 2.75. Claimed output was 140 horsepower at 5,800 rpm and 155 lbs-ft of torque at 3,600 rpm. Compression ratio was 8.2:1. The V-8 had a cast-iron cylinder block, aluminum heads, and oil pan. Note the high camshaft location and twin SU carburetors.
Automotive Industries Magazine

as well as its stiff ride. The flamboyant styling was polarizing; people either loved the SP or loathed it. Even today it appears overwrought compared with its many handsome contemporaries.

And the SP250 was expensive. At £1,495 (about $4,146), it cost £200 (about $500) more than an Austin-Healey 3000 MkI, £300 (about $840) more than a TR4 and was £400 (about $1,120) above the MGA, TR3 and Sunbeam Alpine. Having a V-8 behind that toothy chromed grille did not make up for a premium price.

The Triumph Corporation was the SP250's official U.S. distributor until late 1960 when BSA sold Daimler to Jaguar. On the verge of launching its fabulous E-Type, Jaguar had scant interest in the SP despite giving it two upgrades (Series B and C) that stiffened the chassis and further refined the car.

SP production ended in 1964, after some 2,650 examples were produced—a far cry from BSA's forecast of 3,000 units per year. London's Metropolitan Police purchased 26 SP250s with automatic gearboxes. These were often used to intercept Rocker boys on their fast café racers.

Turner's V-8 lived on, getting a boost to 4.5 liters and powering larger Daimler cars through 1968. His fascination for V-8 engines continued, too. According to Long, before Turner's 1964 retirement he designed a four-cam, 3.0-liter race motor. It was aimed at the 1966 Formula 1 season, but did not progress past the drawing stage.

A Daimler SP250 Dart sports car. Lindsay Brooke

was also made a company director. It was predicted that Turner would hand over Triumph's reigns to Hopwood, a move the BSA board seemed likely to approve when the time came.

The following year, Hopwood stole more talent from Norton when he lured away the brilliant Doug Hele to become Triumph's chief development engineer. At Norton, Hele had further improved the immortal Manx and conceived the 500-cc twin-cylinder Domiracer. He brought design engineer Brian Jones with him; Jones would eventually become Triumph's chief engineer in the last years of the Meriden Co-Op.

Immediately Hele set about bringing Triumph's handling up to par with his former employer's widely respected products. (See sidebar.) His arrival caused the veteran Frank Baker, who had joined Triumph in the late 1930s, to offer his resignation. But Hopwood valued Baker's experience and put him in charge of production-bike development.

"Once there I badgered Hopwood to let me have a rolling road," Baker recalled in a 1993 *Classic Bike*. "The Australian market was very valuable to Triumph and in the winter we weren't allowed to road test the bikes to be exported there because the mud they picked up might carry foot-and-mouth disease." Baker's request was approved and he purchased a British-made Heenan and Froude unit, which quickly paid for itself.

"We were having problems with the 350-cc model Twenty-One seizing, and no one could discover why," said Baker. "Once we got the rolling road, I called in Lucas with their test equipment and they quickly discovered that a maverick spark was causing all the trouble."

Further adoption of rolling road rigs helped Triumph improve its quality, although they never totally replaced the team of test riders, which Meriden continued to employ through 1983.

Hele joined Triumph just as a new 650-cc twin made its debut. The engine was codesigned by Hopwood and Turner, and ET's penchant for lightness was evident throughout. The Bonneville, Trophy, and Thunderbird,

now with gearbox casing and crankcase made as an integral casting, joined their 350-cc and 500-cc cousins in boasting "unit construction," although BSA's A65 had gotten there a year earlier. Turner's original "preunit" powerplant and its separate transmission, after 25 glorious years, were history. So was the hassle of adjusting the gearbox to tension the primary chain.

Numerous other changes graced the new-for-1963 650, including a lighter, stronger crankshaft. The cylinder head had extra finning and redesigned rocker boxes, and it was held down with an additional (ninth) stud. A twin row primary chain replaced the old single-row item. And the electrical system gained coil ignition, its twin contact breakers mounted within an easily accessible pocket in the timing cover. The end of Triumph's magneto era coincided with Lucas ending its magneto production.

In the same way the 500s had changed a few years before, the "unit" 650 was lighter, more compact, and cleaner looking than its pre-unit predecessor. Power steadily rose to a claimed 52 horsepower for the Bonneville and 45 horsepower for the single-carb TR6s; in reality these 1969–1970 figures were probably

Left
The T100S/S was Triumph's hot 500 twin for the British market in 1963, with two-into-one Siamesed exhaust but still with "bikini" rear enclosure. The 350-cc Tiger 90 was virtually identical. *Lindsay Brooke*

Triumph twins, particularly the TR6, ruled the Southern California deserts from the mid-1950s through the mid-1960s. The single-carb 650s, stripped to their essentials and wearing knobby tires and hefty skid plates, won every major cross-country race. This is Pat Owens, service manager at Johnson Motors and tuner for Eddie Mulder and Gene Romero, exercising his "desert sled" somewhere in the Mojave. *Lindsay Brooke archive*

closer to 48 and 42 horsepower respectively. Despite complaints from some zealots that the unit-650 vibrated more than the preunit one, Triumph's "40-incher" (as Americans liked to call the 40-ci powerplant) remained motorcycling's greatest all-around engine. It gave riders a superiority complex, able to doddle through villages in third or fourth gear one minute and smoke Harley Sportsters in stoplight drag races the next.

The problematic duplex frame that lasted just three model years was replaced in 1963. This one reverted to a single front downtube, beefier than in 1959. It was welded into a splayed engine cradle and the rear subframe bolted on as before, but with a stiffer swing arm and stouter engine and swing-arm mounts.

This basic chassis would serve Triumph's 650-cc twins admirably through the 1970 model year, and in similar form was used on the T100s until 1973. Early versions still exhibited stubborn wobbles at speeds over 90 miles per hour, requiring riders to twist the steering damper. A much stronger fork with external springs was added in 1964 and it helped improve stability and ride quality.

But the significant changes that made good twins great were brought by Doug Hele between 1966 and 1968. They included a revised steering head angle; further reinforcement around the swinging arm; two-way fork damping with shuttle-valve internals; an excellent 8-inch front brake with twin-leading shoe; and scores of engine and gearbox improvements. Critics who claim Triumphs "never changed" over the years have not studied a service parts manual!

By the late 1960s, Triumph twins reached their apogee of power, style, and *coolness*. The 500-cc and 650-cc ranges each included low-piped roadsters and high-piped street scramblers, distinguished by single or twin carburetors, slim-line 2 1/2-gallon tanks or 3 1/2-gallon "touring" tanks, painted or polished stainless steel fenders, and paint schemes. Even if you were weaned on a Honda, you probably lusted for a Trophy, Tiger, or Bonneville.

"When I was growing up, Triumphs were the bikes I wanted to own," admitted Thomas Elliott, Honda Motor Co.'s top-ranking American executive at the time this book was written.

The marque's competition successes on Sunday kept the show rooms busy on Monday. A Triumph 650-powered streamliner built by Joe Dudek and piloted by Bill Johnson (no relation to JoMo's founder) raised the world's motorcycle

Left
Contrary to the myth that "Triumphs never changed," the company upgraded its machines through steady evolution. The 1965 T120R Bonneville benefited from an improved fork, a better stand, and the now-classic teardrop "sports" mufflers. This was the last year for the Bonnie's large, 3.5-gallon fuel tank and parcel grid. The Pacific Blue and Silver paint scheme is lovely on this restored machine, seen at Triumph Day in Massachusetts. *Jeff Hackett*

"Come and see the New '65s!" Johnson Motors sales manager Don Brown (right) receives Triumph's first $100,000 order for new bikes from a single dealership—Bill Robertson's shop in Hollywood, California. In 1960s America, having a Triumph-Honda store was like having a license to print money. Many veteran Triumph dealers added Honda, and the Japanese brand brought trade-up customers to Triumph—until the CB750 Four arrived. *Don J. Brown collection*

Trophy 500-riding Bill Baird was U.S. Grand National Enduro champion for seven straight years, from 1962 through 1968. He's shown here at the 1962 Jack Pine Enduro in Michigan. Baird finally won the punishing 500-mile event in 1968, after twice finishing a close second. *Bill Baird collection*

speed record to 230 miles per hour in 1962. Four years later Detroit Triumph dealer and drag-race star Bob Leppan boosted the mark to 245 miles per hour. His spectacular Gyronaut X-1 streamliner was powered by a pair of modified preunit 650 twins.

Triumph notched its first Daytona 200 victory in 1962 at the new Speedway. TriCor-sponsored Don Burnett's T100 racer beat Dick Mann's Matchless G50 by less than 12 feet. Burnett's win came just hours after the announcement that Bill Johnson, the man who put Triumph on the map in America, had passed away.

Triumphs became a favorite Hollywood "extra" in the 1960s, with Tiger, Trophy, and Bonneville twins cast as TV show regulars and movie magnets. Film fans around the world were thrilled by the motorcycle jump scenes that climaxed *The Great Escape*. The most astute viewers of this World War II saga could see that the bike ridden by actor Steve McQueen was not a German army BMW. It was a trusty TR6/A, wearing pseudo-BMW fenders.

What the public didn't know until years later was that off-road racing king and Sherman Oaks, California, Triumph dealer Bud Ekins

Britain's Rickman brothers created a thriving aftermarket business with their Metisse lightweight steel frames for scramblers and road machines.
The excellent off-road chassis kit, which included fiberglass fuel tank and seat unit, became a favorite of motocrossers, who fitted their choice of engine.
An expert racer himself, Don Rickman aviates his Triumph-Metisse to victory in the 1966 British 500-cc GP at Farleigh Castle. *B.R. Nicholls*

Triumph prototyped its first three-cylinder model in 1965, two years before BSA Group executives learned that Honda was developing a 750 Four. Designed by Doug Hele and Bert Hopwood, the P1 employed the long-stroke 63x80-mm dimensions of the preunit 500 twin. The powerplant was fitted to a 1965 T120 Bonneville chassis—the classic "Triumph look" that the production 1969 Trident lacked. This machine was painstakingly re-created from ultrarare factory prototype parts by the Trident and Rocket-3 Owners Club in England. The project was assisted by Bill Crosby, proprietor of the famous Reg Allen Triumph shop in London, where this photo was taken in 1998. *Mick Duckworth*

actually performed the jumps. It was a busy summer for Ekins, who while in Germany to film the movie also contested the ISDT on a factory-prepped TR6/B.

"I got a week off (from filming) and won a gold medal in the 750-cc class on a bike Triumph flew out from England to Munich," Ekins explained in 1992. "It had 6 miles on the clock when I started and 1,200 miles at the end."

Daytona Done Right

Edward Turner retired in 1964. He remained on the BSA board until 1967 while serving as a consultant to the company through his one-man design firm, ET Developments. As an outsider he conceived plans for a four-cylinder machine, and was given the brief to design BSA's 350-cc dohc, five-speed Bandit/Fury twins, which were slated for 1971 but never produced. Turner's 1968 prototype was quick (Percy Tait tested it at MIRA at 112 miles per hour) but so fragile, it had to be totally reengineered at the 11th hour by Hele's team.

Left
Production racing was big business in England during the 1960s, pitting the major factories against each other. Race wins helped sell new machines. In the 1966 500-mile race at Brands Hatch, John Blanchard, on a works-prepared Bonneville, goes around Tony Smith on the factory BSA Lightning. *R.R. Nicholls*

Thruxton Bonnevilles were built by Meriden in very small batches for the factory production racing team, as well as "approved" Triumph dealers. *EMAP archive*

Start of the 1969 Thruxton 500-mile Production Race shows factory-backed riders everywhere. In foreground, No. 53 John Cooper (Triumph Bonneville) gets the jump on No. 60 Peter Williams (Norton Commando), No. 51 Ray Pickrell (Bonneville), and No. 52 Malcolm Uphill (Bonneville). *Mick Woollett archive*

Malcolm Uphill flashes through Governors Bridge on his way to winning the Isle of Man 750-cc Production TT in 1969 on a works 650-cc Bonneville. He averaged 99.99 miles per hour, a record, and achieved a record lap of 100.37 miles per hour—making the Bonnie the first production-based motorcycle to lap the famous TT circuit at over 100 miles per hour. *Mick Woollett archive*

Turner remained the consummate designer until his death in 1973. His natural ingenuity took him into nonmotorcycle areas as well. According to Jeff Clew, who authored Turner's 2000 biography, "He designed a collapsible boat, a fully automated car parking system, and even invented a device for saving soap so that the last remaining sliver was not wasted." Those who worked at Meriden may not be surprised by the latter invention!

Replacing the iconic Turner as Triumph's boss was Harry Sturgeon, who understood the importance of road racing as a marketing tool. He quickly supported the factory's UK Production Racing efforts, which had been kept fairly low key under Turner. Until Sturgeon, Triumph had raced through its British dealers, particularly superenthusiast Syd Lawton.

"Between 1962 and 1966 we'd concentrated virtually all our efforts on the 650," Doug Hele recalled in 1994. "It wasn't until Harry Sturgeon took over as managing director that Triumph made works racing an official focus."

The 500-cc twins were called up into the big leagues in late 1965. TriCor racing manager Rod Coates and his chief tuner, Cliff Guild, had flown to Meriden to discuss the latest Daytona threat: Honda's new 450-cc dohc twin. The Japanese finally had entered middleweight territory.

"What worried us was a Honda factory effort as intense as their international GP program at the time," noted Hele. "Harry Sturgeon gave the directive to go to Daytona with a works effort. So we had to get the job done quickly, which meant using what we had."

Developed in just five months, the new racing 500s were completed just in time for Daytona in early March. They were done in typically economical Triumph fashion. "We only had one man, Jack

DEVELOPMENT GENIUS
Doug Hele

Doug Hele made his mark on street bikes and innovative racing machines at Douglas, Norton, and BSA in the 1940s and 1950s, but his most celebrated successes are forever linked with Triumph. The marque's ascendancy in the 1960s, particularly in international road racing, is the direct result of Hele's intense focus on improving the breed.

Hele was Meriden's chief development engineer from late 1962 through the workers' lockout in 1973. He then left to continue Trident development at NVT. In some ways Hele was the protégé of Bert Hopwood, his old BSA colleague, who invited Doug to join him at Triumph after heading Norton's development department. But Hele was a natural leader himself, and his quiet demeanor, total commitment, and dry humor quickly earned the loyalty of his small team in Experimental, as well as among U.S. technical personnel. He valued and encouraged input from everyone.

With them, Hele put Triumphs into every major road-race winner's circle that mattered—first with the 650-cc Bonneville Production racers in the UK, then with the 500-cc Daytona twins, and finally with the Trident. Meanwhile, he spearheaded the changes that dramatically improved the handling, steering, braking, and durability of the production bikes.

Hele was a degreed mechanical engineer who began his career as a draftsman in the late 1930s. With Hopwood, he conceived the Trident in 1962. Three years later he designed a high-revving 250-cc ohc triple with a six-speed gearbox, and many of its components were prototyped before BSA bosses killed it. Hele rode a motorcycle to work throughout the year.

Racers who rode his machines perhaps paid him the greatest compliments.

"Doug was the engineer every racer wants, but with whom few have the privilege of working," recalled Gene Romero. "He was extremely precise, a careful listener. At Daytona I'd download as much detail about how the bike was behaving and Doug would jot every bit of it down into his notebook. He made improvements happen. It was a highlight of my career to work with Doug on those triples."

Doug Hele in 1994 at his home in the British Midlands, not far from Meriden. Lindsay Brooke

Texan Buddy Elmore won the 1966 Daytona 200, riding a factory T100 at a record speed of 96.38 miles per hour. Starting from the 46th grid position, he crossed the finish line over one minute ahead of the second-place Harley-Davidson. Elmore's machine had been rebuilt six times by a TriCor mechanic during qualifying week, one of five Meriden-prepared racers that experienced catastrophic engine failures prior to the race. It was Triumph's first use of a new cylinder head with narrower valve angles and larger valves, which would appear on Triumph's Daytona 500-cc street bikes in 1967. *Mick Woollett archive*

Shemans, on the test bench at the factory," Hele told the author. "But it wasn't that difficult. I still had the data of what we did to the Domiracer when I was at Norton. I tried to equate that work to the Triumph, with the least possible expense. We did many of the same things, even though the two engines were very different architecturally."

Lightweight, stronger frames, BSA 650 cam forms with nitride hardening (which the Americans brought to Hele's attention) and much cylinder head development equaled a winning machine. Texan Buddy Elmore's 1966 Daytona win was reprised the following year by Gary Nixon on a factory bike of even more advanced specification.

At right are Triumph-Detroit owners Bob Leppan and Jim Bruflodt. Triumph paid for them to bring their record-setting Gyronaut X-1 to the 1966 Earls Court motorcycle show in England. The streamliner had recently raised the World's Motorcycle Speed Record to 245.66 miles per hour at the Bonneville Salt Flats. Driven by Leppan, it held the record until 1970. Note the front suspension with Triumph sprung hub. Gyronaut was powered by two alcohol-fueled, pre-unit 650 twins.
Mick Woollett archive

Nixon went on to win two consecutive AMA Grand National championships in 1967 and 1968, cementing the Triumph legend for a generation.

While Nixon and a host of other top racers led the revitalized Triumph attack on American dirt tracks and road circuits, the factory was engaged in an all-out effort to dominate Production Racing in the UK. In 1964–1966, Meriden built small batches of specially modified Bonnevilles for the extremely popular series. "Proddy racing" wins carried enormous cachet for the brands, and the weekend battles between the very trick works Bonnies, BSA Spitfires, and Norton twins helped boost showroom traffic and new bike sales.

By most accounts, Triumph built 58 of its "Thruxton" Bonneville–8 in 1964, a batch of 52 in 1965, and a final 8 the following year. All of the Thruxtons were standard T120R roadsters pulled from the assembly line and heavily tweaked by Hele's small team in Experimental. The factory rated their output at 54 horsepower, good for over 130 miles per hour. Many of the Thruxton innovations (including exhaust crossover pipes to boost midrange torque, the superb 8.0-inch twin-leading shoe front brake, and an extra oil feed to the exhaust camshaft) became standard on production Bonnies in 1968–1970.

The "proddy racing era" was wildly successful for Triumph. Barry Lawton and Dave Degens took the 1965 Thruxton 500-miler, which Degens reprised the following year with Rex Butcher. In 1967, Percy Tait and Rod Gould made it a 500-miler hat trick for the Bonnie. The same year, John Hartle won the first Isle of Man Production TT

The TT Special switched to the classic 1 3/4-inch downswept exhaust pipes in 1965. A year later, the powerplant was given more aggressive cam profiles and a special cylinder head with 11:1 compression. Larger carburetor adaptors were fitted to mount 1 3/16-inch Amal Monoblocs. The unified air filter canister was fitted to West Coast models. TT Specials sold by TriCor for customers in the eastern United States had separate filters for each carb. *Jay Asquini*

Below
Triumph's U.S. distributors helped Meriden engineers create the TT Special, a racing 650 aimed at American-style TT and scrambles competition. The model was launched in 1963 as a stripped-down Bonneville, with high-level straight pipes, 12:1 compression, and lower gearing. It included numerous unique parts, such as the longer, undrilled rear fender. The TT Special immediately became the bike to beat at California's famed Ascot Park. Many also were used in drag racing. This 1966 example was restored by Michigan Triumph and Ducati expert, Gregg Rammel. *Jay Asquini*

on a Geoff Duke-sponsored Thruxton T120R. In doing so, Hartle humbled the factory BSA Spitfires and Dunstall-equipped Norton 750s.

The Thruxton Bonnie earned legendary status in 1969. After Welshman Malcolm Uphill teamed with Tait to score yet another 500-miler win, he captured the Production TT at a record average speed of 99.99 miles per hour. Thus Triumph's Bonneville became the world's first production motorcycle to lap the famous Isle of Man Mountain Circuit at 100 miles per hour. And it was a rout for Triumph—seven of the top ten riders crossing the finish line behind Uphill were aboard T120Rs!

While the 650s cleaned up in British road racing and American TT action, Triumph's C-range (500-cc) machines also led their segment in sales and competition. Works riders Ray Sayer (3TA) and Roy Peplow (TR5) were the only British riders to

win gold medals in the 1965 ISDT. Along with TR6-mounted team member Ken Heanes, the Triumph squad also captured the Team award.

The following year in Sweden, Triumph fielded two ISDT teams (members included trials legend Sammy Miller plus Meriden's factory champs Giles, Sayer, Peplow and Gordon Farley). Four of the bikes were all-new, built by Henry Vale's Comp Shop and featuring Doug Hele-designed frames with a braced steering head and modified head angle, soon adopted for the factory's Daytona road racers! Sayer, Peplow, and Farley won gold medals and each squad earned Triumph a Manufacturer's Team award.

Triumph twins figured prominently in subsequent Six-Days Trials, with John Giles' TR6 bringing home a gold medal from East Germany in 1967. The bike featured one of Eric Cheney's first lightweight aftermarket frames. Peplow copped gold and silver medals in 1968 and 1969, not the last for Triumph's twins, which continued winning ISDT gold medals well into the Seventies.

Bad Management to the Rescue

The factory's racing support and Doug Hele's tenacity brought literally hundreds of improvements to the twin-cylinder street bikes during the 1960s. Many of these changes were the result of the close communication between Hele and chief tester Percy Tait. The two men's skills were strongly complementary, and they held deep respect for one another.

"Percy was superb in feeding back what he was experiencing on the bike, in any conditions on any model, to our engineering team," Hele told the author in 1994.

In the quest to add steering precision and high-speed stability to the 650-cc range, Hele and Tait initially disagreed over what was the ideal steering-head geometry. To find a solution, five frames were built, each with a different head angle. Early testing narrowed it down to the frame Hele preferred versus Tait's favorite.

To select the best chassis for production, Hele used an unscientific, yet proven, method. He found a place on a road close to the factory where he could observe the handling of each bike, as Tait came zooming past at high speed. The spot was on a corner and the tarmac was extremely bumpy.

"When Percy came 'round the bend, the bike was wobbling violently," Hele recalled. "I thought he was going to lose control! He was coming right toward me, so I rolled toward a shallow gully to protect myself. He didn't crash. Turns out the bike had the frame I thought was better. What I saw convinced me that his frame choice was the one we needed."

By 1968, Triumph's Bonneville had reached the pinnacle of its development. "If you bought one then, or in the following two seasons, you got a machine with the right combination of an engine that didn't overpower its frame, suspension, or brakes," wrote veteran motojournalist Peter Watson in *The Classic Motorcycle*.

A 1967 Nixon won the AMA Grand National Championship and reprised it a year later, giving Triumph its first real American superstar. *Brooke and Gaylin archives; Jeff Hackett photo*

Far left
TR6Cs of 1966 (on left) and 1967 show exhaust system differences. By the late 1960s, motorcycling's most popular "desert sled" had become more of a street scrambler, and those high pipes burned the legs of many a skirted passenger. Triumph's first year for 12-volt electrics was 1966, and in 1967 the TR6 finally gained the Bonneville's larger valves. *Jay Asquini*

Rider's-eye view of 1966 TR6C owned by Michigan vintage bike enthusiast Will Lanesky. VDO speedo with TriCor marking was fitted as standard. "Racing stripe" livery echoed TT Special and Bonneville tanks that year. *Jay Asquini*

Below
The 1966 TR6C weighed slightly less than 400 pounds—a brontosaurus in a growing world of lightweight two-strokes. But the single-carb 650 was tractable, economical, and could exceed 100 miles per hour. *Jay Asquini*

Good it was, but the classic 650 twin's days were numbered. Even before he joined Triumph, Doug Hele had pondered a triple. He and Hopwood had discussed the engineering issues of three-cylinder powerplants as early as 1961, when Hele was still at Norton. At the time Hopwood was finishing development of Triumph's unit-650 twin. Both engineers recognized that even larger-displacement motorcycles were inevitable, particularly for the U.S. market. They knew a triple with a 120-degree firing order would be smoother than a twin of similar displacement, and narrower and lighter than a four-cylinder.

Mick Duckworth's essential book, *Triumph and BSA Triples,* indicates that Hopwood's promise of developing a 750-cc three was one of the reasons Hele left Norton for Meriden in October 1962. When Hele arrived, the concept got off to a slow start. Edward Turner was still in force at Triumph, and he remained a twin-cylinder devotee. Though Triumph was highly profitable and selling every bike it could produce, the company balked at devoting resources to major change.

Between 1964 and 1966, Hele's experimental team at Meriden built two prototype 750-cc triples for road testing. The first, dubbed P1, used the 63x80-mm

An all-original 1967 Tiger 100, owned by Vic Schultz. The single-carb 500 roadster sold alongside the hotter twin-carb T100R Daytona, introduced that year. Paint is Pacific Blue over White. *Jay Asquini*

A 1967 T20M Mountain Cub was the last of the "real" Tiger Cubs before production was switched to BSA for the final (1967–1968) Super Cub models. The Mountain Cub was conceived for the U.S. trail bike market by Johnson Motors sales chief Don Brown. It was catalogued from 1965 to 1967. *Lindsay Brooke*

bore and stroke of the original 500-cc Triumph twin. According to Duckworth's research, it made 58 horsepower—15 percent more than a Bonneville. To handle the extra power, Dunlop began developing a new rear tire specifically for the triple. The result was the excellent K81 series, which was co-named TT100 after carrying Malcolm Uphill's works Thruxton Bonneville to victory in 1969.

The P2 prototype came in 1966. It became top priority, because BSA had learned that Honda was developing a large-displacement four-cylinder. Following Hopwood's interest in modular engine designs, the P2 utilized the 67x70-mm dimensions of BSA's new range of 250-cc singles. Both the single P1 and three P2 prototypes looked

like three-cylinder Bonnevilles, slim and sporty. In fact, during 1966 Percy Tait put many miles on the P2 on the roads around the factory, and even local motorcyclists didn't notice the extra cylinder.

Launched in late 1968, the T150 Trident was genuinely fast. It was more than a full second quicker in the quarter-mile than a sharply tuned Bonneville and had true 120-mile per hour potential. Though heavy at 480 pounds wet, it was a safe, secure handler, albeit with limited lean angle because of low-mounted mufflers and pegs. Compared with its main competitor, the CB750 Honda Four, however, the Trident was born severely handicapped. Its first major letdown was styling. The production designs were the work of Ogle Design, an independent British industrial design firm. Ogle gave the Trident and BSA Rocket 3 big boxy fuel tanks, large fiberglass side covers, and the funniest looking mufflers ever seen on a motorcycle. (Americans nicknamed them "Flash Gordons," and the Brits called them "ray guns.") The bikes resembled overwrought tourers, not sporting superbikes.

But it's unfair to blame Ogle for the early Trident's awkward styling, as has been done endlessly since 1969. The company merely delivered what its client, BSA, asked for—a new look that departed completely from Triumph and BSA tradition. The BSA Group managers endorsed and approved the Ogle work for its new three-cylinder flagships. They could

Restored in 1988, Turner's 350-cc dohc prototype first ran in 1968. Hele and Hopwood were shocked at its flimsy design and how quickly it broke crankshafts. The all-aluminum twin featured a 180-degree firing order and four-speed gearbox. *Mick Duckworth*

Above

The first use of Triumph's famous "scalloped" fuel tank paint scheme appeared in 1969. The sweeping silver scallops, outlined by a white pinstripe, were the perfect accent to the Bonneville's sensuous slimline tank and Olympic Flame metallic base color. The scallop design originated from Bob Leppan's Triumph-Detroit dealership, which had been offering custom-painted fuel tanks to its customers since the mid-1960s. Triumph's Eastern U.S. distributor, TriCor, passed a few examples of the Detroit artwork to the Meriden factory. Two different scalloped paint schemes emerged on 1969 Bonnies—one with long, twin scallops above the tank badge only, and a later version with a second set of scallops below it, as shown on Vic Shultz's expertly restored T120R. *Jay Asquini*

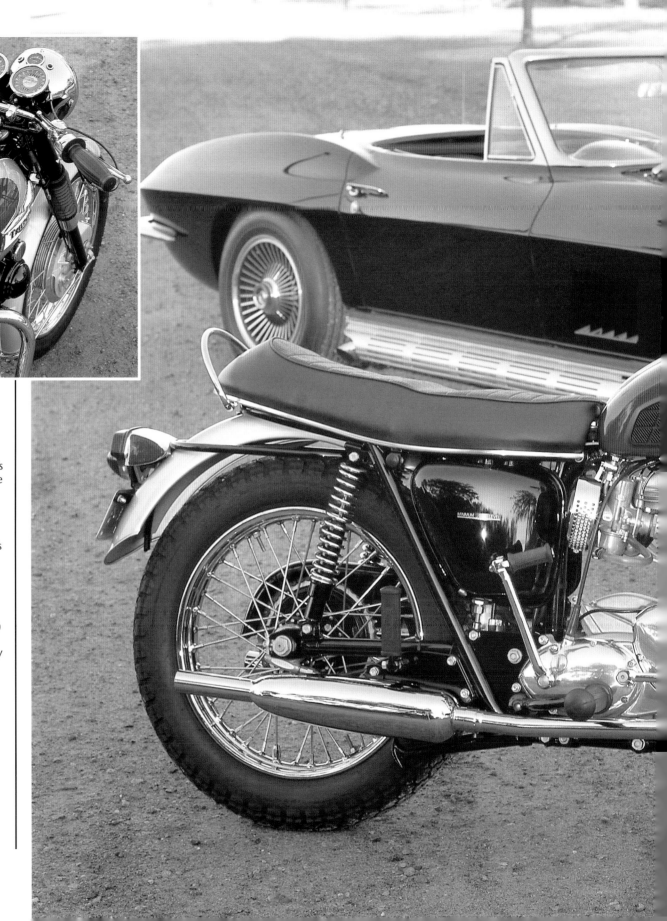

The most desirable stud machines of the 1960s retain every bit of their allure 30 years later. Vic Shultz's 1969 Bonneville is poised to take on Don Sherman's 1967 Corvette 427 roadster. According to period road tests, a stock late-1960s Bonnie would run the quarter-mile in the low 14-second range, with trap speeds in the 90 mile per hour range. The big-block Corvette, with ten times the Bonnie's horsepower, was about a second quicker and could turn an honest 100. *Jay Asquini*

have assigned the Trident's design to Jack Wickes with the brief to create a three-cylinder Bonneville, and they would've sold out the first year's production immediately.

"Most people at Triumph who saw the prototype were shocked when the Ogle bikes were unveiled," recalled Doug Hele in 1994. "But they were exactly what the company wanted."

Of course, feature for feature, the triples suffered painfully against the Honda Four. A four-speed gearbox, drum front brake, kick starting, three individual sets of ignition points to adjust, and leaky, rapid-wearing Amal carbs were simply uncompetitive against the Honda's five speeds, front disc brake, pushbutton starting, overhead cam, and quartet of high-quality Keihin mixers. The Honda also killed the Trident in retail price—$1,500 versus $1,750—even though Don Brown and other industry experts claim the early Four was intentionally "dumped" by Honda, or sold at a price lower than the manufacturer's break-even cost simply to grab U.S. market share as quickly as possible. In Britain, the Honda actually cost more than the Trident.

Far left
The symmetry and style that screams "Triumph." Not a single line or curve is out of place on this 1969 Bonnie. Note, too, the twin Lucas Windtone horns, identified by their domed outer covers and fitted to 1969 and 1970 Bonnevilles only. *Jay Asquini*

BSA-Triumph's new 8-inch, twin-leading shoe, fully ventilated front brake was tested on 1967 factory production racers. It entered Triumph's standard model range in 1968 on 650-cc twins and the 500-cc Daytona. The original straight-pull cable mechanism lacked a firm feel at the lever, so a crank arm was added for 1969 that greatly improved its effectiveness. When properly set up, this drum brake performs as well as many single-disc setups of the 1970s. *Jay Asquini*

The UK-market Triumphs were often more practical rides than their U.S.-market cousins, as motorcycles there were commonly used for transportation rather than just hobby. This Graham Bowen-restored 1968 T120R Bonneville shows its 4.25-gallon fuel tank, which gave it far greater range than the slimline 2.5-gallon tank on U.S. models. Also note long "resonator" mufflers, which quieted the exhaust note considerably. UK-spec machines also came with tire pumps through 1970. The two-tone seat cover had been dropped from U.S.-market models a year earlier. *Mick Duckworth*

One of the first T150 Tridents on test in England, early 1969. Though genuinely quick and fast, the 750-cc triple suffered in the marketplace, particularly in America, for many reasons. It lacked the electric starter, front disc brake, and five-speed gearbox of Honda's stunning new Four. Early models also had quality gremlins, and the bike cost $1,750—$300 more than the Honda. But the 60-horsepower Trident was hobbled most by its styling. It was done by Ogle Design, an independent industrial design house, which sold BSA-Triumph officials on the breadbox fuel tank, square side covers, and "ray gun" mufflers. The world wanted Triumphs that looked like the classic Bonneville. Honda was never challenged, but the triples shined in road racing. *Mick Woollett*

Triumph's sporting image as the motorcycle that could truly "do it all" reached its zenith in the late 1960s. The marque dominated American TT racing at storied venues such as Ascot Park , near Los Angeles, and in Peoria, Illinois. One of Triumph's TT masters was Eddie Mulder, winner of five National TTs and a weekly threat at Ascot. He's shown here at Peoria in 1969. *Bill Delaney*

Above right: Twin-engined Triumph drag bikes began appearing in the late 1950s, challenging and defeating the stroker Harley-Davidsons for both Top Gas and Top Fuel crowns. One of the quickest and fastest was Boris Murray's, which went 9.67 seconds at 157 miles per hour in 1966. Six years later Murray was national champion, with ETs in the 8-second bracket at nearly 175 miles per hour. He's shown heating up the slick at Santa Clara, California. *Norman Mayersohn*

Typical of double-engined Triumph dragsters, Murray's bike was powered by pre-unit T120 engines linked via a single-row chain and driving a Harley clutch. The engines used 750-cc aluminum cylinder barrels supplied by Triumph aftermarket specialist Bob Chantland. Straight-port TR6 cylinder heads were fed a 90 percent nitromethane load through four Amal TT carburetors. The chromemoly steel frame helped pare the bike's total weight to 303 pounds, while a 4.0-inch Avon drag slick and wheelie bars kept 225 horsepower on the pavement—and ahead of the Harleys. *Norman Mayersohn*

BSA-Triumph's clown-suited triples gave the very British-looking Honda Four all the help it needed in getting off to a giddy start. That was unfortunate, because the T150 was essentially a strong engine that became quite robust once Triumph redesigned, modified, or fixed 124 various problems on the 1969–1970 models.

"The Trident was no worse or no better than a 500 twin, in terms of reliability," noted Mike Jackson, former Norton-Villiers Triumph sales director, in a 2001 *Classic Bike* feature. "The triple cost us a third more in warranty claims than the 500 twin and the bean counters were furious," he noted. "It ought to have been a more profitable bike with a price premium, but it wasn't. It was a good stopgap and that's all."

Even with its electric starter in 1975–1976, the Trident was quickly outclassed by legions of new four-cylinder Japanese superbikes and European sporting twins and triples. Between 1975 and 1977, Hele's R&D

World motorcycle GP maestro Giacomo Agostini tries a new Trident (undoubtedly offered to him by Triumph PR boss Ivor Davies for the photo op) at Britain's Oulton Park race circuit in 1969. With no electric starter, Ago had better hope the 470-pound triple fires on the bump. Note the splayed three-into-two exhaust system and the oil cooler mounted under front of fuel tank. *Mick Woollett archives*

TRIDENT WINS 24 HOURS OF NELSON LEDGES

A Triumph 750 Three, piloted by Dick White, Ken Schoville, Bruce Finlayson and Jim Cotherman, won a 24-hour marathon road race at Steel Cities International Raceway, Ohio. During that time, it covered 1,614 miles in 807 laps and the crew reported that the ride was trouble-free, save for two chain adjustments. The bike was prepared by Cotherman, a Triumph dealer from Freeport, Illinois.

The Triumph team picked up the lead in the first 15 minutes of the race and never lost it. They finished 20 laps ahead of 2nd place winners Dick Mankamyer and Dennis Coply (H-D Sportster). Third was a Norton Commando ridden by Skip Eaken and Rowland Kanner. A Honda 450 was 4th.

Cycle World *News Brief, 1970*

It may seem a bit ironic that one of the first Tridents to arrive in the United States also won the first 24-hour motorcycle endurance race in the United States. But that's what happened in July 1970 at the Ohio circuit also known as Nelson Ledges, which has since become famous for 24-hour car and bike events. Triumph's multi had only recently been launched and it was already getting creamed in the sales war by Honda's sensational new 750 Four. As was typical of British bikes in those days, many of the early Tridents were plagued with oil leaks and spotty assembly quality. But they were fast, steered accurately and offered rock-solid handling.

So when *Cycle* managing editor Phil Schilling went looking for a machine to win America's first all-day bike race, the big triple seemed a good bet. Schilling selected and organized the four-rider team centered around Cotherman, who was the "C" of C&D Inc., a legendary Midwestern Triumph and BMW shop. Two of his co-riders (Finlayson and Schoville) were motorcycle-crazed University of Wisconsin students who both held AMA licenses and club-raced on weekends. Richard White was probably the fastest of the quartet, a Canadian who successfully campaigned a Ducati single. Besides Cotherman, none of the team had raced anything bigger than a 250 until then.

Cotherman took a new Trident from his inventory, rode it 500 miles, then disassembled it entirely. Its nearly new engine revealed the beginnings of trouble: a fractured inner valve spring, several loose cylinder stud bolts, an off-center pushrod, and an inner primary-cover oil seal that had been installed backwards at the factory. Typical 1970 Triumph stuff, but nothing that couldn't be corrected.

He replaced the stock British valve springs with American S&W's and matched the carburetor manifolds and gaskets to the intake ports. He narrowed the valve seats to 0.045-inch for better gas flow, balanced the con-rods and pistons, and meticulously reassembled the engine. Cotherman pulled up the stock "Flash Gordon" mufflers slightly and removed both stands to improve cornering clearance. Lower handlebars were fitted. Otherwise the Trident was 100 percent stock, including its Dunlop K81/TT100 tires, which were state-of-the-art production rubber at the time.

At 3:00 P.M. on Saturday it was time to race. The team divided the riding duties into one-hour stints. Fast-guy Richard White would start and would try to grab the lead for the team if he could. With the bikes and riders lined up Le Mans-style, the starter flag dipped and White ran for the Trident. Leaping aboard he cranked the throttle and flooded the engine. He was still kicking away madly trying to fire it as the entire field roared off down the track.

But within 20 minutes White had the ugly-duckling Triumph howling into the lead, riding so hard that he ground the exhaust headers away. "There was a possibility that we might hole a pipe in the next 23 hours," noted Schilling in a 1971 feature story on the race. "So the riders adopted the Continental style of racing as much as they could: hang way off the bike to get through corners," rather than lean it over and risk scraping those thin headers.

The tactic worked. "The race was pretty uneventful for us, as we'd hoped but certainly never expected," recalled Finlayson in 1998. "We gassed up at every second rider change, and made chain adjustments at many of them. We changed the rear wheel in the early morning darkness, replacing it with one wearing a fresh tire. Sometime around mid-morning we realized there was no rear brake shoe material left; Cotherman disabled the linkage to the pedal so we wouldn't grind the brake shoe backing plates into the drum liner."

During the night, Schoville had overdriven his headlight, went wide in a corner and left the track at 75 miles per hour. He went down in the grass and was okay, cracking the headlamp lens.

While other teams on allegedly reliable Japanese machines, including Honda Fours, were replacing broken parts and rebuilding engines under lantern lights, the metallic-green Trident ran through the night like an express locomotive. "It was easy; the bald results reflect a crushing victory for the Triumph," said Finlayson. "The only bike we really raced with was an H1 Kawasaki triple, with the fast ex-Brit racer John Samways on it half the time. But even when the two bikes ran close, the Trident was laps ahead."

When the race was over at 3:00 P.M. on Sunday, Cotherman took the winning machine back to Freeport and made the few changes required to sell it as a used bike. It ran on for years in the local area, with no troubles.

"Jim Cotherman now has a powerful sales pitch to lay on potential customers who come into his shop to look at Tridents," concluded Schilling's race story. "His three-cylinder demonstrator had done us proud."

Bruce Finlayson passes a Honda on the inside as he pilots the C&D Trident to victory at Nelson Ledges in 1970. Bruce Finlayson

The winning C&D Trident was stock except for a careful blueprinting. Here the pistons and connecting rods are balanced. Bruce Finlayson group made numerous explorations to enlarge and modernize the Trident. An electric-start 870-cc T180 prototype was virtually ready for production. A sohc version was built but made no more power than the pushrod engine. There was a T160 fitted to an oil-bearing Triumph twin chassis, and the T180 was likewise tried in Norton's rubber-mounted Commando frame. And the 1,000-cc four-cylinder Quadrant was basically a T150 with an extra cylinder.

None made it beyond the prototype test stage. The Quadrant showed plenty of midrange torque and good speed and handling, but development was finally halted by NVT because the company felt its two other "engines of the future," the rotary and the Cosworth twin, would be cheaper to produce.

The Trident's launch was but one of a series of shortsighted BSA blunders in the late 1960s that set Triumph on a calamitous course. Harry Sturgeon's 1965–1967 plan to merge the Triumph and BSA brands had been met with near-mutiny from Triumph's American dealers, who wanted no part of Beeza's "watermelon" twins, so named because of their oval engine cases. When Sturgeon passed away unexpectedly in 1967, his replacement, Eric Turner, (no relation to Edward) and BSA chairman Lionel Jofeh, continued to rely on marketing glitz, rather than new, competitive products, to move Triumph and BSA forward.

Under Jofeh, BSA purchased a stately manor house in the English countryside and converted it into a corporate engineering center. Umberslade Hall opened in early 1968, with the goal of developing fresh products for both brands using new thinking and methods. Jofeh, who publicly admitted he cared little for motorcycles or their owners, was an aerospace industry refugee and he staffed Umberslade with many of his former colleagues. The facility produced very little except the P39 oil-bearing frames discussed in chapter 5 while costing the company millions of pounds each year.

As Triumph's most profitable decade came to a close, Edward Turner's vertical twins and their two most popular British competitors were still atop the big-bike heap. Triumphs were "the bikes to beat," their winning image affirmed by supremacy in nearly every form of motorcycle sport. Meriden's bulging assembly lines were cranking out a record 900 bikes a week, most of them Bonnevilles and TR6s for U.S. export.

Japan's success in smaller machines had been a blessing to the British; according to Don Brown's data, annual U.S. sales of motorcycles increased from less than 60,000 units to 750,000.

The tide helped Triumph, BSA, and Norton hold nearly 50 percent of the over-500-cc market in America.

Within three years, that share stood at 9 percent and Triumph would be fighting for its life.

BSA-Triumph made an all-out assault to win the 1970 Daytona 200, bringing seven works-prepared Trident and Rocket 3 road racers, chief engineer Doug Hele, a BSA Group aerodynamicist, and specialists from Lucas and Dunlop. Team Triumph riders were Gary Nixon, Gene Romero, and Don Castro, plus factory development rider Percy Tait, shown here in the paddock. Minus its fairing, Tait's machine wears sheet metal cooling shrouds, designed to route air inside the fairings. Note the 250-mm Fontana front brake and 3-into-1 exhaust header. The British triples, with their Rob North-built frames, dominated qualifying. Romero and Castro placed second and third in the big race, behind Dick Mann's Honda four. *Mick Woollett*

OIL IN THE FRAME

A Hurricane named Vetter
the story of the last BSA motorcycle
by Joe Parkhurst

"**O**nly the best get sold out early, and a Triumph is worth waiting for," concluded the one-page letter that ran in U.S. motorcycle magazines during late spring 1970. This unusual advertisement was just plain text with the Triumph logo at the top and Peter Thornton's signature at the bottom. The boss of BSA-Triumph's U.S. operation was admitting that his company had a serious problem.

The 1970 sales season was still far from over but Triumph's dealer network was basically out of motorcycles, particularly the ever-popular Bonneville and Tiger 650 models.

"We are disappointed that we have not been able to supply our dealers fast enough to keep them stocked," lamented Thornton. "We know that when you order a bike you want to start enjoying it as soon as possible, not at some time in the future." The letter spoke of a "temporary shortage" and noted that since December 1969, the factory had doubled its production rate. Meriden was cranking out more than 900 bikes per week, a record. And Triumph was using every means possible to get its products to dealers quickly—including costly air freighting when necessary.

Thornton's message was more than an apology, however. It was also a subtle attempt to keep Triumph customers in the fold. With the 650-cc twins sold out and the expensive, funky-looking Trident not attracting many trade-ups, some Triumph riders were beginning to migrate to Honda's new CB750. The revolutionary four retailed for $200 more than a Bonnie. It was the first serious sales threat to Triumph's big moneymaker. Luckily for the British, the Japanese also had miscalculated demand. The Honda four sold out early, too.

The industry's acute 1970 product shortage sparked an insightful feature story in *Cycle* magazine. The article by Frank Conner keenly summed up the cause of Triumph's (and the British industry's) long-festering problem:

"British stockholders never have gotten interested in the American 'growth company' concept, where the company plows money into expanding the company and increasing the value of its stock, rather than paying out each year's profits as dividends to the stockholders," wrote Conner. "The British investor prefers to build the cheapest factory possible, to make a sure-fire product, and then milk out all of the profits as dividends each year—without putting anything back into the company to modernize or expand it."

Don Brown attended high-level product planning meetings where the British executives told him every new model was expected to recoup its total investment—R&D, tooling, marketing—within 12 months. "This was absurd, and it forced them into a corner," noted the former Triumph and BSA sales executive. "Their thinking was extremely short term, while the Japanese took the long view."

The slow, predictable sales demand of the 1950s had been perfect for the British motorcycle industry's way of doing business. Indeed, Edward Turner and Bill Johnson had believed demand for new Triumphs should always exceed supply. The strategy worked through the 1960s, before the British 500-cc and 650-cc twins felt the hot breath of the Japanese.

By the decade's end, however, Japan's makers were turning the tables. The Superbike Era had begun, and they were deploying their tremendous R&D and production prowess into the big-bike segment. Meanwhile Triumph, along with BSA and Norton, was drifting with the tide.

Almost Slain by Slumberglades

By 1971, Triumph's Experimental department at Meriden effectively had become a race shop, tending to both Triumph and BSA triples. "We were stretched quite thin," reflected Doug Hele in 1995. "The works triples program and an international race schedule demanded more and more of our time."

New bike development, including the total redesign of Edward Turner's dohc 350-cc twin, was in the hands of BSA Group engineers at Umberslade Hall. The first sweeping changes were planned for both BSA's and Triumph's 1971 ranges.

The research facility has been justifiably criticized as a white elephant that reportedly gobbled up $2.1 million per year in operational costs alone. Hele and Bert Hopwood both refused to move their offices there. The Meriden engineering staff jokingly dubbed the old manor house "Slumberglades" and they often made fun of the Umbersladers' favorite terminology—"critical-path analysis" was turned into "typical crap analysis" by the Meriden men, recalled Hele with a chuckle. But some of the R&D center's efforts were positive. The most important of these was a stout new frame. See the sidebar on page 132.

By eliminating the separate oil tank, Umberslade's engineers were able to package a cast-aluminum airbox assembly. This was necessary for the engines to meet increasingly stringent noise legislation that was coming in the United States and Europe. Enclosing the twin filter canisters and the battery, coils, and electrics mounted between them were flat side panels—the "modern" alternative to the glossy, voluptuous oil tank and toolbox that had been a Triumph visual hallmark since the 1950s.

Offsetting the motorcycle's plain flanks were long megaphone mufflers. With their graceful taper and rounded end-caps, these units resembled the famous Dunstall Decibel aftermarket pipes. They were marginally quieter than the traditional "snake-ate-a-rabbit" Burgess mufflers they replaced, but still uncorked that vertical-twin snarl under hard throttle.

Nearly all of the running gear and ancillary hardware also was revamped for 1971, designed for Triumph and BSA common use. New front fork assemblies on every model except the Daytona and Trophy 500s gave 6.5 inches of double-damped travel. The forks rode in tapered roller bearings on the steering stem, a much-needed improvement. Their appearance followed the slimline Ceriani pattern that was sweeping the industry—exposed stanchions, internal springs, cast-aluminum sliders, and black rubber scrapers instead of gaiters.

Flat-backed Lucas headlamps as used on the first Trident were suspended on trendy chromed wire mounts attached to each triple clamp (a la Ducati's 750GT). Smiths instruments nestled in rubber pods widely spaced atop

Early-1971 oil-bearing frames were a disaster on the assembly line and on the show room floor. Engines couldn't be installed unless their rocker boxes were removed, and the bikes' 34.5-inch seat height (3 inches taller than the 1970 models!) turned off scores of customers. Besides its tall saddle, this restored TR6C also shows the conical brake hubs, internally sprung "Ceriani-type" forks, turn signals, and grotesque tail lamp assemblies, also new in 1971. *Jeff Hackett*

Above
Two years after Honda introduced the disc brake to motorcycle mass production, BSA-Triumph responded with . . . yet another drum brake. The 8-inch, twin-leading shoe binder was used on 650 twins and the Trident. It was tricky to set up properly and its arms were too short to deliver strong stopping power. Luckily, the 500-cc twins retained the excellent 1969–1970-type brake. Note the thin wire fender mounts used on all 250s, 650s, and the Trident in 1971–1972.
Jeff Hackett

each fork leg. Shortened fenders fore and aft, rubber isolated on thin-gauge wire rods, added to the Italianesque tackle.

Umberslade designers also gave all models except the 500s new front and rear brakes. Both featured conical aluminum wheel hubs. The 8-inch front units were cooled by a large air scoop cast into their back plate, mimicking the John Tickle aftermarket brakes popular with British café racers in the 1960s. The attractive 7-inch rear hub was easily mistaken for a Manx Norton unit. (Triton builders often use these cheap and plentiful rear hubs today as a substitute for the genuine Manx item.)

The aim of BSA Group's ground-up redesign was "to make the motorcycle look like a whole machine, rather than a collection of bits and pieces," reasoned Stephan Mettam, the 29-year-old styling chief at Umberslade. Motojournalists on both sides of the Atlantic seemed to agree. Many of them welcomed the new, contemporary look.

"At last Triumph have achieved a 'with it' modern appearance—urgently needed to keep them in with the best sellers," wrote John Brown in *Motor Cycle News*. The bikes' style was 'truly exciting,' opined *Motorcycle Sport Quarterly* writer Bob Greene. And *Cycle* gave thumbs-up to the "cleaner, lighter look" of the new 650s and Trident. It "doesn't do violence to the time-honored Triumph shape," the editors argued.

Top
The factory Trident and Rocket 3 racers ruled international Formula 750 road racing in 1971, giving the British industry its last hurrah. One of Triumph's stars was Paul Smart, a pioneer of the "hanging off" style of cornering that's universal today. He's shown here at Clearways, on the Brands Hatch circuit. *Jim Greening photo; Brooke archive*

Far left
Team Triumph group photo, 1971 Daytona 200. The impressive lineup of riders and machines included (from left) Gene Romero, Don Castro, Tom Rockwood, Gary Nixon, and British road race ace Paul Smart. Romero and Smart are aboard new, lowered versions of the superb Rob North-framed Trident, while the others used the 1970-type North chassis. Smart was the fastest qualifier and Romero finished second, again behind Dick Mann on a similar BSA triple. *Mick Woollett*

Heroes to Triumph racing fans worldwide, No. 33 Paul Smart, No. 34 Ray Pickrell, and No. 29 Percy Tait head for the starting grid at Britain's Snetterton circuit, 1971. The works lowboy triples show their "letterbox" oil cooler slots and twin Lockheed front disc brakes. The fairings were developed in a Royal Aircraft Establishment wind tunnel. Note the three helmet styles. *B.R. Nicholls*

THE P39
OIL-BEARING FRAME

Destined for use on 1971 Triumph and BSA 650-cc models, the new frame was first penned by Triumph draftsman Brian Jones when he was assigned to Umberslade Hall in 1969. According to an interview with Jones in Mick Duckworth's essential book *Triumph and BSA Triples*, his drawings caught the eye of Dr. Stefan Bauer, an Umberslade honcho and formerly Norton's director of engineering during Commando development. It was Bauer who shepherded the concept toward production.

The new frame was Triumph's first twin-loop frame since 1960–1962 and the company's first all-welded production frame. Until 1971, Triumph lagged BSA, Norton, and most of the motorcycle industry by not having a modern, welded frame. Its previous frames with their cast-iron lugs, furnace-brazed construction, and bolt-on rear sections were expensive and time consuming to produce.

The new frame, code-named P39, featured a 4-inch-diameter central backbone tube. This giant "spine" served two purposes. First, it made the overall structure far stronger than its predecessors. Second, it doubled as the engine oil reservoir. Carrying the lubricant internally, like the proven Trackmaster, Cheney, and Rickman racing frames, would theoretically help keep the oil cooler due to the increased surface area of the tubing, compared with a separate oil tank.

In the real world, however, the new "oil-in-the-frame" Triumphs (as they've been nicknamed through the final 750-cc T140 series) tended to run hotter than the oil-tank bikes. This was partly due to the location of the filler neck. The original frame design had the oil filler neck just below the steering head, giving a 3.0-quart capacity. But to accommodate both Triumph and BSA engines for production, the neck was moved farther down the main tube, between the gas tank and seat. This reduced oil capacity to a marginal 2.2 quarts.

Today, riders who regularly use their oil-in-the-frame twins can choose from a wide selection of aftermarket oil coolers and automotive-type cartridge filters, for improved cooling and longer engine life.

Despite the high seats, the early oil-in-frame 650s' handling was quite good. It improved as Series 2 and Series 3 versions of the frame with lower seat rails arrived in 1972. The T140 750-cc models brought far better rider

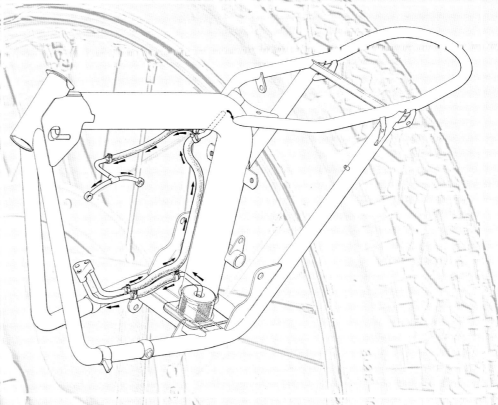

Introduced for 1971, the BSA-Triumph oil-bearing frame was influenced by successful aftermarket competition frames from Rickman, Trackmaster, and others. The 4 inch diameter backbone held the lubricant and provided a base for the oil filter element. It was Triumph's first duplex frame since 1962 and stayed in production on 650-cc and 750-cc twins through the Harris Bonneville era. It also was the company's first all-welded steel frame, with no iron lugs. It proved to be a strong, stable design, once early problems were overcome. Factory drawing; Brooke archive

ergonomics and tires (Dunlop TT100s, then Avon Roadrunners), vindicating what had been a flawed but solid design.

"Cars and vans are mopped up with blasts of instant acceleration," wrote Mick Duckworth about an oil-in-frame Bonneville he tested for *Classic Bike*, "and bends taken by simply feathering the throttle, heeling the buzzing Bonnie over, and snapping the power back on as soon as the exit is sighted."

London-area Triumph dealer Boyer of Bromley raced Tridents with great success in both short-circuit and long-distance events. This Seeley-framed F750 racer, ridden by Dave Nixon and Peter Butler in 1972–1973, was equipped with the famous Boyer-Bransden electronic ignition. It is shown here at the 1972 Barcelona 24-hour race, an event Triumph won in 1969. Note mounting for Zener diode heat sink next to primary cover. *B.R. Nicholls*

Whether Triumph's classic signature remained can be debated, but most of the 1971 changes sacrificed function for style. Fitting new front drum brakes to the 650s and particularly to the 125-mile per hour, 470-pound Trident was a mistake. Honda already had its groundbreaking disc brake on middleweight bikes.

There was plenty more "new" to stew about. Standard turn indicators were a safety benefit, but the poorly designed Lucas switchgear made them difficult to use. Sharp-bladed aluminum clutch and brake levers were uncomfortable to squeeze. Chopped fenders were unloved in rain-soaked Britain. The front fenders' frail, pretzel-thin wire mounts often fractured in use.

Moving the ignition switch from the left headlamp bracket (where it had been since 1968) to the right side cover was obviously done by someone who never rode a motorcycle. And the 1971 models were screwed together with a hodgepodge of British and American nuts and bolts.

The 1971 250-cc singles were redesigned as extensively as the 650-cc twins. Their oil-bearing frames were influenced by BSA's excellent world-championship Victor motocross frames. It was a last-ditch stab at making the little thumpers competitive with the shiploads of lightweight Japanese trail bikes flooding America. Built at BSA's Small Heath factory like their predecessors, the 250s didn't gain much of a following, due to their underwhelming engines—the only part of the bike that was unchanged from 1970.

By early 1972, Gene Romero and Dick Mann were the only remaining factory-supported riders on the BSA-Triumph American team. At Daytona, both bikes were 10 miles per hour slower than the new Suzuki two-stroke triples. *Daytona Speedway Archives*

At the other end of the spectrum, the mighty 750 Trident "shed its Jumpin' Jack Flash outfit and now—finally—it looks like a Triumph," declared *Cycle* in a July 1971 cover story. Triumph's superbike no longer needed its dealer-installed "beauty kit." It now left the factory slim and trim, with a proper teardrop fuel tank and added the new corporate fork, fenders, mufflers, and conical brakes.

The T150 also sported an optional five-speed gearbox that was perfectly matched to the engine's power characteristics. In 1970 BSA Group had bought production rights to the five-speed gearsets made by British transmission specialist Rod Quaife, who supplied the factory's road racers. With the new 'box the triple earned the "world's quickest stock motorcycle" title, according to *Cycle*. Consistent 12.9-second, 102-mile per hour dragstrip runs "will pin your navel to your spine," wrote the testers. The Trident also handled superbly, but would ground its pegs, stands, and exhaust system at extreme lean angles.

Five speeds transformed the Trident, but the gearbox cost $200 extra when it should've been standard. And the bike still lacked an electric starter and disc brake! For every Trident sold in 1971, Honda sold six of its less-expensive, better-equipped CB750s.

The outrageous X75 Hurricane was conceived in 1969 by BSA Inc. executive Don Brown, who commissioned Craig Vetter to design and build the prototype. Their combined vision resulted in one of the first "factory customs." By the time production began at BSA's Small Heath factory in June 1972, the exciting Rocket-3-based triple had been badged a Triumph. Reportedly 1,175 examples were built, most of them with five-speed gearboxes. The X75's fork tubes were 2 inches longer than standard and made the bike a slow steerer. *Jeff Hackett*

Overhead view of Vetter's wasp-waisted X75 bodywork reveals the Hurricane's unique cylinder head, specially cast with extended cooling fins. Vetter was elated that his design made it to production with few changes. His only gripe was that the prototype's one-piece molded bodywork had become a two-piece affair, with a central trim strip covering the panel joints. *Jeff Hackett*

In 1969, BSA Group began developing a Wankel rotary-engined motorcycle. The project began with a 300-cc single-rotor powerplant, and by 1974, Norton-Villiers-Triumph was testing the 600-cc twin-rotor, air-cooled prototype shown here. *Cycle* magazine editor Cook Neilson sampled the test mule, declaring it "as smooth as a Honda CB500 Four," with performance "capable of jerking the eyes out of a good-running 750 Trident." The project slowly evolved into the Norton Rotaries, built in low volumes in the 1980s and early 1990s. *Mick Woollett archive*

The only street bikes that escaped Umberslade's heavy hand in 1971 were the venerable 500-cc twins. Both the T100R and T100C remained basically in 1969–1970 spec, except for abbreviated rear fenders, turn indicators, and the universally reviled BSA Group sheet metal taillamp unit—dubbed "the gargoyle" by Triumph historian David Gaylin. They even wore scalloped paint jobs. Carrying over the sweet-handling Daytona and Trophy 500s turned out to be a lucky decision for Triumph, because when it came time to start 1971 production in August 1970, things went horribly wrong.

Umberslade Hall's "experts" had not sent the new P39 frame's blueprints to Meriden in time for tooling to be built and checked. More than three months passed and the 650 production line didn't build a single bike. To keep busy, the workers cranked out their entire year's production run of 500-cc models. This became a savior for dealers—Daytonas and Trophies were the only twins they had to sell for months. Then more waiting.

When the first 1971 frames finally arrived on the assembly line, it was discovered that engines could not be installed into the chassis without first removing the rocker boxes! More costly time passed before the engine components were redesigned to fit the frame. It wasn't until January 1971 that 650-cc Bonnevilles, Tigers, and Trophies finally began rolling out of the factory.

Five months had been wasted. Triumph's most popular and profitable models didn't reach U.S. dealerships until well into the 1971 sales season. British customers found few 650s available, and to make matters worse, the Bonneville's UK price had been raised 30 percent.

Once in show rooms, another malady was exposed: The seats were sky high! Riders sat 34.5 inches above ground, making the new 650s unwieldy for even average-height riders. The too-tall saddles were widely criticized in magazine road tests, turning off scores of potential customers.

Then dealers began finding that the early-1971 frames were not thoroughly flushed out at the factory. Debris from the welding process ended up in oil pumps, sometimes with catastrophic results. A quick-fix solution was put into action by BSA service staff in the United States. Using a pressurized pump (nicknamed the "tampon") they were able to flush out the frames while the new bikes were still in their shipping crates.

Was this the best that BSA Group's "fresh thinkers" and aerospace refugees at Umberslade Hall could do? Many motorcyclists were puzzled. No one had questioned the enduring art form that was the late-1960s Triumph twin. Those beautiful bikes fit most riders like a glove.

What customers wanted in a "new" Triumph was an end to the headaches—the leaky engines, electrical maladies, and generally inconsistent build quality. They would've loved front disc brakes, five-speed gearboxes, and reliable electric starters. Such upgrades were within the financial resources of an extremely profitable Triumph in the late 1960s. They could've been part of the ongoing product evolution. But why spend money when your annual production is selling out year after year?

"Until the Honda Four's debut, there was no real pressure from BSA top management to make important product changes," notes former BSA vice president Don Brown. "The Four shocked them into action, but by then it was too late."

Doug Hele admitted that remarkably, it wasn't until 1971 that Meriden actually purchased a Japanese motorcycle (Honda's brand new CB500 Four) to tear down and analyze.

"When we took the Honda apart I realized that it would be impossible to compete directly with them," Hele told the author. "Our manufacturing capabilities wouldn't permit things like horizontally split, pressure-die-cast engine cases."

The 1971 650s reflected those limitations. The bikes were alternately praised and damned by the magazines. *Cycle World* concluded that the T120R Bonneville still was "one of Triumph's best," even after gaining 20 pounds versus the 1970 edition. The testers blasted the tall seat ("two of our shorter staffers found it impossible to plant both feet squarely on the ground"), the lousy Lucas handlebar switches, and the "bulbous" 3.5-gallon fuel tank.

But they lauded the Bonnie's new chassis—"hairline steering and good ride," with "one of the best-operating fork assemblies available." Clutch and gearbox action were superb, the headlamp threw a powerful beam, and overall finish quality was "excellent."

A change in AMA racing rules in 1969 allowed U.S. Triumph dirt track racers to use lightweight, aftermarket frames. The oil-bearing frames made by Trackmaster, Red Line, C&J, and others became the standard for AMA Grand National competitors. This is Gene Romero's Trackmaster 750-cc twin, which he used to win the 1972 and 1973 San Jose National races—the last British twin to win an AMA National mile dirt track race. The 270-pound bike used a C&J swing arm. Its C.R. Axtell-tuned engine produced 72 horsepower. *Jeff Allen*

The 1973 TR5T Trophy Trail mated a single-carb T100 engine with BSA's oil-bearing Victor frame. Designed to recapture the Trophy 500's street scrambler glory, it was enlisted into the 1973 International Six-Days Trials, held in Massachusetts. Batches of stock TR5Ts were modified at Meriden and at Triumph's California distributor for British and American Triumph teams. Major upgrades for the ISDT included Spanish-made Betor forks, Rickman wheels, and waterproofed dual-ignition systems. Though the 306 pound twins weighed 60 pounds more than most two-strokes, the British team earned a second-place silver medal, behind the factory CZ team. This is one of the team's TR5Ts, now displayed at Britain's National Motorcycle Museum. *Jim Davies*

At the drag strip the reframed Bonnie delivered a best run of 14.2 seconds at 92 miles per hour, and a 112-miles per hour top speed—no quicker or faster than the 1969 model. Braking performance was disappointing. It took 140 feet for the new conical binders to haul the bike down from 60 miles per hour. The front brake quickly gained a reputation for needing very careful setup and frequent adjustment. Proving the point, a year later a *Cycle World* 1972 test Bonneville with the same brakes stopped from 60 miles per hour in just 118 feet.

Britain's *Motorcycle Sport* echoed the Americans' findings, heaping scorn on the new Bonnie's high perch and third-rate switchgear. "It was impossible for the rider to operate the indicators without releasing his grip on the throttle," the editors reported. "We pretty soon gave up using the indicators."

Handling was considered "absolutely first class," although the British testers cursed the high-rise U.S.-spec handlebars that were now standard on home-market models, too. But *Motor Cycle News'* Mike Nicks put the torquey twin into perspective.

"In this age of racy two-strokes and three- and four-cylinder superbikes, it's a genuine pleasure to find a machine that doesn't need to be coaxed along with constant stabs at the gear lever," Nicks reflected. The Bonneville, he noted, "will pull steadily in top gear from as low as 1,700 rpm (about 28 miles per hour) and once you get out of town, it becomes almost a two-gear machine."

With so many things compromised on the street bikes, Triumph fans could at least point to outright glory on the racetrack. The brilliant triples prepared at Meriden absolutely dominated road racing in 1971. Percy Tait won every round of the British Superbike Championship. On the Isle of Man, Tony Jefferies won the Formula 750 TT and Ray Pickrell rode the famous Trident nicknamed *Slippery Sam* to its first of five consecutive Production TT victories.

At Thruxton, Tait teamed with Dave Croxford to win the grueling 500-miler. Paul Smart aced the Hutchinson 100 at Brands Hatch then won the Silverstone F750 event. Tait, Pickrell, and Meriden race shop manager Les Williams took a North-framed machine to Le Mans and beat Europe's best Hondas and Laverdas in the 24-hour Bol d'Or. It was Triumph's second consecutive win at the French endurance race. What the works Tridents didn't win in 1971 were won by BSA Rocket 3s.

In the United States, Gene Romero's Trident road racer and 750-cc twin dirt tracker carried his AMA No. 1 plate into battle against the archrival BSA squad. Romero ended up second in the season's points to Daytona-winning Beeza ace Dick Mann. The last pavement race of the year at the Ontario, California, superspeedway saw a pair of Doug Hele's latest triples ridden by Gary Nixon (Triumph) and John "Mooneyes" Cooper (BSA) each win one 125-mile leg of the 250-mile event. Cooper got the overall victory. The factory team also launched the popular Anglo-American Transatlantic Match Race series, which formed the basis of Formula 750 racing.

Over $2 million reportedly was spent on BSA Group racing in the United States, Britain, and Europe during 1970–1971. It was a lavish outlay but the results speak for themselves.

One of the world's most famous racing motorcycles, and certainly the best-known Triumph racer, is *Slippery Sam*. The factory-prepared Trident won five consecutive Isle of Man Production TT races from 1971 and 1975. This is Tony Jefferies banking *Sam* past the Quarter Bridge Hotel in the 1973 TT. He averaged 95.62 miles per hour over 151 miles. *B.R. Nicholls*

BSA Group's plans to meet demand for its motorcycles went up in smoke in 1971. Of the 50,000 machines that Triumph's U.S. distributors planned to sell in 1971, roughly 30,000 were actually imported. But the botched launch of the 650s ended up jamming U.S. warehouses with nearly 11,000 unsold machines (mostly BSAs) at season's end. Coupled with the big-bucks racing program, an expensive advertising campaign, and £2 million ($4.2 million) wasted developing a commuter trike—the 50-cc two-stroke Ariel 3 that went virtually unsold—the company suffered multi-million-pound losses. BSA stock plummeted.

Another victim of the collapse was the twin-cam 350-cc, five-speed Bandit twin. It first had been promised "by March," then "sometime in summer." Edward Turner's poorly engineered swan song had been totally redesigned under Doug Hele's supervision on a very compressed timetable. The new version had dealers' appetites whetted with 34 horsepower, optional electric starting, and a lightweight twin-loop frame similar to the Rob North racing frames. One of the dozen prototypes built for road testing had clocked 103 miles per hour.

Over £2 million ($4.2 million) worth of tooling and components had been produced for the Bandit and its BSA Fury brother, including 26,000 pistons and con-rods. Production was ready to commence; advertising had begun. But when a retail price was finally calculated, the project was killed by the frantic BSA managers.

"They said that the least the 350 could have sold for in the United States was $1,500, and that a reasonable price was $1,600!" recalled Don Brown. At the time Honda's wildly popular 350-cc twins retailed for about $800. Britain's last great hope in the middleweight segment died without a chance to prove itself.

In 1971 BSA Group lost £8.5 million (about $18 million), a near repeat of the year before. The debacle earned the boot for Managing Director Lionel Jofeh; Chairman Eric Turner and U.S. boss Thornton left soon after. Umberslade Hall was closed, the racing budget slashed and thousands of BSA workers fired. A new management board was formed and it replaced Jofeh with Brian Eustace, an experienced executive from industrial giant GKN. After securing an £11 million (roughly $23 million) loan from Barclay's Bank, one of Eustace's first actions was to bring back Bert Hopwood as chief engineer.

The veteran Hopwood, now close to retirement age, had left the company in frustration in 1970. His first priority upon rejoining was to correct the worst of Umberslade's mistakes.

The oil-bearing frame went under the torch to have its seat rail lowered by nearly 3 inches. Combined with a redesigned saddle, this dropped seat height to a reasonable 31 inches. The 650s' rockerboxes were redesigned with one-piece, finned tappet covers. British home-market bikes were finally given larger 4.2-gallon (U.S.) fuel tanks and low handlebars. Durability problems with the optional new five-speed gearboxes were cured. The Trophy 500 was dropped and development began on the TR5T Trophy Trail—a factory "Tribsa" hybrid launched in 1973. It combined the T100C motor in the BSA Victor oil-bearing frame.

By summer 1972, BSA Group decided to end BSA motorcycle production after 66 years. Only one model, the 500-cc B50MX motocrosser, was catalogued for 1973; it would be rebadged as the Triumph TR5MX Avenger for the 1974 season. The dying giant didn't pull Triumph down with it, because Meriden had remained profitable, despite all the problems of the past two years. It was by far the stronger of the two marques. Jack Sangster's 1951 sell-out to BSA finally was exposed as the folly that Triumph fans had known it to be all along.

Also clear was how far, and how fast, Britain's bikemakers had fallen in the marketplace. At the close of 1971, Triumph held just 11 percent of the U.S. market's heavyweight (over 500-cc) segment, despite sales of over 21,000 machines. BSA sold slightly fewer than 9,000 big bikes for a woeful 4.6 percent share, according to R.L. Polk registration data. Norton's speedy Commando was a hit, but its 6,100 total sales equaled a measly 3.2 percent share.

By comparison, Japan now controlled over 90 percent of the American motorcycle market. In the big-bike segment, Honda ruled supreme. Sales of 70,000 CB750 and CB500 Fours gave it a 37.2 percent share.

Slippery Sam changed to twin disc front brakes in 1974, the year the bike's paint scheme switched to Norton-Villiers–Triumph's red, white, and blue livery. Production Trident "ray gun" silencers gave the broadest power band. *Sam* tipped the scales at 405 pounds, using twin six-volt batteries and many other tricks to save weight. The legendary road racer is now displayed at Britain's National Motorcycle Museum and is occasionally run at vintage race events and Trident and Rocket 3 Owners Club meetings. *Jim Davies*

For Triumph, the future now depended on the extensive changes ordered by Hopwood and Hele for the 1973 model range. The upgrades helped the company pull itself out of the deep hole BSA dug for it in 1971–1972. They also set the mold for Turner's classic Triumph twin through its final hour in 1988.

Survival by 750

Hele's team focused on two priority programs—a 750-cc version of the twin, and a second-generation Trident. And handed over from BSA was an air-cooled Wankel rotary project that ultimately evolved into a Norton in the 1980s and won the Isle of Man Senior TT.

The 750-cc T140 was spurred by the American distributors. It was critical for Triumph to keep pace with bigger, faster, and more sophisticated Japanese and European machines entering the market. This meant abandoning the 650-cc segment that the company had created in 1950 and owned ever since.

But progress rarely came to Triumph on a totally clean sheet of drafting paper. Although various new twin concepts were prototyped during the early '70s, including versions with overhead cams and a third piston acting as a crankshaft counterbalancer, what finally entered production was an evolution of Hopwood's classic 1963 ohv "unit" motor.

The extra displacement was achieved using a new top end with larger cylinder bores. There were two versions: first a 75-mm bore (the very early T140s were actually 726 cc) then 76 mm (744 cc). The stroke remained at the old 650's 82 mm. There was an extra stud holding down the top end, bringing the total to 10. The T140 got 1/2-inch shorter connecting rods, new camshafts with a milder profile, and a lower 8.5:1 compression ratio. The primary drive gained a triple-row chain. Overall, the larger engine was stronger, quieter and more user friendly. But performance didn't suffer, thanks to the extra displacement and now-standard five-speed gearbox.

"We wanted a meaty twin, able to pull like a steam engine," explained Bert Hopwood in his memoir. "So we cut down on rpm and worked to make the power curve fatter at the bottom end of the rev scale."

The new T140RV Bonneville and its single-carb brother, the TR7RV Tiger—the "V" signified the five cogs—were genuinely quicker and faster than the legendary 650s of the late-1960s. Meriden continued to build 650-cc Bonnies and Tigers, with the new running gear, through summer 1973 for the British market and general export.

A standard 10-inch Lockheed front disc brake brought the 750 twins and Trident triple into modern times. And quality was the best to come out of Meriden in many years. Upgraded gaskets, more and better fasteners, and a new 8-psi static air check of every engine before it left the assembly line vastly improved oil tightness. A host of styling changes made the six 1973 models look like classic Triumphs again.

Cycle editor Cook Neilson tested the new Tiger 750 and rated it as the best Triumph since the 1960s. Neilson lauded the Tiger's engine, handling, and braking performance. But his praise was balanced with many caveats, reflecting Triumph's challenges in a rapidly changing big-bike market.

"The Triumph . . . has all the technical design qualities of an efficient machine—light weight, simple power-plant, a minimum of luxury or convenience features, easy maintenance, superior fuel economy (49 miles per gallon), inexpensive manufacturing procedures, and especially well-rounded performance in stopping, acceleration, top speed and handling. And then it demands that the rider put up with the side-effects of such a package: more than moderate vibration, maintenance on certain outdated design features such as the primary chain, some oil leaks, a stiff ride, less than ideal seating position, etc.

"The Japanese go at it the other way," Neilson continued, "and they go at it with trainloads of money. And what comes out the other end for the most part is a succession of motorcycles with extraordinary engines and comfort and indifferent handling and 90 percent of the American market. Can Triumph copy? No. Triumph simply doesn't have the resources."

Final version of the "factory" Trident road racer, as campaigned by Triumph's American distributor in 1973–1974. New frames patterned after the Rob North originals were fabricated by Wenco Industries in California. Wenco used thin-gauge 4130 tubing and heli-arc welding, rather than brazing, to reduce frame weight by six pounds. Other changes include Morris cast wheels and specialist-built oil and fuel tanks. Gene Romero, Gary Scott, Dick Mann, Mike Kidd, and John Hateley rode these machines to some high placings, but the winning days were over. *Larry Willett*

By the 1973 model year, Triumph had corrected the early faults of the oil-in-frame chassis, launched a 750-cc twin, and finally added front disc brakes. The 1973s looked like classic Triumphs again. A new range of modular engines was being planned. Then, in September, Norton-Villiers Triumph boss Dennis Poore shocked the industry by announcing his scheme to close Triumph's Meriden plant, thus eliminating 1,750 jobs. The workers took over the plant and the 18-month Meriden Blockade began. *EMAP archive*

Below
The Meriden siege left an assembly track full of 1974-model twins in various stages of completion. It also cut off the lifeblood of Triumph dealers worldwide, a catastrophic blow from which they never fully recovered. The famous factory that produced 900 motorcycles per week in the late 1960s stands silent in this mid-1974 photo. The lockout gave birth to the employee-owned Triumph Motorcycles (Meriden) Ltd. *EMAP archive*

It was true. In 1972 Honda alone spent $8.1 million on advertising alone in the United States, while the combined ad budgets of Triumph, BSA, and Norton totaled $1.3 million. Product development money was equally scarce, though Hopwood and Hele had plenty of ideas for new motorcycles. Since the 1950s Hopwood had envisioned a range of "modular" machines that would share common engine architectures and key components, saving development time and tooling costs and creating huge economies of scale for the company.

When he returned to Triumph in 1972, Hopwood rekindled the idea in earnest. He hoped the cosmetic and mechanical upgrades for the 1973 season would be the last major effort with the old Turner twins he himself had helped originate back in 1936!

The basis of Hopwood's modular lineup was a sohc 200-cc single, which would then be multiplied to create a 400-cc twin, a 600-cc triple, and ultimately, a 1,200-cc V-5—the latter predating Honda's 2003 GP engine configuration by 30 years. The visionary designs would feature pressure-die-cast engine cases, belt-driven

camshafts, two- or four-valve cylinder heads, single-sided swingarms, and cast-alloy wheels with tubeless tires. Also planned for further development was the Wankel rotary.

If approved by BSA Group management, Hopwood reckoned the first prototype could be ready within a year and the bike launched in 1975. Others would be phased in annually, until the Turner-era Triumphs were ultimately replaced around 1978–1979.

At least that was the plan. Total investment for the ambitious project reportedly was pegged at £20 million (over $40 million)—a "trainload of money," as Cook Neilson would say. And its success was contingent upon achieving production volumes never imagined in the British motorcycle industry—twenty-thousand bikes per week, or one million annually. Such output would put Triumph back into serious contention with the Japanese. But Hopwood's dream was not realized until 1990, when John Bloor's resurrected Triumphs, based on the modular concept, first appeared.

Battleground Meriden

Revolution was not to be in 1973; however, one model genuinely surprised the public. This was the X75 Hurricane, credited with pioneering the "factory custom" trend that continues today. The Hurricane was originally intended to be a BSA. It was developed in secret in 1969 by independent American designer Craig Vetter, from a design brief by BSA executive Don Brown. The flamboyant triple created a buzz for Triumph when it finally entered production in June 1972.

Based on the A75 Rocket 3 engine and frame, the Hurricane's raked fork, three-megaphone exhaust, and sexy one-piece tank/seat unit (painted in bright orange with a yellow stripe) helped bring customers back into the company's dealerships, even though fewer than twelve-hundred examples were built. Most were exported to the United States, where their high price ($2,300) and outrageous looks made them slow sellers. Today the X75 is the most collectible BSA-Triumph triple. It still looks modern and turns heads.

The rest of Triumph's models were much more competitively priced, due in part to a favorable dollar/pound exchange rate. But the optimism that had returned to Triumph lovers everywhere could not mask the serious problems that were about to undermine the company yet again.

Although BSA had ended its motorcycle production (except for Trident engines and the B50MX), the parent company was in financial chaos. More new management was brought in but, as *Cycle* columnist Jim Greening observed, "only the costumes changed." A clear lack of leadership in the boardroom, a militant workforce at Meriden that was causing costly work stoppages and slowdowns, and the effects of many product blunders since 1968 had the giant conglomerate in a tailspin. The escalating interest on its bank loan alone cost BSA £20,000 ($48,000) per week!

And in the United States, the distributors' warehouses were jammed with unsold 1971 and 1972 motorcycles; these had to be sold at a loss. American dealers were stuck with "T120Vs sitting stripped of parts, and had drip pans underneath them," recalled veteran Massachusetts Triumph stalwart John Healy. He added that many of those bikes sat "with an open cavity where the transmission once was," a reference to the fragile early five-speed gearsets that were a warranty nightmare.

BSA's long-suffering, complacent shareholders had been told that 1973 would be a "breakeven" year. Now they were warned to expect another multimillion loss. After losing over £15 million (over $30 million) since 1970, BSA's plight was a national issue. Unfortunately Triumph's fortunes were tied to it.

In late 1972, Barclays Bank informed Britain's Department of Trade and Industry that if BSA did not receive financial assistance, the bank would force the company into receivership. Indeed, the latest BSA Chairman, Lord Shawcross, had quietly floated the need for financial support to a few key government types. This was a time when socialist Britain was reeling economically. Workers in many industries racked by the oil crisis, low-cost competition from abroad, and sagging productivity were facing massive job cuts. Strikes dominated the news.

The Conservative government had already broken its election promises not to spend taxpayers' money on propping up failing industries, and was nationalizing or subsidizing many of them. But motorcycles were considered a key export, given the superbike boom in the United States, and BSA was a famous name. Rather than bail it out directly, the government went to Dennis Poore.

The chairman of Manganese Bronze, a specialist metals company, and owner of Norton-Villiers, Poore was respected as the man who had "saved" Norton from doom in 1966 and turned it into a modestly profitable company with only the Commando. With BSA, the banks and the British government, Poore eventually hammered out a scheme: Norton-Villiers would take over BSA, a company many times its size.

Rumors of the plan were leaked a few days before the deal was to be announced, causing shock selling of BSA shares on the London Stock Exchange. The share price crashed dramatically, wiping another £2.5 million ($6 million) off the company's value.

Amidst the calamity, Triumph was rebounding on its own. Monthly revenue jumped to £400,000 (nearly $900,000) on sales of the smash-hit 1973 twins and triple. It looked to be a strong year. Then in July came the formation of a new

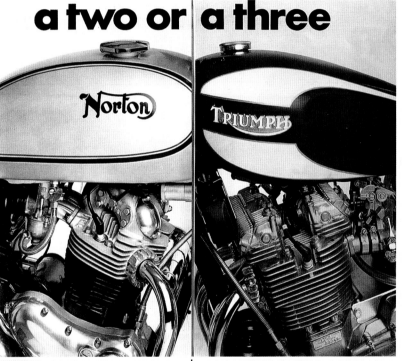

a two or a three

Some critics of Dennis Poore allege that the Norton boss' ulterior motive for closing Meriden was to kill the Triumph twin. With the plant blockaded in 1974, the NVT product strategy focused on the Trident and Norton Commando. Both gained electric starters for 1975. *Jeff Hackett photo; David Gaylin archive*

Worker-owned Triumph made the T140 twin in many flavors. One specialty model was the T140J, or Silver Jubilee edition. Built for the 1977 model year, to celebrate 25 years of Queen Elizabeth II's reign, the Silver Jubilee was basically a standard Bonnie with special paintwork and badges, a blue seat with red piping, chromed timing and primary covers and taillamp housing, and a $200 higher price tag. The U.S. and UK markets each received 1,000 examples, with another 400 built for general export. This UK version is identified by its breadbox fuel tank. In the United States, many Silver Jubilees went unsold through the early 1980s. Today, only unused, zero mileage examples are actually worth more than a regular T140. *EMAP archive*

Right: A wave of new American safety and emissions regulations in the 1970s forced Triumph to adapt the venerable 750 twin and Trident. Both models gained left-side gearshifts to comply with 1975 standards, a move that finally brought British bikes into line with European and Japanese models. In 1978, stricter U.S. evaporative emissions laws finally rendered obsolete the tickler on Amal carburetors. The Bonneville added Amal MKII carburetors, a new cylinder head with straight intake ports, and a revised airbox. The changes created the T140E (the E is for EPA), introduced as a 1978 1/2 model. That year, Triumph also offered a Chocolate-brown paint color and brown vinyl seat, a combination that was so unpopular in the United States that 500 chocolate T140Es were shipped back to Britain. They're a rare find today. *Jeff Hackett*

company—Norton Villiers Triumph (NVT). In effect, it consolidated the remains of Britain's once-huge motorcycle industry. Half of NVT's £10 million ($21 million) start-up capital came from Manganese Bronze (in exchange for BSA's non-motorcycle businesses—quite a bargain) and half came from the British taxpayer. The politicians reasoned that injecting public funds into the ailing bike industry was no different than in Japan and Germany, where government collaborated with the banks and private industry to capture world markets.

The British public and media generally viewed NVT's founding with cautious optimism. Those familiar with the company's current products had greater doubts. The newest bike in the range, Triumph's Trident, was conceived a decade earlier. Norton's 850 twin started life as a 500 in 1949, and the Bonneville hailed directly from Turner's 1937 Speed Twin. This aged fleet would have to carry the flag until NVT could develop a new line-up—within five years, reckoned Poore. Meanwhile the hyperbike stampede was beginning, led by Kawasaki's 900-cc Z-1—an 85-horsepower, dohc four-cylinder sledgehammer.

Poore was made NVT chairman. He established two manufacturing divisions, one at the former BSA Small Heath works in Birmingham, the other at Norton's Commando plant in Wolverhampton.

Small Heath would build Bonnevilles and Tridents, Poore decided. Meriden would be closed due to high cost; Triumph's profitability since 1950 had ensured it was the highest staffed, highest paid factory in the British bike industry. Its workers were notorious for walking off the job over the slightest grievance—in August 1973 they struck over holiday pay, right after returning from holiday! But they were also renowned for their pride in Triumph. Even the *Financial Times* lauded them for "a tremendous loyalty to the product, the Triumph motorbike."

More pragmatic than loyal was Bert Hopwood. The legendary engineer quit Triumph for the last time in August, when Dennis Poore refused to approve his modular plan. It is unlikely Hopwood would have remained at Triumph one month later. On September 14, 1973, Poore hastily called a meeting of Meriden's union stewards in the factory cafeteria. He told them he intended to shut down the Triumph plant and shift tooling to Small Heath, as was his right as company owner. Until then, he expected them to continue full production of the 1974 models, which had been under way for only a month.

What followed was the gloomiest period in Triumph history—an immediate sit-in strike by the Meriden workforce and their subsequent blockading of the plant for the next 18 months. Pickets manned the iron gates in front of the famous factory 24 hours a day, seven days a week. No materials arrived; no new bikes left. The supply of service parts that was critical for Triumph owners and dealers around the world was decimated. Unfortunately, the blokes behind the blockade either didn't consider this effect of their action, or didn't care.

Triumph's spares shortage had been a growing problem since 1971, when a large chunk of that year's 650-cc model output was lost due to the P39 frame debacle. To try to catch up in 1972–1973, Meriden's priority was building motorcycles, not spares. So when the workers cut off the supply of new machines, dealers literally had nothing to sell. Many of them quit Triumph.

The siege of Meriden and the formation of the worker's cooperative—Triumph Motorcycles (Meriden) Ltd.—was a political tragedy that pitted socialistic idealism against the realities of capitalism. The lockout ended in 1975, only when the British government allowed Triumph's workers to purchase the factory from NVT. The Co-Op, as it is often called, sold its finished Bonnevilles and Tigers back to NVT, which handled worldwide marketing and distribution.

(Interestingly, legal rights to the valuable Triumph logo were actually held by the Meriden District Council, which kept it as collateral for loans made to the Co-Op. The logo's ownership eventually transferred to John Bloor during Triumph's bankruptcy proceedings in 1983.)

For Triumph twin lovers who ride their bikes on a regular basis, the late 1970s and early 1980s T140s offer the best reliability and comfort. And they're easier to upgrade for greater overall performance and practicality, thanks to a thriving parts aftermarket. One T140 advocate is American enthusiast Mark Zimmerman, shown here enjoying his 1979 Bonnie on New England back roads. The bike wears Norton "peashooter" silencers, a popular modification. *Jeff Hackett*

In hindsight there were no real winners. NVT hung on to the Trident and was able to get the triple back into production in 1974. Though complete engines and some cycle parts were produced at the BSA Small Heath works, much of the Trident tooling and blueprints were locked in at Meriden. The only resort was to spend £500,000 ($1.1 million) to create new tooling, which was done in record time. The 1974 T150s were virtually identical to the 1973s, except for the color of their fuel-tank scallop. In Britain they were given considerable media attention as having beaten the blockade.

Prototype testing of a vastly revamped Trident had been under way since 1972. It featured a new frame derived from the factory's high-ground-clearance T150 production road racing frame. Other significant changes included new sheet metal, left-side gearchange, rear disc brake, and quieter muffling and air induction. Most importantly, electric starting was added behind BSA-style inclined cylinders.

The original intent was to name it Thunderbird III and stretch the motor out to 830 cc, but ultimately it remained a 750. When launched late in 1974, it was badged the T160 Trident. Heavier than its predecessor, the T160 is generally considered the best-looking Trident. Craig Vetter designed its slimline fuel tank and up-tilted instrument cluster for a prototype Bonneville TT custom project that followed his Hurricane work.

The new Trident's "intermittent" Lucas electric starting made the triple only slightly more sophisticated than its predecessor, in an era where smooth, fast 1,000-cc triples and fours, and sporting Ducati and BMW twins were capturing enthusiasts' hearts. As a competitive motorcycle the T160 was a flawed gem: beautiful to look at, tenacious on a twisty road, decently quick, but still cursed with drippy Amal Concentric carbs, a fiddly maintenance routine, and poor fuel economy.

More promising Trident spin-offs were in the works by Doug Hele's tiny engineering group at Kitts Green in Birmingham during 1974–1975. Among them were the 870-cc T180 Trident and the big, torquey 1,000-cc Quadrant four—the latter a Trident with an extra cylinder added, housed in a Rocket 3 chassis. But NVT's impending financial doom ensured neither bike would be built. Norton died in 1976 and the Wolverhampton plant closed. NVT itself sputtered out in 1977.

Fighting to the Finish

The Co-Op struggled from year to year, trying to pay down its debt while continuing to improve and refine the Bonneville. That it did, building more than 55,000 new 750-cc twins (and a handful of short-stroke 650-cc Thunderbird models) between 1976 and 1983.

"The message is clear," wrote *Cycle Guide* editor Steve Thompson in the first U.S. road test of the post-blockade 1976 Bonneville. "To some people, a narrow, 400-pound, competitively priced 750 twin that handles and steers lightly makes sense. If it happens to vibrate more than a multi, leak a bit of oil, or require more frequent routine maintenance, it's still a fair trade to obtain the kind of responsive handling and lean styling that currently isn't available anywhere else."

In a way the revamped Bonnie and Tiger, with left-side gearchange (to meet new U.S. regulations) and 10-inch rear disc brake, shared certain qualities of their old American nemesis, the Harley Sportster. Both were honest, true-grit motorcycles that refused to die in the face of technologically superior machines from Japan and Europe. And both enjoyed perhaps the fiercest owner adoration in motorcycling.

Frank Baker, the veteran engineer who was Triumph's experimental department chief before Doug Hele in the early 1960s, returned to that post after the Co-Op was launched. He explained the Triumph twin this way: "There is a world market for simplicity, and that's something our bike has always had."

In its first two seasons, the Co-Op concentrated on satisfying worldwide pent-up demand for new Triumphs—and paying its government loans on time. As befitting a true cooperative, there was little demarcation between jobs in the plant. Employees learned to work where needed and even do each other's tasks, something that was never permitted by the plant's strident unions before the blockade.

By 1978, sales growth in the United States had quietly pushed Triumph into sixth place in the market, ahead of BMW. Meriden was producing 60 bikes per day, about 300 every week. While this was hardly one-third of the factory's output in the heady late 1960s, it was the best since 1973, when the company had a six-model lineup. The marque was even winning races—UK dealer A. Bennett and Sons' T140 convincingly won Britain's 1978 Avon Tyres Production Bike championship. The near-stock Bonnie stunned the field of four-cylinder Japanese superbikes, Laverdas, and Ducatis with its reliability and impeccable handling.

Unfortunately, the Co-Op was losing money. Cash flow was an annual problem and low volumes put it at the mercy of international currency swings, particularly the dollar/pound exchange rate.

There was scarce funding for investment. No matter that Triumph continued to cut overhead by reducing its staff on both sides of the Atlantic. The bikes were becoming closer to hand-built rather than mass produced, which was actually used as a selling point. Without money for an all-new product, Meriden maximized its only platform, the T140/TR7.

More than a dozen variations of the Bonneville and Tiger were produced during the Co-Op's seven-year existence. In 1977 the twenty-fifth anniversary of Queen Elizabeth's reign was celebrated by a limited run (about 2,000) of Silver Jubilee Bonnies (T140J), decked out in special red, white, blue, and silver paint schemes with chromed timing and primary cases. The T140D Bonneville Special appeared in 1979, with its American-made Lester cast alloy wheels, classy black and gold paint and a two-into-one exhaust.

The sport-touring Bonneville Executive with cockpit fairing and hard luggage came in 1980, followed by 1981's Royal Wedding model that honored the marriage of Prince Charles and Diana Spencer. The 1981 TR7T

Tiger Trail aimed to capture some of the old Trophies' off-roader style, and the 1983 TSX was Meriden's answer to Yamaha's wildly successful XS650 Custom series.

Besides the many changes in paint scheme, fuel tanks, seats, and handlebars were hundreds of important engineering changes—from the belated switch to negative-ground electrics, to French-made Veglia instruments, powder-coat frame paint, stronger swing arms, Bing carburetors, 180-watt alternators, halogen headlamps, Magura controls, exhaust valve oil seals, Marzocchi forks, and Paioli shocks, to name a few.

In 1982 Triumph even built a few hundred TSS models (the T140W) with an updated version of the old Weslake eight-valve head, plus aluminum barrels, a stronger crank, costly American Morris cast wheels, and twin front disc brakes with Lockheed aluminum racing calipers. And a handful of AV Bonnevilles and single-carb Tigers, with special antivibration engine mounts, were among the company's final products.

Most significant of the later models were the 1979 T140E, and the 1980 T140ES Electro. The "E" signified compliance to the latest U.S. Environmental Protection Agency emissions standards. The increasingly strict pollution and noise regulations in the United States and Europe were frightful for a small company like Triumph because they consumed precious R&D resources, chief engineer Brian Jones noted in a 1979 *Classic Bike* interview. Jones' entire design and development team comprised just 14 people, but they made Turner's evergreen twin smog-compliant.

The "E" model unveiled for 1978 1/2 adopted a new cylinder head with parallel inlet ports and Amal MkII carburetors. It was the square-bodied MkII's that made the Triumph "cleaner" in the eyes of the EPA, because this Mikuni-like mixer had an lever for enriching, instead of the old Concentric's gasoline-dribbling tickler. For this reason, Triumph could no longer export the single-carb TR7 Tiger to the United States. The centrally mounted MkII carb and its airbox would not fit the Tiger because it interfered with the frame's backbone tube.

Along with its new induction setup, the T140E brought reliable Lucas Rita electronic ignition, a three-phase alternator, redesigned side covers, seat and handlebar switchgear, and Girling gas-charged shocks.

Triumph could have sold boxcar loads of electric-start twins years before, but it wasn't until 1980 that the concept entered production. On the ES models, the Lucas starter motor was fitted behind the cylinders, in the same place as the magneto on the original Speed Twin. *Cycle World* tested a 1981 "electric-leg" Bonnie and found much to like.

"The Bonneville manages to be a good all-purpose bike," wrote the editors. "It's both fun to ride and convenient at the same time. The light weight, electric start and quick warm-up made the Triumph the obvious and inviting choice for short trips and errands."

The Electro's stiff suspension was punishing on California's choppy freeways, but the stiff springing also contributed to "the Triumph's traditional feeling of tightness and solidness ... a sensation of agility and steering precision well known to British bike buffs."

The testers praised the Bonneville's classic dimensions—at 444 pounds with a half-tank of fuel it was the lightest 750 available, weighing 16 pounds less than a Kawasaki GPz550 Four. And its drag strip performance was virtually identical to the first Bonneville road tested by the magazine in 1962.

More civilized than the 650-cc twins of the 1960s, with satisfying power, decent rider comfort (for a British twin), and good handling and braking, the T140 series is by far the most popular classic Triumph today. The series is favored by enthusiasts who prefer to ride their machines. The fact that thousands of oil-in-the-frame models are still ridden regularly has helped create a multi-million-dollar parts and aftermarket industry that caters to the 750-cc twins. There's a long list of components and modifications available from Triumph specialists worldwide that will easily improve the bikes' function, reliability, and performance.

Though the Meriden Co-Operative was doomed from the start, and devoured more than £25 million ($50 million) in British taxpayers' money before the 1983 demise, its products continue to uphold Triumph's enduring virtues everywhere they are ridden.

The electric-start T140ES Electro was launched in 1980, its Lucas M3 starter motor mounted behind the cylinders where the pre-unit magneto once resided. The starter drive necessitated a new, wider timing cover. A year later, tighter emissions regulations brought Bing type-94 constant-velocity carburetors. Their complex linkages were an eyesore, so Triumph extended the T140's side cover molding to hide the Bings. The large gas tanks were now made in Italy, and "smoked" paint schemes were standard, as seen on this unrestored 1982 T140ES. *Jeff Hackett*

chapter
SIX

THE REBIRTH OF TRIUMPH

In the end, it was the workers themselves who decided Meriden's fate, and on August 26, 1983, they voted to declare bankruptcy of Triumph Motorcycles (Meriden) Ltd. Three months later, the factory that had been built for Jack Sangster and Edward Turner with government funds during World War II finally shut its doors.

Numerous schemes were proposed for use of the legendary plant and its 22-acre property, but eventually it was bulldozed to make way for a suburban housing development. (Its street names include Bonneville Close and Daytona Drive). Major artifacts were claimed and disbursed; the factory's iron gates and signage ended up at Norman Hyde's Triumph parts business. Andover Norton acquired over 150 tons of spares and motorcycle inventory.

But what really mattered—ownership of the timeless Triumph logo, patents, and manufacturing rights—was purchased by an obscure 40-year-old British businessman who hadn't ridden a motorcycle since his youth.

Nor had John Bloor prior experience in the motorcycle industry. He isn't a Triumph enthusiast per se, although he learned to ride on a Tiger Cub and later commuted on a 6T Thunderbird. Bloor is a self-made multimillionaire who grew up in the Midlands. He began his career as a plasterer's apprentice. From that skilled trade he built a small empire of construction companies, which he then parlayed into real estate development. His company, J.S. Bloor Holdings, builds about 2,000 homes per year.

The first time he visited the empty Meriden factory site, Bloor was considering purchasing it to develop as a housing estate. In 1984, he told *Classic Bike Magazine's* Mike Nicks that he had no emotional attachment to the Triumph brand. Acquiring it was just a business project.

"I saw that it was for sale," he noted. "If you don't have a go, you never achieve anything."

Eighteen years later in an interview with *Fortune* magazine, Bloor reflected that his motive was simple. "I'm interested in seeing things put together well," he said. "I had just a little hankering to build some kind of product."

Bloor purchased Triumph's key assets from the liquidators for a reported $300,000 (£120,000 at the time). The iconic "swooping R" logo actually came to him via the Meriden District Council, which held it as collateral for loans made to the workers' Co-Op.

The package included all of Meriden's final R&D projects including the Diana—a dohc eight-valve, liquid-cooled vertical twin. The Co-Op had hoped to produce this engine in a machine tentatively named Phoenix, with monoshock rear suspension. There were plans to make the bike in 600-cc, 750-cc, and 900-cc versions and in two styles—a European standard and a U.S.-custom lowrider. It had reached the running prototype stage and was generally assumed to be the T140 Bonneville's successor.

Also vying for the Triumph marque was L.F. "Les" Harris, an independent parts maker and importer. Harris' company, Racing Spares, had been producing Triumph components since the 1960s. He had a serious business interest in keeping the T140 in production. Thousands were in regular use throughout the world and it was the source of most of his parts business.

Harris' ambition actually fit Bloor's plan nicely. Soon after he had the assets in hand, Bloor granted Harris a five-year license to assemble electric-start T140ES Bonnies at his small Devon plant. The deal accomplished two things: it kept the Triumph name alive and bought Bloor time to develop his company and a range of new Triumph models. The license also prohibited Harris from further evolving the old Bonneville with any of Meriden's latest upgrades—the fully machined TSS crankshaft, eight-valve head, and antivibration engine mounts were off limits.

The first Racing Spares-built Bonnies were launched in 1985. They were mostly identical to the 1983 Meriden machines but many of their components came from continental Europe—the traditional British supply base had dried up. Harris went to Italy to purchase front forks and rear shock absorbers (from Paioli), mufflers (Lafranconi), and brake calipers and master cylinders (Brembo). From Germany came Magura switchgear.

Ironically, the carburetors reverted back to Amal MkI Concentrics. This move illustrated one of Harris's problems—he couldn't sell Triumphs in the United States. In order to export to the world's largest motorcycle market, every bike maker must carry costly product liability insurance. And since Harris was not allowed to develop the Bonneville under his deal with Bloor, he was unable to keep pace with U.S. noise and emissions laws. These regulations were not nearly as stringent in the UK, so the roughly 2,000 Harris-built T140s remained mostly a home-market product (some also went to Australia) during the bike's 1985–1988 production run.

Bloor did not renew Harris' assembly contract in 1988. Thirty years after the original T120 left the Meriden assembly track, the air-cooled Bonneville was dead. In the end, over 300,000 650-cc and 750-cc versions were made.

Daytona Super III arrived in 1994 as a tuned version of the standard Daytona sports triple. With hotter camshafts and a bump in compression, it produced a claimed 113 horsepower. The limited-production model also featured six-piston Alcon front brake calipers and carbon-fiber styling touches. The Super III's price was intimidating—about $16,000 in the United States. *Jeff Hackett*

Modular Triples and Fours

Meanwhile, the methodical Bloor had quietly established his new company, Triumph Motorcycles Limited. He purchased a 10-acre, greenfield site at Hinckley, Leicestershire, 15 miles east of Meriden and not far from Triumph's original Coventry works. There construction began on a 90,000 square-foot, single-story factory to be filled with computer-controlled precision tooling (much of it sourced from Japan and Germany) and an eager, young, and decidedly nonunion workforce. A few veterans of the "old" company were asked to join Bloor's team, including David Green, a skilled draftsman who began his career at Triumph in 1944.

The first-generation Speed Triple, launched in 1994, immediately accounted for half of Triumph's European sales. The aim was to recapture the unfaired café racer look, feel, and performance—a Triton for the 1990s. Powered by a 100-horsepower 885-cc triple with five-speed gearbox, the Speed Triple gained "street cred" through its low clip-on bars and taut suspension. The fork is a 43-mm Japanese Kayaba. *EMAP archive*

Green picked up where he'd left off at Meriden, except now a computer-aided design (CAD) terminal replaced his old drawing board and blueprints. "John Bloor assured me I could master CAD and he gave me breathing space to get used to it," Green said in a 1995 interview just after retiring. "The confidence he showed in us before there was ever a product was amazing."

Bloor's small team had inspected the prototype Diana engine and the Phoenix, but deemed them hopelessly obsolete. From that point on, Triumph looked forward. Led by chief engineer Martin Roberts, the team was given all the time it needed. Bloor realized that remaking Triumph had to be done right, regardless of whether it took four years or the actual eight. Bloor established Triumph as a privately held company, of which he owns 100 percent. His pockets were deep enough to bankroll the entire development process without feeling pressure from shareholders or bankers.

After visiting Kawasaki, Suzuki, and Yamaha plants in Japan, and closely analyzing those makers' motorcycles, the Triumph men settled on a range of modern three- and four-cylinder, liquid-cooled machines. Their ultimate design was most closely influenced by Kawasaki's much-respected GPz series, marketing chief Michael Lock admitted later, but with improved durability built in.

The strategy was not to fight the Japanese head on, which would be too costly for a tiny company like Triumph. Instead, Bloor adopted a "modular" strategy similar to the one Bert Hopwood advocated 20 years before.

Because going "modular" means making many parts common to save development cost and maximize production volumes, it has some disadvantages in the fast-paced motorcycle industry. Frequent product redesigns in the bike world are often critical, especially for sports models. In the hyper-competitive 600-cc sport bike category, for example, three-year-old engines are considered old. Cylinder heads are often thoroughly revamped every two years to gain the slightest power advantage and sales edge.

Soichiro Irimajiri, the famous Honda engineer who designed many of that company's championship Grand Prix engines in the 1960s as well as the 1979 six-cylinder CBX road bike, told the author that Honda

had considered its own modular-engine plan. "We quickly abandoned the concept—it had too many compromises," he explained.

But to a new company starting from scratch, the modular approach has many advantages. Sharing engine dimensions and components, chassis and running gear, and cycle parts among various models greatly reduces investment cost, Spare parts inventory is minimized. Service training is simplified. John Bloor needed the greatest bang for his investment buck, and he got it with modularized design

The first engines to emerge from Triumph's CAD screens were a family of triples and fours. All featured a common 76-mm cylinder bore and either 55-mm or 65-mm strokes, depending on the required displacement. The triples were 749 cc and 885 cc, and the fours displaced 1,190 cc All of the engines used dohc, four-valves-per-cylinder architecture, with common 28-mm and 32-mm valve diameters, chain-driven camshafts, inverted bucket-type tappets with shim lash adjustment, and 36-mm flat-slide Mikuni carburetors. Each engine was given its own distinct power characteristics and "feel" by mixing and matching compression ratios and camshaft profiles.

To quell vibration, the triples and fours employed balance shafts in their horizontally split cases. The wet-sump triples had a single shaft located ahead of the crankshaft, and the dry-sump four had twin counter-rotating shafts below the crank, with oil carried in a reservoir below the gearbox.

Depending on model, gearboxes were either five or six speeds, with a stout 6-inch multiplate wet clutch. The overall impression of the new Triumph powerplants was of strength and robustness. They also were blessed with an abundance of power; the 750-cc triples offered 90 horsepower at 10,500 rpm and the 1,200-cc four claimed a brutish 147 horsepower at 9,500.

Modularity also extended to the new bikes' chassis. The engine served as a stressed member in the steel-tube frames that incorporated a large backbone tube as a strengthening spine. The extruded aluminum swing arm was suspended by a rising-rate Japanese Kayaba monoshock. To make chain adjustment easy the arm featured large, eccentric chain adjusters at the axle end. Up front, the new Triumphs wore Kayaba forks, and most models were stopped with Japanese Nissin disc brakes.

The modular strategy allowed Triumph to launch a multimodel range—standard Tridents, Daytona sport bikes, and a fully faired Trophy sport-tourer—from a common "platform." More than 85 percent of the parts were shared among the models. This approach is used with great success in the auto industry and continues to serve Triumph well as it moves forward.

Remarkably, Bloor kept his project secret until early 1989, when the first evidence of the modular engine range was uncovered by an astute Triumph owner/enthusiast attending an auto engineering show in Detroit. At the show one of Triumph's engine casting suppliers had on display a few components, including a dohc, four-valve cylinder head. The Triumph fan, John Hubbard, spotted the new "swooping R" logo embossed on each casting and hurried home to get his camera. His photos were first published by England's *Classic Bike* magazine. Bloor's cover had been blown.

Nearly 18 months later, Bloor launched his reborn products at the Cologne Motorcycle Show. Once again, new Triumphs were under the lights in front of the world's media! Bloor decided to launch in Germany because it is perhaps the world's most demanding motorcycle market. German customers are famously finicky about quality. Their stamp of approval means a new machine generally can succeed in any market.

New for 1998, the Sprint Executive was an 885-cc triple equipped for sport touring, with dual-headlamp half fairing, 6.6-gallon fuel tank, and standard Italian-made Givi hard luggage. Best of all, it sold in the United States for just $8,995—$1,500 less than the 1997 Sprint that came without the hard bags. *David Dewhurst*

"It sounds strange to be at a race and hear over the PA that a Triumph is in the lead … are we stuck in some weird time warp here? Is that Gary Nixon?" wrote moto-journalist John Burns about rider Curtis Adams and the T595 Daytona road racer built by Orange County Triumph. Adams and the Daytona became the combination to beat in the AMA's Sound of Thunder race series in 1998. *Motorcyclist*

The 1998 Thunderbird Sport resurrected more classic Triumph styling cues. Compared with the standard T-bird, the 72-horsepower Sport featured new Keihin carburetors, an X75 Hurricane-influenced three-into-two exhaust system, 1960s-style humped back seat, and flat-track handlebars. While *Cycle World* tested its Sport against Harley's Sportster Sport (the Triumph proved to be the better machine), *Classic Bike* compared its with a genuine 1973 Hurricane, seen here on the right. *EMAP archive*

While the first-generation Speed Triple echoed the 1960s café racer, the 1998 version was Triumph's reply to the "streetfighter" trend then popular among British motorcyclists. Streetfighter machines were basically sport bikes that had been stripped of their fairings, usually after a wreck, and put back on the street naked. The new S-triple was a stripped Daytona with twin bug-eye headlamps and a standard handlebar. U.S. magazines rated it highly as a "hooligan" bike, capable of power-wheelies with ease. *Jay Asquini*

Bloor was also preparing to face the home crowd. He knew the jaded mainstream British motorcycling press would be ruthless in its criticism of new Triumphs that didn't measure up to the best from Japan and Europe. Few of them had cried over Meriden's demise. To them, the Co-Op's struggle to survive was just a memory of "the bad old days" they wanted to forget. The media also was convinced that Britain would never again be a volume motorcycle producer. A reborn Triumph would be a tough sell indeed, even to the most fervent Union Jack-waving riders.

Bloor had much to prove. But when the first published road tests appeared, the naysayers were all but silenced. Here were competitive machines with bags full of useful grunt, exemplary fit and finish, plenty of speed, powerful brakes, and excellent road manners.

In his road test of an early Trident 900, *Motorcycle International*'s Dave Minton called the triple "astonishingly well mannered and magnificently finished. It's a little raw and all the better for it," Minton gushed. "They don't build 'em as handsomely rugged as this in Japan, nor as crammed with torque."

The new Triumphs were good bikes, as customers soon found out. Yes, there were areas needing improvement—the greatest complaint was rust-prone chrome plating. Seat heights were higher than average, due to the spine-frame design, making the motorcycles feel top-heavy at slow speeds.

Triumph's fully equipped Trophy 1200 was the only four-cylinder model remaining in the lineup prior to the TT600's debut. It's rated highly among sport-touring riders. Journalist Chris Cimino rode one in the 1997 Iron Butt Rally, which traversed 11,000 miles across the United States in 11 days. His Trophy was fitted with a 4-gallon auxiliary fuel tank, taller gearing, 32-liter Givi hard bags, Tiger 900 fork springs, and a Speed Triple rear shock absorber. He was sponsored by Engle Motors, a Triumph dealer in Kansas City, Missouri. *Motorcyclist*

Stylistically the bikes were a bit dated. Die-hard fans of the "classic" Triumphs jokingly described the early Hinckley-built machines as "last year's Kawasakis." They also noted that the new engines had an "attractive" side (the right side) and an "ugly" side on the left, with exposed water pump, cooling hoses, faux covers over unsightly plumbing and wiring and, on some models, a chrome horn hanging from the cylinder head. And the radiators on the naked Tridents looked large enough to cool a small car.

It was a fair criticism. But when customers sounded off, Triumph listened—and acted quickly. It diligently corrected early problems, even to the point of bringing all paint work and chrome plating in-house. The factory's new chrome shop was an expensive investment but one that has paid off in a durable, lustrous finish.

The combination of stoutly engineered, well-made, fun-to-ride motorcycles and a customer-focused company put Triumph back into the game faster than most observers imagined. Reports of the new models turning in some fantastic mileages began to appear; one British owner's 1992 Trident covered 250,000 well-documented miles with little more than regular maintenance.

By early 1992 the brand had taken over the big-bike sales lead in the UK and had begun to expand into major world markets. Led by international marketing manager Michael Lock, an enthusiastic dynamo whom Bloor hired away from Honda UK, Triumph set up distributors and sales networks across Europe, Australia, Canada, and Japan. Annual production jumped from 5,000 bikes in 1992 to 12,000 in 1995, and the Hinckley plant was doubled in size to satisfy demand.

Bloor now had all of the key pieces of the puzzle in place, except one: the United States. Returning to the scene of Triumph's greatest sales and speed glories was intentionally reserved until the right moment. Since

Triumph jumped back into the World's Fastest record books in August 1998, when Brad Scheire rode a Daytona triple to a record in the Stock Production class. Average speed was 173.735 miles per hour. The machine was prepared by Matt Capri's South Bay Triumph dealership in Lomita, California. *Matt Capri*

1984, Bloor had monitored the U.S. market as it split into two major segments: cruisers (dominated in styling influence and sales by Harley-Davidson) and sport bikes, the realm of Japan and the Italians. Clearly there was room for a revitalized Triumph, if the bikes were done properly.

The brand's identity remained strong—perhaps stronger in America than anywhere else in the world. Americans revered the bikes that carried names like Nixon, Romero, and McQueen to stardom. Michael Lock, whom Bloor promoted to president of the U.S. operation, began by checking the pulse of the American public with a poll about motorcycles.

"The results floored me," Lock told the author in 1995. "It was a decade after the last Meriden-built Bonnies were sold, and people who weren't even bike enthusiasts told us that the Triumph name was still the third most-recognized motorcycle brand, after Honda and Harley."

When the U.S. operation was in the planning stage, Bloor considered a number of distribution options. Links with Kawasaki (including a joint manufacturing scheme at Kawi's Lincoln, Nebraska, factory) and Cagiva North America were discussed. The spirit of cooperation also led old rivals Triumph and Harley-Davidson to help get each other's motorcycles through U.S. and European emissions certification.

But as the U.S. launch deadline approached, Bloor finally decided that a wholly owned distributor—Triumph Motorcycles America Ltd.—based near Atlanta, Georgia (close to eastern U.S. ports), was the way to go. It was the same basic business model that Edward Turner had established so successfully with TriCor some 40 years earlier. And in late 1994, the company officially landed back in America with a 10-model lineup—everything except the 750-cc Trident—and a starter network of 60 dealers.

The much-anticipated U.S. debut was timed to coincide with the first major expansion of Triumph's product portfolio. Leading the thrust was the Speed Triple, basically an 885-cc Daytona triple minus its fairing and sporting five ratios, rather than six, in its gearbox. The name played off of the legendary Speed Twin, and the new bike was no less a sensation.

Available in either gloss black or the shocking Fireball Orange, the Speed Triple was Triumph's reincarnation of the mighty Laverda Jotas of the 1970s. It was a modern café racer in the purist idiom, devoid of any frills. With low clip-on handlebars and high rearset pegs, it forced its rider into jockeylike obedience. And just as its acceleration and lusty three-cylinder howl pumped adrenaline into riders' veins, the big, bad Speed Triple brought serious attitude back to Triumph.

Also part of the American beachhead was the Tiger 900, Triumph's entry into the "adventure bike" or "trailie" market that was so popular in Europe. With long-travel suspension, plastic fenders, raised exhaust, and a tuned for low-end torque 885-cc triple, the Tiger was a sport-utility motorcycle. Like most four-wheeled SUVs, it was far more at home on the street than the trail, but it injected some of the old TR6C's go-anywhere spirit into the brand.

The star of the 1995 U.S. invasion, however, was the Thunderbird. Once again Triumph loaded its three-cylinder gun to create a new model, but this time its blast was aimed as much toward the past as the present. Bloor had waited patiently for this moment to occur, as he admitted later.

"If we had gone into the retro stuff first, we would have been seen purely as a niche retro-builder," Bloor told writer Stuart Brown in 2001. "We would have found difficulty being accepted later on three- and four-cylinder sport bikes. That was the strategy behind it at the time. If we had started just in the retro market, we might have gone only halfway."

Like the Golden Spike that connected U.S. eastern and western railroads in 1869, the Thunderbird rejoined Triumph with its fabulous heritage. Here was a cruiser-segment bike adorned in classic British shapes—rounded black side covers, teardrop fuel tank, wire-spoke wheels, a low seat height, and plenty of polished alloy and chrome. It even wore authentic Burgess "snake-ate-a-rabbit" mufflers and an updated version of the 1957–1965 "mouth organ" tank badge.

The T-bird was retuned (via cam profiles and lower compression) to deliver "just" 70 horsepower, but it also cranked out 90 percent of its total 55 lbs-ft of torque across a 2,800 rpm spread. Best of all, the Thunderbird was not another V-twin Harley clone. Customers flocked to the $9,995 machine. It quickly became Triumph's hottest model in America, capturing one-quarter of U.S. sales and earning *Motorcyclist's* "Motorcycle of the Year" honors.

Underneath its Brando-era skin, the reborn Bird was designed to give Triumph a multimodel platform. By once again swapping cycle parts and other hardware, and tweaking the engine tune, the 1995 model soon spawned the '97 Thunderbird Sport (with low 'bars, six-speed gearbox, and flat-track inspired three-pipe exhaust), the '98 Legend TT (a lower-priced version with an even lower seat height) and the Adventurer. The latter was a grotesque British interpretation of an American custom—Austin Powers' wardrobe transformed into a motorcycle!

Hinckley's output crested 30,000 bikes in 1996; exports accounted for 80 percent of sales, just like in the golden 1960s but now divided more equally to markets beyond the United States. The UK market had become a bigger slice of revenues. Triumphs' performance, quality, and ever-stronger brand image helped the company grow to a 22 percent share of the UK's big-bike (over-700-cc) segment by 1997—a rise of 8 percent in two years.

That year came the company's first all-new models since the 1991 relaunch. The T509 Speed Triple and T595 Daytona cast a new mold for Triumph, in terms of design and performance. Both proved the

South Bay Triumph's Daytona Streetfighter project. The hairy-chested screamer produces over 300 horsepower with a Garrett turbo. *Matt Capri*

Triumph's Atlanta-based U.S. distributor takes this 45-foot custom semitrailer to major motorcycle races and rallies across the country each year. The company offers rides and product information, and the lines of people waiting to try a new Trumpet are always long. Here, the road ride saddles up during the 1999 AMA vintage festival at Mid-Ohio Race Course. *Lindsay Brooke*

Far right
The 955i Daytona continues to get refinements to keep it firmly in the superbike game. The 490-pound triple's fuel injection was remapped for 2000 and its engine received significant design changes in 2002. Suspension is by Showa. With 105 horsepower at the rear wheel, the Daytona runs the quarter-mile in 10.8 seconds at 127 miles per hour. Top speed is 156 miles per hour. *Jay Asquinit*

Triumph finally entered the ultracompetitive 600-cc sport bike market in 2000, with its new TT600. An aluminum-beam frame helped pare weight to 375 pounds, and the fuel-injected four-cylinder packed a claimed 110 horsepower at the crankshaft. Here, the TT600 makes its world debut at the 1999 British Motorcycle Show in Birmingham. *Mick Duckworth*

brilliance of Triumph's charismatic, three-cylinder powerplant and sported fresh thinking everywhere. (Triumph's decision to carry the bikes' 509 and 595 project codes into their production model names was unfortunate; to the public the numbers indicated engine displacement, while the new motors displaced 955 cc!)

The new black-painted engines were lighter, more compact, and more powerful. Their cylinder heads were developed with airflow and combustion input from F1 car experts Lotus Engineering. Fuel injection, by a French Sagem electronically controlled system, replaced the carburetors. Oil coolers hung alongside the crankcases to help keep oil temperatures low.

A 955i Daytona in final assembly at Hinckley, 2000. The factory's young workforce uses the latest automotive production techniques and performs much subassembly work in-house, including the entire powertrain, chrome plating, and injection molding. Note the TIG-welded oval frame tubing and how densely packed these machines are under the fairing. *Triumph Motorcycles Ltd.*

Owners began personalizing the new Bonneville almost immediately after the bike's 2001 launch. The aftermarket is serving up plenty of goodies for the 800-cc dohc twin, many of which improve its rather sedate performance and help give the bike a leaner, 1960s look. The owner of this 2002 Bonnie had it repainted to include matching fender stripes. He also fitted flat, 1-inch Flanders handlebars for a more sporting stance. Next priority is CR Keihin smoothbore carbs and airbox, and replacing that "blob" taillamp. *Lindsay Brooke*

Above
Triumph plans to squeeze many variants from the new Bonnie's platform. The 2002 model year saw two limited-edition versions of the basic Bonneville: the T100 Centennial Edition, painted to resemble a 1969 T120R, and the Golden Jubilee, shown here. This bike's name commemorates the fiftieth year of Queen Elizabeth's reign, while its livery recalls the 1977 T140J Silver Jubilee. *Lindsay Brooke*

167

The 2002 Golden Jubilee model was actually a dealer-installed kit. For roughly $1,000 over the price of a new Bonnie, the owner got a special fuel tank paint job, fenders, side panels, and optional headlamp flyscreen. Only a handful of Jubilee-kitted Bonnies were sold. Lovers of Triumph's reborn parallel twin were lucky that most of the season's Bonneville production was already built before a serious fire in March 2002 crippled Hinckley production for most of the season. *Lindsay Brooke*

"A great alternative to the mongrel hordes" is how *Sport Rider* described the new-for-2002 Daytona. Still not truly competitive with Japan's hottest open-class sportbikes in power ("only" 128 horsepower) and weight (a hefty 478 pounds), the triple offers neck-snapping performance, excellent brakes, fine handling, and a spine-tingling sound. This is the limited-production Centennial version, with special green paintwork and single-sided swingarm. Standard 2002 Daytonas got a new twin-sided arm. *Factory photo*

The new engines served as a stressed member in the bikes' radical frames. Their oval-section aluminum tube was beautifully welded to cast-aluminum steering heads and upright members that supported the rear of the gearbox and the single-sided, aluminum swing arm. The rear disc brake was mounted Ducati 916 style, inboard of the final drive sprocket.

The T595 Daytona was Hinckley's first sport bike that could hold its own in comparison tests with the latest from Japan and Italy. Though still not quite rapid enough to win tests by the radar gun alone, the new Daytona was widely praised and won thousands of satisfied customers who weren't concerned about max-speed bragging rights.

While the Daytona owed the shape of its fairing upper and "cats-eye" headlamps to the trend-setting Ducati, the second-generation Speed Triple set a new style of its own. Like its predecessor, the "Rippo Trippo" basically was a

naked Daytona, endowed with 102 horsepower and nearly 80 ft-lb of torque. Its visual signature is twin bullet-shaped headlamps that protrude from the fork like a stripper's brassiere.

Fitted with a lowish handlebar instead of clip-ons, the S-triple quickly gained a reputation as a wheelie king and "hooligan" bike, able to smoke its rear tire between city stoplights or carve through curvy mountain roads with equal finesse. As Triumph's sporting flagships, the S-triple and Daytona top the development-priority list. They were again thoroughly revamped for 2002, with new lighter, stronger pressure-die-cast engine cases, smaller bearing journals (for reduced internal friction), new cylinder heads, and 12:1 compression. The new motors howl out 113 rear-wheel horsepower (S-triple) and 127 horsepower (Daytona). The engine in retuned form also went into a new Tiger 900 trailie in 2001.

The '02 S-Triple kept the single-sided swingarm, while its fully faired cousin reverted to a new, lighter twin-sided 'arm. And Triumph is focused on weight reduction for its sporting models; at 477 pounds fully gassed, the '02 Speed Triple is 37 pounds lighter than Yamaha's FZ1 and nearly 70 pounds leaner than Kawasaki's ZRX1200R.

The Bonnie Returns

As the twenty-first century approached, Triumph was rapidly filling market segments with new entries. While the Trophy 1200 tourer gained a new fairing and features, it retained its old-generation four-pot engine. Another new platform was added in 1999 to update the three-cylinder Sprint series sport tourer. This one featured a new chassis with extruded-aluminum beam frame and a retuned T595 powerplant.

It was Triumph's answer to Honda's excellent VFR Interceptor, and with an integrated full fairing and optional hard luggage, the Sprint was so good that many journalists rated it on a par or better. The ST sparked a half-faired RS version in 2000 and picked up the die-cast 955 engine in '02.

In 1999, Bloor took a major leap into the most hotly contested market segment: the 600-cc sport bike. Triumph's TT600 had been in development since 1996 and its 108-horsepower four-cylinder engine was developed in conjunction with F1 maestros Cosworth Engineering. At 374 pounds dry, the TT600 handled superbly and had the best brakes in its class.

But ongoing glitches with the control mapping of its Sagem fuel-injection system, a first in the 600-cc segment, continued for 18 months. This caused a lot of lukewarm road tests and coupled with a rather high price tag ($8,500 in the United States) and further advances by the Japanese competition, the TT was not an initial success. By 2002 the bugs were gone, development continued (Bloor's not giving up on this model!), and a naked Speed Four variant was launched.

While development of the 600 four and the revamped Sprint series were under way, Hinckley's R&D department was simultaneously working on the gem of Triumph's "classic" range. As far back as 1994, U.S. boss Michael Lock had noted his company's investigation of a new Bonneville. "It absolutely has to be right," he told the author. "We're playing with at least two concepts, but we're taking our time."

Through the late 1990s, the UK bike media speculated wildly about the reborn Bonnie's specification, and many artists' renderings were published. In 1997, U.S. dealers got their first indication of the company's intentions.

"A Triumph guy from England visited our shop looking for an accurately restored late-1960s Bonnie," recalled Keith Martin, a veteran Triumph dealer and tuner in Dallas, Texas. "We thought it was strange that the factory didn't have one a little closer to home."

Martin and other dealers in the United States and in the UK were solicited for their input on a new Bonneville's styling and specification. Most all agreed that the 1969–1970 T120R was the best reference. So a restored 1970 model was purchased in America and shipped to Hinckley to serve as the benchmark for the 908MD project—the 2001 Bonneville. Bloor's engineers decided upon a 790-cc dohc, eight-valve parallel twin,

TALKING TRIUMPH WITH CHAIRMAN JOHN BLOOR

In the 10 years since the official rebirth Triumph Motorcycles Ltd., you could readily count the published interviews with company chairman John Bloor. That's been by design. Unlike self-promoting titan Edward Turner, Bloor is a soft-spoken man who's not interested in the media spotlight. He prefers to let his products do the talking. But to mark the company's first decade (and the one-hundredth anniversary of the Triumph brand), Bloor decided to grant a few interviews with select reporters to discuss the state of his business—where it's been and where it's going.

Fortune magazine's industrial technology writer Stuart Brown was indeed fortunate to sit down with Bloor in New York City in November 2001. The reporter and his subject were a perfect fit: Brown is a veteran motorcyclist who owns an '02 Speed Triple and rode a 1968 TR6/R in his youth. He says Bloor "is by nature very shy and not at all into ego, despite the worldwide fame of his achievement. But he's extremely proud of Triumph and loves manufacturing. He'll talk to you all day about the details of how things are built."

Brown was armed with many questions for Bloor, including the following, which were earmarked specifically for this book.

Is Triumph profitable?

Bloor: Triumph is a subsidiary of Bloor Holdings, and the strategy right from the start has been to get a spread of product into the marketplace, and not to be vertical—not to offer just a three-cylinder engine or just a twin. By having a spread of product we can cater to different segments of the market.

It's more appealing to our dealerships to cater to several segments, because they can make their living with one or two franchises instead of three or four. This enables us to have less switch-selling and less pressure on the dealers for floor space. If there are four franchises in a shop (for example, a Triumph/Honda/Kawasaki/Ducati store), there's probably one flooring contract coming to an end and pressure to sell those bikes out. Somebody's going to get a bad display.

Fewer franchises in the dealership gives us a better market penetration. But to get to that stage we've needed a broader product spread. For our size, we spend a disproportionate amount of money on R&D—about £10 million (about $15 million) per year. That's been fairly steady over the last three years.

Our R&D has been treated as a revenue item, so it's written off the year that we incur the cost. It's not amortized, which would be the industry norm. We have a design team that is quite large also, in reference to the R&D costs.

But now we're getting to the point that with our product spread, we are achieving a volume that puts us in the black. We're not running a charity this year. We turned the corner into black ink for 2001, on sales of $245 million.

We design our own engines, and we manufacture our own engines in-house. And the gestation period of designing and developing an engine is about 2½ years. We try to be focused. Our volume for model-year 2001 will be 33,000 motorcycles. Over 10 years the cumulative sales have been, including 2001, about 170,000 units.

What are Triumph's biggest world markets?

Bloor: Europe is 60 percent of our business. America is 30 percent. The rest (Australia, Japan, etc.) accounts for 10 percent. This year the UK will take about 5,000 units, same as Germany. The Tiger and the sport bikes sell better in Germany, the Bonneville and the retro bikes sell better in America, the UK and Australia.

Our largest selling model across all these markets has been the Sprint ST over the last two years. We've put a new engine in it for 2002 and it's about 12 kilos (25 pounds) lighter.

Demand for new Triumphs has forced you to expand the factory?

Bloor: We've actually got two plants, next to each other in an industrial park in Hinckley, with a capacity of 45,000 to 50,000 units per year. There is more space if we need to expand further. Our expansion is incremental. We have grown each year; this year was about 18 percent growth from last year. Total factory space is now 40,000 square meters.

Triumph's workforce totals 400 people in production, and about 90 in engineering and development. Most of our people are young and homegrown. The average age on the R&D side is about 30 years old.

How do you decide what parts to make in-house and what to purchase?

Bloor: We design everything ourselves, but with input from specialist manufacturers like suspension makers Showa and Kayaba. Electrics are Denso and Kokushin. All the critical pieces on the engineering side we keep in-house, so we have absolute control over them and can modify them as we need. We would feel uncomfortable putting outside things like cylinder heads, crankshafts, crankcases, and camshafts; we make those things 100 percent in-house. We plan to continue to design and build our own engines and chassis.

One of the reasons we control most of our subsidiaries, the distributors in the United States, Japan, Germany, and France, is that we want direct feedback from our customers. We need that intelligence gathering. If you want to stay in business you have to keep moving.

[Bloor showed a reader survey from a fall 2001 issue of Germany's *Motorrad* magazine, which ranked Triumphs at or near the top in initial owner satisfaction.]

Are you planning any new powerplants?

Bloor: We will stay for the foreseeable future with a twin-, three-, and four-cylinder lineup, having a spread of engine designs.

Why challenge the Japanese 600s?

Bloor: Because it's a large segment of the market, and we have to give our dealers a spread of product. We have to have a middle-sized sport bike.

Do you feel the TT600 is different than the Japanese offerings?

Bloor: I would say we are on the way. This year's 600 model (2002) is much improved. We do the engine mapping internally now, which we were contracting out previously. We buy the hardware, but the software is developed internally.

Care to comment about a big-displacement three-cylinder, shaft-driven sport tourer we've heard about?

Bloor: [smiling]There may be an element of truth in those rumors.

British businessman John Bloor made his fortune in construction and real estate. Soon after Meriden closed in 1983, he bought the Triumph name, manufacturing rights, and remaining assets for a reported $300,000. With that start, Bloor resurrected the company. Roland Brown

with a 360-degree crankshaft (to give the traditional Triumph sound) but featuring twin gear-drive balance shafts to quell vibration.

The oversquare (86x68-mm bore and stroke) twin was tuned to deliver broad, usable power—the new Bonnie was categorized as a "beginner bike" in Triumph's portfolio. Output was finalized at 62 horsepower at a rather revvy 7,400 rpm, and max torque of 42 ft-lb at 3,500 rpm. Engine styling was an important element to the 908MD program. The wet-sump engine has horizontally split crankcases, with chromed exterior covers gracing its faux timing chest, five-speed gearbox casing, and gear-driven primary. The drive chain is on the right side, not the left as on the T120 and T140 twins. A nice classic touch is the chromed oil-drain tube placed vertically in front of the cylinder barrels, mimicking the exhaust pushrod tube on the old engines.

The new motor is mounted as a semistressed member in the frame, which does not include a front cradle. Chassis and sheet metal are obviously critical to evoking the T120's form, and the Hinckley twin is perhaps 85 percent faithful. It employs traditional twin-shock rear suspension, laced wire wheels, and single disc brakes front and rear. The overall package, at 477 pounds wet, is about 85 pounds heavier than the 1960s 650s.

Triumph reprised its original Sprint sport tourer in 1999 with an all-new version. Aimed directly at Honda's do-it-all VFR Interceptor, the new Sprint achieved parity or better, quickly earning *Cycle World's* "Best Sport Tourer" award due to its overall balance, comfy ergonomics, torquey new injected 955i triple, and optional hard luggage. *Factory photo*

A few styling areas have been roundly criticized since the new Bonnie first broke cover in 2000. (Triumph strategically leaked a profile photo onto the Internet, to gauge public reaction and stoke demand.) The exhaust system raised the greatest guffaws; its "kink" between the end of the head pipes and the trad-look mufflers spoils the bike's lines. Triumph claims the kink is needed for cornering clearance, but aftermarket pipes that eliminate the kink are already flooding the market.

Other not-quite-right visuals: The fuel tank has too wide a flange on its underside. The rear shocks, wheel hubs, and high-crowned wheel rims look as if they were pulled from a Harley-Davidson parts bin. The blob-like taillamp is freakishly out of place, and the rear fender is too deeply valanced for a lean Bonneville. The bike lacks a tachometer as standard equipment. And where are the rubber fork gaiters?

But Triumph did not intend to produce a perfect copy of the T120R. As Peter Egan astutely noted in a 2001 *Cycle World* test, the new Bonnie is "a modern bike in the visual and dynamic spirit of the old girl—what the Bonneville might have become, had it stayed in production all these years, with sensible updates, while keeping the price ($7,200) reasonable."

Egan and other testers praised the Bonnie's roomy ergonomics and chuckability, its 4.3-gallon fuel tank (available in three two-tone paint schemes), and 45-mile per gallon economy. The engine, Egan wrote, is "muscular and

Few Triumph buffs will believe Hinckley's claim that the 2002 Bonneville America was styled to resemble a late-1940s Trumpet that's seen the dealer's accessories counter. But this "cruiser" Bonnie, with its kicked-out front end and tank-top control panel, gives buyers seeking the chopped look an alternative to V-twin conformity. A new 270-degree crankshaft and reprofiled camshafts create a rumpity-rumpity exhaust note, and Triumph offers loads of customizing gear. *Factory photo*

sweet-running," with enough grunt to troll through town in the higher gear ratios. The exhaust note with standard silencers is too muted (especially compared with Kawasaki's Bonnie clone, the W650) and many buyers are fitting Triumph's throatier aftermarket muffler kit, good for an extra 10 horsepower.

Handling is solid if not outright sporting, unaffected by rough pavement, and cornering clearance is excellent. Compared with the W650 and Harley's base 883 Sportster, the Triumph is "the easiest to ride fast on a winding road," reported Egan, "and has the most drive coming off a corner. It also feels the safest and most stable at speed." (The magazine clocked a top-speed run of 105 miles per hour, about 5 to 7 miles per hour down on a strong T120R.)

The Bonnie adds yet another "platform" to Bloor's stable and has already spawned a U.S.-custom version, the Bonneville America. It's a cruiser styled to mimic a chopped late-1940s Tiger (with questionable results) and features a 270-degree crankshaft, to add a bit of lope to the exhaust note. As this book was written, the Triumph rumor mill was filled with other Bonnie spin-offs, including a high-piped T120C-influenced version and a café racer.

While the new Bonnie brought the light, simple, twin back, Bloor was also preparing something for the opposite end of the spectrum. This was Triumph's ultimate statement—a 2,200-cc inline three with shaft drive. The engine is mounted longitudinally in the frame, like a 1950s Sunbeam twin, and carries its lubricant in a tank mounted to the side of the crankcase. Early unofficial photos indicate a megacruiser aimed directly at Honda's Valkyrie. Certainly the bike will give Triumph bragging rights to the "world's biggest production motorcycle engine" title when it leaves its drydock in late 2002.

By January 2000 John Bloor's enterprise had become the industry's greatest success story. Hinckley had built over 100,000 machines in its first decade and a new facility nearby was slated to go on line in early 2003. Bloor had even inked a deal to make components in Thailand, where quality is high and costs low.

Hinckley's production was set at 33,000 motorcycles (100 per day) for 2002, but that wasn't Triumph's most important driver. The marque has rekindled the value of what "Made in England" means to motorcycling, in its most positive sense. Enthusiasts can only believe that the spirit of Siegfried Bettmann, Edward Turner, and a host of Triumph engineers, racers, dealers, and owners are smiling on Britain's legendary machines as they move forward into the millennium.

THE
TRIUMPH LIFE

Mick Duckworth

What makes a Triumph enthusiast? The answer resides in the machines themselves. The versatility, mechanical honesty, and stylistic flair of a Triumph twin or triple create an ideal platform for personal expression. Generations of owners have transformed their stock machines into *exactly* the bike they want to ride—from race-replicas and high-mileage tourers to chopped, raked, and metal-flaked monstrosities.

Ingenuity and taste (or lack thereof) are their starting points; welding rigs, spray guns, and a healthy parts aftermarket are the tools that turn their dream bikes into reality. Truth is, there are as many variations of Triumph motorcycles as there are Triumph riders, tuners, and equipment vendors. And if you like stock, Triumphs continue to anchor the classic-bike restoration hobby.

The Heart of a Triton

Since the advent of the 1938 Speed Twin, the marque has always been a magnet for "specials" builders who wanted the ultimate combination of powerplant and chassis. The most famous among them were independent British frame specialists Eric Cheney and Derek and Don Rickman, who fitted Triumph's popular twin-cylinder engines into their own custom-built frames for road, off-road, and track use.

Others, including Paul Dunstall, marketed their own supersport bikes based on standard T120 Bonnevilles, with racy fairings, tanks, exhaust systems, and disc brakes. In Italy, Leopold Tartarini sold Bonneville-powered sport bikes under his Italjet brand during the 1960s and early 1970s. The Italjet-Triumphs featured the company's own twin-loop, full-cradle frames, and unique running gear.

In the United States, Triumph owners enjoyed a dizzying selection of personalizing options. For 13 years beginning in 1957, the Triumph Corporation published its own catalogue of factory and aftermarket goodies, from which owners could order through their local dealer. Some Triumph shops built their own customs, too. Detroit dealer and speed king Bob Leppan sold scores of new Triumphs with beautiful custom-painted fuel tanks, which he farmed

Standard 1960s Triumphs are easily converted into tasty café racers, as this 1967 T120R photographed at Triumph Day in Massachusetts proves. Slimline aftermarket fork, clip-on handlebars, uptilted instruments, solo seat, and classic sweptback exhausts with big reverse-cone megaphones make this a raucous, fun machine for twisty back roads. *Jeff Hackett*

out to a local car painter. One of Triumph-Detroit's most popular tank motifs featured twin scallops of a contrasting color, rising from each tank badge and flaring back into a point toward the seat. The scallops were outlined in pinstripes. Meriden styling chief Jack Wickes liked this design so much he adopted it for the standard Bonneville paint job during the 1969 model year. It's been a Triumph hallmark ever since.

If you wanted a race-ready "desert sled" in the 1960s, you could buy one brand new from Los Angeles Triumph dealer Ted Lapadakis. He converted Trophy 500s and 650s right out of the crate and sold them from his show room. Or, if the chopper scene was your "bag" in the early 1970s, Van Nuys Cycle would construct a brand new, custom Triumph exactly to your specification. Just walk into the dealership, sign the paperwork for a new 650 and check off the "righteous" hardware on the shop's options list—fork extensions up to 12 inches over stock; custom gas tanks, pipes, handlebars, lights and sissy bars; any style of paint and acres of chrome.

The Van Nuys mechanics then rolled the stock bike into the service area and went to work. They'd even remove the rear shock absorbers and replace them with hard-tail "struts." When your dream chopper was completed, Van Nuys Cycle would deliver it right to your door.

Even in hindsight, the chopper craze is still difficult to reconcile with Triumphs and other British bikes. To the backyard "artist" armed with a few hand tools and a blowtorch, the chopper was all about self-expression

In the early 1960s, rock-and-roll, British motorcycles, and a new generation of youth looking for excitement collided, and the "Rockers" lifestyle was born. It's still a state of mind, and style, for many Triumph enthusiasts, including these two, who rode into London for the annual Rocker's Run celebration in 1989. The rider at left is on the quintessential Rocker's machine, a Triton, with a pre-unit 650 motor. His friend has a customized TR7 from the late 1970s. Each wears an array of enameled pins that would be a major "ouch" in the event of a spill. *EMAP archive*

and freedom. To riders who valued road holding, braking, and safe ergonomics, choppers were all about turning a perfectly good motorcycle into junk. It's hard to believe that as Doug Hele's team of factory engineers was dramatically improving the standard Triumph's chassis and brakes in the late 1960s, the chopper crowd was plying the opposite course. They could've saved a lot of time and bought Harley Sportsters instead.

But for those who wanted the ideal blend of power and handling, there was only one Triumph-engined special: the legendary Triton. Whoever built the first Triton in mid-1950s Britain is unknown. As the name implies it married the era's best overall engine—Triumph's torquey 650-cc Tiger 110 or Thunderbird, usually tweaked for more power—with Norton's legendary twin-loop, all-welded Featherbed frame and Roadholder forks. Gearbox could be either Triumph's Slickshift or the Norton-AMC four-speed. The resulting hybrid delivered Triumph thrust with the rock-solid handling and pinpoint steering that made Nortons unbeatable on the Isle of Man.

Meriden's twin-carburetor "Delta" cylinder head immediately became the crowning glory for Triton builders. The most revered of these machines employ pre-unit engines, which visually fill out the big frame more completely than the later unit-construction motors. By the time the Triton craze had reached its zenith in the late 1960s, it was being fed by an ample supply of donor T120 Bonneville powerplants and Featherbed frames.

"Around town, where many of them spent their lives, the Triton was intended to outrage the uptight, impress anything squeezed into a short, tight skirt, and taunt the constabulary," wrote Peter Watson in a 1991 *Classic Bike* test of a restored pre-unit machine. "As a racer on the road, even today it identifies its owner as a tear-away, albeit one liable to be complimented by misty-eyed middle-aged men driving Ford Sierras."

With the look of a Manx Norton on steroids and no concessions to rider comfort, Tritons are all business. "The fact that (during extreme cornering) you can come close to scraping the frame rails on road tires should tell the would-be café racer all he needs to know about Triton handling," noted Watson. "With the right suspension it's simply the best there is."

Watson's test bike had been restored by Dave Degens, whose Dresda Autos company in Britain is the world's most experienced Triton builder. Dresda has completed over 1,000 Tritons for customers all over the world since the 1960s. It was still producing them to a long waiting list when this book was written. Degens, a Triumph stalwart, boosted the Triton mystique when he and co-riders won the 1965 and 1970 Barcelona 24-Hour endurance races with a 650 Triton of his own construction. The Barcelona wins helped cement this mixed-breed thoroughbred as the premier over-the-counter café racer with the heart of a Triumph.

But for every Triton that's engineered by Degens and other pros, there are many iffy ones pieced together by amateurs. "Tritons are the British bike equivalent of the American hot-rod car," explains moto-journalist and veteran Triton owner Mick Duckworth. "There are so many details to get right if you want a properly engineered machine—engine and gearbox position, chain alignment, battery placement, how you anchor the exhaust pipes, how you sort out the electrics, and how you isolate the critical parts from vibration. A Triton is much more than the sum of its parts. A poorly built one can be a bloody disaster."

Just as the answer to who built the first Triton is lost in history, so too is the originator of the term "café racer." Certainly it was born in Britain, probably in the 1950s. A café racer has come to define a fast street bike with road-racer styling, but during Triumph's heyday it represented the working-class youth culture of black leather, rock-and-roll music, and a new status symbol—the motorcycle. The culture may have been spawned in 1953 when the infamous American outlaw-biker movie, *The Wild One*, was banned in Britain. Of course, censoring the film only helped make rebel-heroes of the film's main characters, Triumph Thunderbird-riding Marlon Brando and his nemesis, Harley-mounted tough guy Lee Marvin.

Left
Anyone owning a Triton built by Jerry Cartwright is lucky indeed, and Ron Pruette agrees. He ordered this beauty from Cartwright's Peninsula Classics shop in North Wales and was delighted with the result. Pruette specified a pre-unit 650-cc motor in a slimline Norton Featherbed frame, "because the separate engine and gearbox fill out the space better than the unit-construction motors—and it just looks more authentic." Drum brakes are a double-sided Grimeca 230 mm in front and a Manx look-alike BSA-Triumph conical rear hub. The slender alloy fuel tank is the short-circuit Manx type. *Jay Asquini*

Right
They may look simple, but building a dirt-track special for the street takes patience in getting the details right. Don Miller's Trackmaster Triumph is set up like a TT racer, with Ceriani forks and triple disc brakes. Both the frame and engine come from 1969. The tuned Bonneville engine features a 750-cc Routt cylinder barrel, Routt-modified head with 32-mm Mikuni carburetors and Megacycle cams. Period racing hardware includes Barnes quick-change hubs, brake rotors by flat-track veteran Neil Keen, and Airheart brake calipers. A small box behind the engine hides the tiny Yuasa battery and Boyer electronic ignition. Total weight for this flyer is 290 pounds. *Jeff Hackett*

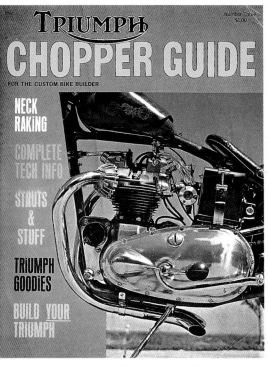

In the 1960s and 1970s, Triumphs fell victim to that cruelest of custom bike trends—the chopper. It is sad how quickly a blowtorch and a few tools in the wrong hands can butcher the work of skilled factory engineers into evil handling, brakeless monstrosities. Special-focus magazines were even published for the "chopper freaks." *David Gaylin archive; Jeff Hackett photo*

Above right
Derek and Don Rickman began building "Street Metisse" versions of their beautiful lightweight chassis kits in the late 1960s. Buyers provided their own power unit, and many chose Triumph twins. Derek is astride a Bonneville-engined Metisse in 1968. Note semienclosed Lockheed front disc brake and stout Metal Profile forks, both Rickman trademarks. *Mick Woollett*

Former Johnson Motors service manager Pat Owens and wife Donna and their amazing T120RT Bonneville, photographed in the 1970s. Twenty years later, the Owens' had ridden the Bonnie over 420,000 miles throughout North America. This was the very first 1970 Bonneville converted to 750-cc for AMA racing homologation. Soon after purchasing the bike from JoMo, Owens removed the original Routt iron cylinder barrels and replaced them with an aluminum 750-cc barrel kit, made by aftermarket big-bore specialist Bob Chantland. Owens still owned the rare RT Bonnie in 2002, its handlebars wearing a cluster of four Smiths speedometers—each with 99,999 miles on it. *Lindsay Brooke archive*

As the British public's spending power rose in the late 1950s, so did motorcycle sales. The truckers' cafés and coffee bars became popular hangouts for motorcyclists. On any given night leather-clad riders with evocative aliases such as Chilly Willy, the Rapido Kid, and Big Ginger, their bikes fitted with clip-on 'bars, sweptback exhausts, racing fuel tanks, and personalized with nicknames like *Voodoo*, *Genghis Khan*, and *Meggas*, would race from café to café. Or the kids would put a raucous 45-rpm record on the café's jukebox, jump on their bikes and attempt to ride a predetermined street course and return before the record was finished playing!

It was called "record racing" and the riders were labeled "Rockers" by the British press. Among their infamous exploits was "doing the ton"—burning up the public roads at 100 miles per hour or faster. That was easy on a Tiger 110, Bonnie, or Triton. Along with BSA's Clubman Gold Star and Norton's 650SS, the big Triumphs were the stars of the café scene. Some of the places became almost as legendary as the bikes—London's Ace Café on the North Circular Road and the hot-dog stand at Chelsea Bridge; the Busy Bee café on the A41; Johnson's on the A20 just south of the Brands Hatch race circuit, the Tip Top café on the Kingston by-pass, and The Nightingale near Biggin Hill, to name a few of the most popular spots.

At these joints on a Saturday night, the parking lot would be packed with bikes. The mood among those with the hottest machines was that of Wild West gunfighters squaring off in the middle of Main Street at high noon. So you've got a quick Trumpet, eh mate? Prove it!

To beat an Eddie Cochran or Chuck Berry tune at the Ace, for example, you had to cover a 3 1/2-mile course over often wet, greasy pavement—behind the burning arc of your six-volt Lucas headlamp.

"Turning left out of the car park onto the North Circular, the contestant would immediately dive under a conglomeration of railway viaducts before hitting the traffic lights at Stonebridge Park," recalls Mike Clay in his superb 1988 book *Café Racers*. "A good clear view to either side made shooting these lights on red an acceptable risk to many, before chinning the tank for nearly three-quarters of a mile into a 90-mile per hour right-hander. This led into the climbing left-hander that marks the entry to the infamous Iron Bridge. Exiting this at 80 miles per hour, a strong heave on the brakes was required to bring the speed down to the 65 miles per hour or so necessary to negotiate the downhill left-hander which, with its tightening radius and adverse camber, spelt trouble for anyone who mucked it up." (Try that on your chopper...)

"Honest, officer, you're *supposed* to ride 'em this way!" Triumph-engined dirt-track replicas are gaining popularity in both America and Britain, and they don't get any better than Don Miller's Trackmaster-framed T120, seen here with Miller doing a Gene Romero imitation on a rural New England road. *Jeff Hackett*

Above left
Fans of the fabulous BSA-Triumph F750 factory racers erupt in glee when they hear Eric Parr's works replica Trident howl past them on British motorways. Miles Engineering (now NWS) in Britain builds complete chassis kits for the triples that feature the Rob North road race frame. While most are sold for vintage racing, a few of the Miles kits are put on the street. To make it legal, Parr's machine wears twin Cibie car headlamps outside the fairing, though a fairing nose with a headlamp opening molded in is also offered. *EMAP archive*

This twin-engined curiosity was created in the early 1960s by TriCor's Rod Coates. It used unit-construction T100 engines, the front one with its gearbox sawed off. A single Amal Monobloc carburetor was fitted at a 90-degree angle on each side of the bike, feeding split manifolds. Note cobby use of saucepan for front crankcase cover. The frame wears a TriCor center-mount racing oil tank. This machine has surfaced on the U.S. auction circuit in recent years. *Lindsay Brooke archive*

Before converting this 1957 Tiger Cub into a road racer in 1961, Teddy Colligan used it as a daily commuter bike in his native Belfast, Ireland. He scored a trio of 200-cc Irish championships with it during the 1960s and has campaigned the little single continuously ever since. The Cub runs a 1.0-inch Monobloc carburetor on both single- and dual-plug cylinder heads modified by Colligan. With a special aluminum fuel tank, NSU moped oil tank and a Yamaha roadster front brake, the highly developed Cub still competes successfully in European vintage races against Spanish two-strokes and Ducati singles. Colligan revs it to 8,000 rpm, good for over 110 miles per hour. It is shown here at a 1996 race meeting in Belgium. *Mick Duckworth*

"A gentle quarter-mile right-hand bend followed," Clay explains, "leading into the Neasden roundabout, which marked the halfway stage, where the rider would turn and come back."

Meanwhile, the jukebox back at the Ace is still wailing and the crowd—which could number in the hundreds on a good night—is anxiously watching for your headlamp to appear. Your reputation is on the line. There are people to impress—mainly your archrivals with their own fast bikes, and the local girls, of course. You've have to do the return leg at 70 miles per hour or faster if you aim to beat the last chords of *Summertime Blues* or *Johnny B. Goode*. And you'd better punctuate your arrival with the right blend of speed, noise, and style—a Brando-meets-Hailwood grand entrance.

The Rocker era had more than its share of spills and fatalities, and the British police did what they could to protect the citizenry from the scourge. Triumph Speed Twins had always been the standard motorcycle of the London Metropolitan Police, and by the 1960s the coppers were patrolling on TR6P's. Nicknamed the Saint—from the acronym Stops Anything In No Time—these white Trophy 650s could rarely catch a well-ridden Triton, but their sirens and radio gear made up for top speed. Also out to nab café racers was a fleet of 26 black Daimler SP250 sports cars purchased by London's finest from 1961 through 1964 (see chapter 4).

The café tradition continues today, with Triumph enthusiasts stuffing modified twins and triples into various chassis that reflect their owners' views of what a proper "special" should be. Rickman Metisses remain a favorite everywhere. In the United States, various lightweight frames originally built for mile and half-mile dirt track racing have become America's version of the Triton. The nickel-plated Trackmaster, Champion, and Red Line frames are made from stout chrome-moly tubing, and carry the engine oil within the top tube or backbone. They're a superb platform for a tuned 650-cc or 750-cc twin.

Custom touches inspired by the 1950s abound on this nifty single-carb T100, built by Detroit, Michigan, Triumph specialist Ken Lanoo. The frame's seat rails were carefully bent to bring the seat height down so Lanoo's wife could plant her feet flat on the ground when she rides the machine. Note the shrouded fork springs and rear shocks, and aircraft-quality fasteners. *Jay Asquini*

Below
Italian stylist Leopold Tartarini designed the Grifon in the late 1960s for his motorcycle and scooter company, Italjet. The machine used 650-cc Bonneville engines, purchased directly from Triumph and installed in Tartarini's own duplex frame. The first Italjet Grifons were sold in Italy in 1967 and undercut the price of a standard Bonnie by 10 percent. The model, which used Italian forks, brakes, and bodywork, was sold in small batches through 1971. None were officially imported to the United States. Chain guard location is odd.
Mick Duckworth archive

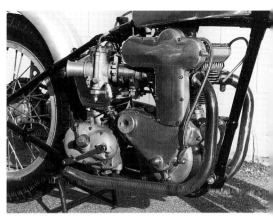

Various overhead-camshaft cylinder heads made by highly committed speed enthusiasts were fitted to Triumph engines in both Britain and the United States. This T100-based dohc special was built by California machinist Ralph Gaebel in the late 1950s, for use on the salt flats and on drag strips. It was campaigned by racer "Digger" Helm, but proved no faster than a well-tuned pushrod setup. *Lindsay Brooke*

Left
The Triumph Owners Motorcycle club is one of the worlds largest, best organized, and most active bike enthusiasts organizations. Members of the Bexley, UK, chapter enjoy themselves during a rainswept Rally of the Tigers in 1998. *Jim Davies*

Fitted with all the "right stuff"—slimline Ceriani or Betor forks, Barnes quick-change wheels shod with modern disc brakes and tires, low and wide handlebars, and a racing saddle, a Trackmaster street Triumph is beautiful to look at and a joy to ride on a twisty road. With 50 to 70 horsepower (depending on state of tune) motivating a 320-pound package, it's easy to imagine you're Gene Romero aboard one.

A similar feeling can be had on a howling Triumph Trident that's built to look, handle, and sound like the championship 1971 works racers. That's because replica Rob North chassis for F750 vintage racing have been manufactured in Britain for over 20 years, first by Miles Engineering and recently by NWS (who took over from Miles in 2001). A number of these machines have been put on the road in Britain and elsewhere. With headlamps added above the "letterbox" oil cooler slot in the fairing and small batteries tucked into the tailpieces to power the electrics, a North triple like those made famous by Romero and Paul Smart makes a unique café racer.

The popularity of the Hinckley-built bikes and the plethora of accessories being made for them ensures that Triumphs will continue to be tailored to their owners' personal tastes and riding styles. While it's unlikely that a 2002 Daytona will be chopped or converted into a flat-track lookalike, the new Bonneville already shows signs of picking up where the T140 left off.

The new Bonnie is turning out to be popular for modification. Aftermarket parts from the UK, Europe, and the United States are available to create boulevard cruisers and café racers. There's a 900-cc big-bore kit from California and components from Italy that can transform your low-piped Bonneville into a very credible knockoff of a 1965 T120C high-piper!

MEGA-MILE TRIUMPHS

During the last decade, owners of the "new" Triumphs have racked up mileages that would have been almost impossible to achieve on the Meriden-era machines without numerous rebuilds. Chris Cimino's 1997 Trophy Tour covered 11,000 miles in 11 days when he criss-crossed the United States during that year's Iron Butt Rally. Sure, the bike's 4-gallon auxiliary fuel tank helped keep Cimino's armor-plated posterior in the saddle. But the new-generation Triumphs mostly are blessed with car-like robustness.

While the same generally cannot be said for the "old" Triumphs, many of them delivered reliable service in all types of operating conditions. Like most British vehicles of the post-World War II era, Triumphs suffered from inconsistent build quality. Those lucky enough to have bought a "good one" and who followed the factory maintenance drill religiously thereafter could expect a faithful steed.

Perhaps the world's most famous high-mileage Triumph is the 1970 T120RT owned by Pat Owens. The former Johnson Motors service manager and race tuner for Gene Romero's championship season has put over 420,000 miles on his Bonneville. He and his wife, Donna, have ridden their trusted friend across North America, including three tours of Alaska. They've been through Mexico and Central America on it, covering 8,000 mostly trouble-free miles in six weeks on one trip.

Owens' bike has averaged 25,000 miles between top-end overhauls. He's replaced the cylinder barrels once every 100,000 miles. His many service recommendations include use of a Trident oil cooler and Purolator spin-on filter. He mixes Kal-Gard engine protectant with the Texaco Formula 3 20/50 engine oil and changes the oil every 1,500 miles. Owens lubricates the big Bonnie's gearbox with a pint of STP blended with 140-weight gear lube. As this book was written, Owens and Bonnie were headed toward the half-million-mile mark.

Like Owens, London artist Dave Spurring is a strict disciple of 1,500-mile oil changes. His preferred lube is Castrol GTX multigrade. Fresh oil is one reason his modified 1965 Bonnie had done 175,000 miles with only a single engine rebuild when *Classic Bike* caught up with him in the mid-1980s. Spurring's key to keeping the well-worn Triumph in regular use was careful maintenance. He was avid about warming up the engine before each morning's ride and keeping the engine in sharp tune. He added extra breathers in the rocker boxes to aid oil-tightness. He also welded reinforcing washers behind all sheet-metal mounting points, to minimize stress cracks from vibration.

In winter, Spurring kept the Bonnie in daily use. It was coated with Finnegan's Waxoyl protectant, which kept corrosion at bay but made the bike look rather tatty. It was a small price to pay for such dependability.

But high-mileage Triumphs can be showroom-spotless, too. Such was the condition of Dan Cooley's 1969 Trident when *Cycle* magazine writer Jess Thomas profiled the bike in 1975. At the time the triple's odometer read 98,464 miles. The engine's lower end had not been touched, and it was only on its second set of ignition breaker points! Through six years of ownership, Cooley, a professional mechanic at Brattin Motors in San Diego, had done mostly top-end work. He replaced piston rings at 27,000 miles; two transmission gears at 30,000, and pistons, rings and valves at 50,000.

The triple, which wore an early Vetter Phantom touring fairing, was still on its original rear sprocket and chain at nearly 99,000 miles. Its whereabouts are unknown today, but it's likely the bike went well beyond 100,000 miles.

Triumphs dominate the landscape at the many British bike rallies held in North America each year. Jay Cohen rode this stock 1966 6T Thunderbird over 800 miles roundtrip to the All-British Motorcycle Meet in Auburn, Massachusetts. The event is one of the largest annual Britbike gatherings in the United States. *Lindsay Brooke*

Far left
California road racer and motorcycle dealer Sonny Angel on *Hurd Bird*—his Vincent H.R.D.–framed Triumph Thunderbird special. Note Burman gearbox, flame paint scheme, and one-piece seat/tail unit. The photo was taken in 1957 outside Angel's shop in National City, California. *Gordon Menzie collection*

These "before" and "after" photos show a 1971 T100R Daytona transformed from its sadly neglected, as-purchased state, into a tasteful custom. Owner-restorer Don Sherman wanted to blend a flat-track look with the classic Triumph lines. He also likes the sheen of polished metal, and his Daytona has plenty of it. Sherman had the frame nickel plated, and commissioned the aluminum tank from Don Woodward, the British sheet metal expert who fabricated Triumph's factory road race tanks in 1971. Alloy rims, custom seat, a 6-inch Trophy 500 headlamp, and TT pipes complete the showstopper. *Aaron Kiley*

APPENDIX
SOURCES AND RESOURCES

Few motorcycle marques have had as much written about them as Triumph. Sitting on my own bookshelves are forty-two titles covering this company and its machines. My archive is by no means complete, nor does it include the various grease-smudged service manuals and parts books in my workshop, the large filing cabinet filled with Triumph-related magazine articles, or the binders full of sales literature.

Many books on Triumph are available from the extensive Motorbooks International catalog and Web site, www.motorbooks.com. Others that are out of print can be found, along with original copies of old motorcycle magazines, through diligent hunting at swap meets, auto-jumbles, and various used-literature sources.

Memberships to The Triumph Owners' Club (U.K.) and Triumph International Owners Club (U.S.) include magazines that are wonderful historical resources. And no enthusiast should be without subscriptions to the contemporary magazines covering the vintage and classic motorcycling scene.

Triumph's recorded history is a continuum, and this book is only the latest step in the journey. The literature listed below was essential research material for this book, and I highly recommend all of it to Triumph fans and those interested in general motorcycle history.

Books

Bonnie: The Development History of the Triumph Bonneville. Nelson, J.R. Haynes; 1979.

British Motor Cycles Volume 5 (Triumph: The Company). Wilson, Steve. Patrick Stephens Ltd.; 1991.

British Motor Cycles Volume 6 (Triumph: The Bikes). Wilson, Steve. Patrick Stephens Ltd.; 1992.

The British Motor Industry, 1945-94: A Case Study in Industrial Decline. Whisler, Timothy. Oxford University Press; 1999.

The British Motorcycle Industry: Interview with Edward Turner. (tape recording). Lee, Jim. 1973.

BSA and Triumph Triples: The Complete Story. Duckworth, Mick. Crowood; 1997.

Café Racers: Rockers, Rock n' Roll and The Coffee Bar Cult. Clay, Mike. Osprey; 1988.

Daimler V8/SP250. Long, Brian. Veloce; 1994.

It's A Triumph. Davies, Ivor. Haynes; 1980.

It's Easy On A Triumph. Davies, Ivor. Haynes; 1990.

The Ricardo Story. Ricardo, Sir Harry. Society of Automotive Engineers; 1990.

Tales of Triumph Motorcycles and the Meriden Factory. Hancox, Hughie. Veloce; 1996.

Triumph Bonneville and TR6 Restoration Guide. Gaylin, David. Motorbooks International; 1997.

Triumph: The Complete Story. Davies, Ivor. Crowood; 1991.

Triumph Motorcycles in America. Brooke, Lindsay and Gaylin, David. Motorbooks International; 1993.

Triumph Racing Motorcycles in America. Brooke, Lindsay. Motorbooks International; 1995.

Triumph: Return of the Legend. Minton, Dave. Chartwell; 1995.

Triumph T120/T140 Bonneville. Wilson, Steve. Haynes; 2000.

Triumph Tiger Cub Bible. Estall, Mike. Veloce; 2000.

Triumph Twins and Triples. Bacon, Roy. Osprey; 1981.

Turner's Triumphs: Edward Turner and His Triumph Motorcycles. Clew, Jeff. Veloce; 2000.

Whatever Happened to the British Motorcycle Industry? Hopwood, Bert. Haynes; 1981.

Magazines

Classic Bike
The Classic Motorcycle
Classic Bike Guide
Cycle
Cycle World
Motor Cycling
The Motor Cycle
Motorcyclist
Vintage Bike (Triumph International Owners Club quarterly newsletter)
The Nacelle (Triumph Owners Club magazine)